THE 5 AM CLUB

ALSO BY ROBIN SHARMA

The Monk Who Sold His Ferrari
The Greatness Guide
The Greatness Guide, Book 2
The Leader Who Had No Title
Who Will Cry When You Die?
Leadership Wisdom from The Monk Who Sold His Ferrari
Family Wisdom from The Monk Who Sold His Ferrari
Discover Your Destiny with The Monk Who Sold His Ferrari
The Secret Letters of The Monk Who Sold His Ferrari
The Mastery Manual
The Little Black Book for Stunning Success
The Saint, the Surfer, and the CEO

THE 5 AM CLUB

OWN YOUR MORNING. ELEVATE YOUR LIFE.

ROBIN SHARMA

HarperCollins*Publishers*Ltd

Published by HarperCollins Publishers Ltd

First edition

HarperCollins books may be purchased for educational, business
or sales promotional use through our Special Markets Department.

HarperCollins Publishers Ltd
Bay Adelaide Centre, East Tower
22 Adelaide Street West, 41st Floor
Toronto, Ontario, Canada
M5H 4E3

www.harpercollins.ca

Interior illustrations by Mae Besom (pages 21, 40, 109, 123, 200 and 274)
and Lola Landekic (pages 176 and 280).

Library and Archives Canada Cataloguing in Publication
information is available upon request.

ISBN 978-1-4434-5662-3

Printed and bound in the United States
LSC/H 9 8 7

Message from the Author + Dedication

I'm immensely grateful that this book is in your hands. My deep hope is that it serves the full expression of your gifts and talents beautifully. And causes revolutions of heroic transformation within your creativity, productivity, prosperity and service to the world.

The 5 AM Club is based on a concept and method that I've been teaching to celebrated entrepreneurs, CEOs of legendary companies, sports superstars, music icons and members of royalty—with extraordinary success—for over twenty years.

I wrote this book over a four-year period, in Italy, South Africa, Canada, Switzerland, Russia, Brazil and Mauritius. Sometimes the words flowed effortlessly as if a gentle summer breeze was at my back and at other times, I struggled to move ahead. Sometimes I felt like waving the white flag of creative depletion and during other periods of this intensely spiritual process, a responsibility higher than my own needs encouraged me to continue.

I've given all I have to give in the writing of this book for you. And I greatly thank all the very good people from around the planet who have stood with me to the completion of The 5 AM Club.

And so, with a full heart, I humbly dedicate this work to you, the reader. The world needs more heroes and why wait for them—when you have it in you to become one. Starting today.

With love + respect,

CONTENTS

"We will have eternity to celebrate the victories but only a few hours before sunset to win them." —Amy Carmichael

"For what it's worth, it's never too late or, in my case, too early to be whoever you want to be . . . I hope you live a life you're proud of. If you find that you're not, I hope you have the strength to start all over again." —F. Scott Fitzgerald

"And those who were seen dancing were thought to be insane by those who could not hear the music." —Friedrich Nietzsche

THE 5 AM CLUB

CHAPTER 1

The Dangerous Deed

A gun would be too violent. A noose would be too ancient. And a knife blade to the wrist would be too silent. So, the question became, *How could a once-glorious life be ended swiftly and precisely, with minimum mess yet maximum impact?*

Only a year ago, circumstances had been dramatically more hopeful. The entrepreneur had been widely celebrated as a titan of her industry, a leader of society and a philanthropist. She was in her late thirties, steering the technology company she founded in her dorm room in college to ever-increasing levels of marketplace dominance while producing products that her customers revered.

Yet now she was being blindsided, facing a mean-spirited and jealousy-fueled coup that would significantly dilute her ownership stake in the business she'd invested most of her life building, forcing her to find a new job.

The cruelty of this remarkable turn of events was proving to be unbearable for the entrepreneur. Beneath her regularly icy exterior beat a caring, compassionate and deeply loving heart. She felt life itself had betrayed her. And that she deserved so much better.

She considered swallowing a gigantic bottle of sleeping pills. The dangerous deed would be cleaner this way. Just take them all and get the job done fast, she thought. I need to escape this pain.

Then, she spotted something on the stylish oak dresser in her all-white bedroom—a ticket to a personal optimization conference that her mother had given her. The entrepreneur usually laughed at people who attended such events, calling them "broken winged" and saying they were seeking the answers of a pseudo guru when everything they needed to live a prolific and successful life was already within them.

Maybe it was time to rethink her opinion. She couldn't see many options. Either she'd go to the seminar—and experience some breakthrough that would save her life. Or she'd find her peace. Via a quick death.

CHAPTER 2

A Daily Philosophy
on Becoming Legendary

"Do not allow your fire to go out, spark by irreplaceable spark in the
hopeless swamps of the not-quite, the not-yet, and the not at all. Do not let the
hero in your soul perish in lonely frustration for the life you deserved and have
never been able to reach. The world you desire can be won. It exists.
It is real. It is possible. It is yours." **—Ayn Rand**

He was a speaker of the finest kind. A genuine Spellbinder.

Nearing the end of a fabled career and now in his eighties, he had
become revered throughout the world as a grandmaster of inspiration,
a legend of leadership and a sincere statesman helping everyday people
realize their greatest gifts.

In a culture filled with volatility, uncertainty and insecurity, The
Spellbinder's events drew stadium-sized numbers of human beings who
longed not only to lead masterful lives filled with creativity, productivity
and prosperity but also to exist in a way that passionately elevated humanity. So that, at the end, they would feel confident they had left a wonderful
legacy and made their mark on the generations that would follow.

This man's work was unique. It blended insights that fortified the warrior within our characters with ideas that honored the soulful poet who
resides inside the heart. His messaging showed ordinary individuals

3

how to succeed at the highest levels of the business realm yet reclaim the magic of a life richly lived. So, we return to the sense of awe we once knew before a hard and cold world placed our natural genius into bondage by an orgy of complexity, superficiality and technological distraction.

Though The Spellbinder was tall, his advanced years left him slightly bent over. As he walked the platform, he stepped carefully yet gracefully. A precisely fitted charcoal gray suit with soft white pinstripes gave him an elegant look. And a pair of blue-tinted eyeglasses added just the right amount of cool.

"Life's too short to play small with your talents," The Spellbinder spoke to the room of thousands. "You were born into the opportunity as well as the responsibility to become legendary. You've been built to achieve masterwork-level projects, designed to realize unusually important pursuits and constructed to be a force for good on this tiny planet. You have it in you to reclaim sovereignty over your primal greatness in a civilization that has become fairly uncivilized. To restore your nobility in a global community where the majority shops for nice shoes and acquires expensive things yet rarely invests in a better self. Your personal leadership requires—no, demands—that you stop being a cyber-zombie relentlessly attracted to digital devices and restructure your life to model mastery, exemplify decency and relinquish the self-centeredness that keeps good people limited. The great women and men of the world were all givers, not takers. Renounce the common delusion that those who accumulate the most win. Instead, do work that is heroic—that staggers your marketplace by the quality of its originality as well as from the helpfulness it provides. While you do so, my recommendation is that you also create a private life strong in ethics, rich with marvelous beauty and unyielding when it comes to the protection of your inner peace. This, my friends, is how you soar with the angels. And walk alongside the gods."

The Spellbinder paused. He drew in a gulp of air, as big as a mountain. His breathing grew strained and made a *whooshing* noise as he inhaled. He looked down at his stylish black boots that had been polished up to a military grade.

Those in the front row saw a single tear drizzle down the timeworn yet once-handsome face.

His gaze remained downward. His silence was thunderous. The Spellbinder appeared unsteady.

After a series of stressful moments that had some in the audience shifting in their seats, The Spellbinder put down the microphone he had been holding in his left hand. With his free hand, he tenderly reached into a pocket of his trousers and pulled out a crisply folded linen handkerchief. He wiped his cheek.

"Each of you has a call on your lives. Every one of you carries an instinct for excellence within your spirits. No one in this room needs to stay frozen in average and succumb to the mass mediocratization of behavior evident in society along with the collective de-professionalization of business so apparent in industry. Limitation is nothing more than a mentality that too many good people practice daily until they believe it's reality. It breaks my heart to see so many potentially powerful human beings stuck in a story about why they can't be extraordinary, professionally and personally. You need to remember that your excuses are seducers, your fears are liars and your doubts are thieves."

Many nodded. A few clapped. Then many more applauded.

"I understand you. I really do," continued The Spellbinder.

"I know you've had some difficult times in your life. We all have. I get that you might be feeling things haven't turned out the way you thought they would when you were a little kid, full of fire, desire and wonder. You didn't plan on each day looking the same, did you? In a job that might be smothering your soul. Dealing with stressful worries and endless responsibilities that stifle your originality and steal your energy. Lusting after unimportant pursuits and hungry for the instant fulfillment of trivial desires, often driven by a technology that enslaves us instead of liberating us. Living the same week a few thousand times and calling it a life.

5

I need to tell you that too many among us die at thirty and are buried at eighty. So, I do get you. You hoped things would be different. More interesting. More exciting. More fulfilling, special and magical."

The Spellbinder's voice trembled as he spoke these last words. He struggled to breathe for an instant. A look of concern caused his brow to crinkle. He sat down on a cream-colored chair that had been carefully placed at the side of the stage by one of his assistants.

"And, yes, I am aware that there are also many in this room who are currently leading lives you love. You're an epic success in the world, fully on your game and enriching your families and communities with an electricity that borders on otherworldly. Nice work. Bravo. And, yet, you too have experienced seasons where you've been lost in the frigid and dangerous valley of darkness. You, too, have known the collapse of your creative magnificence as well as your productive eminence into a tiny circle of comfortableness, fearfulness and numbness that betrayed the mansions of mastery and reservoirs of bravery inside of you. You, too, have been disappointed by the barren winters of a life weakly lived. You, too, have been denied many of your most inspired childhood dreams. You, too, have been hurt by people you trusted. You, too, have had your ideals destroyed. You, too, have had your innocent heart devastated, leaving your life decimated, like a ruined country after ambitious foreign invaders infiltrated it."

The cavernous conference hall was severely still.

"No matter where you are on the pathway of your life, please don't let the pain of an imperfect past hinder the glory of your fabulous future. You are so much more powerful than you may currently understand. Splendid victories—and outright blessings—are coming your way. And you're exactly where you need to be to receive the growth necessary for you to lead the unusually productive, extremely prodigious and exceptionally influential life that you've earned through your harshest trials. Nothing is wrong at this moment, even if it feels like everything's falling apart. If you sense your life's a mess right now, this is simply because your fears are just a little stronger than your faith. With practice, you can turn down the volume of the voice of your scared self. And increase the tone of your most triumphant side. The truth is that every challenging event you've experienced, each toxic person that you've encountered and all the trials you've endured have been perfect preparation to make you into the person that you now are. You needed these lessons to activate the treasures, talents and powers that are now awakening within you. Nothing was an accident. Zero was a waste. You're definitely exactly where you need to be to begin the life of your most supreme desires. One that can make you an empire-builder along with a world-changer. And perhaps even a history-maker."

"This all sounds easy but it's a lot harder in reality," shouted a man in a red baseball cap, seated in the fifth row. He sported a gray t-shirt and ripped jeans, the type you can buy torn at your local shopping mall. Though this outburst could have seemed disrespectful, the pitch of the participant's voice and his body language displayed genuine admiration for The Spellbinder.

"I agree with you, you wonderful human being," responded The Spellbinder, his grace influencing all participants and his voice sounding somewhat stronger, as he stood up from his chair. "Ideas are worth nothing unless backed by application. The smallest of implementations is always worth more than the grandest of intentions. And if being an amazing person and developing a legendary life was easy, everyone would be doing it. Know what I mean?"

"Sure, dude," replied the man in the red cap as he rubbed his lower lip with a finger.

"Society has sold us a series of mistruths," The Spellbinder continued. "That pleasure is preferable to the terrifying yet majestic fact that all possibility requires hard work, regular reinvention and a dedication as deep as the sea to leaving our harbors of safety, daily. I believe that the seduction of complacency and an easy life is one hundred times more brutal, ultimately, than a life where you go all in and take an unconquerable stand for your brightest dreams. *World-class begins where your comfort zone ends* is a rule the successful, the influential and the happiest always remember."

The man nodded. Groups of people in the audience were doing the same.

"From a young age, we are programmed into thinking that moving through life loyal to the values of mastery, ingenuity and decency should need little effort. And so, if the road gets tough and requires some patience, we think we're on the wrong path," commented The Spellbinder as he grasped an arm of the wooden chair and folded his thin frame into the seat again.

"We've encouraged a culture of soft, weak and delicate people who can't keep promises, who bail on commitments and who quit on their aspirations the moment the smallest obstacle shows up."

The orator then sighed loudly.

"Hard is good. Real greatness and the realization of your inherent genius is meant to be a difficult sport. Only those devoted enough to go to the fiery edges of their highest limits will expand them. And the suffering that happens along the journey of materializing your special powers, strongest abilities and most inspiring ambitions is one of the largest sources of human satisfaction. A major key to happiness—and internal peace—is knowing you've done whatever it took to earn your rewards and passionately invested the effortful audacity to become your best. Jazz legend Miles Davis stretched himself ferociously past the normal his field knew to fully exploit his magnificent potential. Michelangelo sacrificed enormously mentally, emotionally, physically and spiritually as he produced his awesome art. Rosa Parks, a simple seamstress with outstanding courage, endured blunt humiliation when she was arrested for not giving up her seat on a segregated bus, igniting the civil rights movement. Charles Darwin demonstrated the kind of resolve that virtuosity demands by studying barnacles—yes, barnacles—for eight long years as he formulated his famed Theory of Evolution. This kind of dedication to the optimization of expertise would now be labeled as 'crazy' by the majority in our modern world that spends huge amounts of their irreplaceable lifetime watching streams of selfies, the breakfasts of virtual friends and violent video games," noted The Spellbinder as he peered around the hall as if committed to looking each of the attendees straight in the eye.

"Stephen King worked as a high school writing teacher and in an industrial laundry before selling *Carrie*, the novel that made him famous," the aging presenter continued. "Oh, and please know that King was so discouraged by the rejections and denials that he threw the manuscript he wrote in his rundown trailer into the garbage, surrendering to the struggle. It was only when his wife, Tabitha, discovered the work while her husband was away, wiped off his cigarette ashes, read the book and then told its author that it was brilliant that King submitted it for publication. Even then, his advance for hardcover rights was a paltry twenty-five hundred dollars."

"Are you serious?" murmured a woman seated near the stage. She wore a lush green hat with a big scarlet feather sticking out of it and was clearly content with marching to her own drumbeat.

"I am," said The Spellbinder. "And while Vincent van Gogh created nine hundred paintings and over one thousand drawings in his lifetime, his celebrity started after his death. His drive to produce wasn't inspired by the ego fuel of popular applause but by a wiser instinct that enticed him to see just how much of his creative power he could unlock, no matter how much hardship he had to endure. Becoming legendary is never easy. But I'd prefer that journey to the heartbreak of being stuck in ordinary that so many potentially heroic people deal with constantly," articulated The Spellbinder firmly.

"Anyway, let me simply say that the place where your greatest discomfort lies is also the spot where your largest opportunity lives. The beliefs that disturb you, the feelings that threaten you, the projects that unnerve you and the unfoldments of your talents that the insecure part of you is resisting are precisely where you need to go to. Lean deeply toward these doorways into your bigness as a creative producer, seeker of personal freedom and possibilitarian. And then embrace these beliefs, feelings and projects quickly instead of structuring your life in a way that's designed to dismiss them. Walking into the very things that scare you is how you reclaim your forgotten power. And how you get back the innocence and awe you lost after childhood."

Suddenly, The Spellbinder started to cough. Mildly at first. Then violently, like he'd been possessed by a demon hell-bent on revenge.

In the wings, a man in a black suit with an aggressive crew cut spoke into a mouthpiece tucked discreetly into his shirt cuff. The lights began to flicker, then dim. A few audience members who were located near the platform stood, unsure of what to do.

A uniquely pretty woman with her hair in a crisp bun, a clenched smile and a tight black dress with an embroidered white collar rushed up the metal staircase that The Spellbinder had ascended at the beginning of his talk. She carried a phone in one hand and a well-worn notebook in another. Her red high heels made a "click clack, click clack" sound as she raced toward her employer.

Yet, the woman was too late.

The Spellbinder crumpled to the floor like a punch-drunk boxer with a large heart but weak skills in the final round of a once-glorious career that he should have ended many years earlier. The old presenter lay still. A tiny river of blood escaped from a cut to his head, sustained on his fall. His glasses sat next to him. The handkerchief was still in his hand. His once-sparkling eyes remained closed.

CHAPTER 3

An Unexpected Encounter with a Surprising Stranger

"Do not live as if you have ten thousand years left. Your fate hangs over you. While you are still living, while you still exist on this Earth, strive to become a genuinely great person." —Marcus Aurelius, Roman emperor

The entrepreneur lied to the people she met at the seminar, telling them she was in the room to learn The Spellbinder's fabulous formulas for exponential productivity as well as to discover the neuroscience beneath personal mastery that he had been sharing with leaders of industry. She mused that her expectation was that the guru's methodology would give her an unmatchable edge over her firm's competition, allowing the business to swiftly scale toward indisputable dominance. You know the real reason she was there: she needed her hope restored. And her life saved.

The artist had come to the event to understand how to fuel his creativity and multiply his capability so he could make an enduring mark on his field by the paintings he generated.

And the homeless man appeared to have sneaked into the conference hall while no one was watching.

The entrepreneur and the artist had been seated together. This was the first time they'd met.

"Do you think he's dead?" she asked as the artist fidgeted with his dangling Bob Marley dreadlocks.

The entrepreneur's face was angular and long. A wealth of wrinkles and weighty crevices ran along her forehead like ruts in a farmer's fresh field. Her brown hair was medium in length and styled in an "I mean business and dare not mess with me" kind of a way. She was lean, like a long-distance runner, with thin arms and lithe legs that emerged from a sensible blue designer skirt. Her eyes looked sad, from old hurts that had never been healed. And from the current chaos that was infecting her beloved company.

"Not sure. He's old. He fell hard. God, that was wild. Never seen anything like it," the artist said anxiously as he tugged on an earring.

"I'm new to his work. I'm not into this sort of thing," the entrepreneur explained. She stayed seated, her arms folded over a cream-colored blouse with a colossal floppy black bow tie perched fashionably at the neckline. "But I liked a lot of his information on productivity in this era of devices destroying our focus and our ability to think deeply. His words made me realize I have to guard my cognitive assets in a far better way," she carried on, fairly formally. She had no real interest in sharing what she was going through, and she obviously wanted to protect her facade of an illustrious businesswoman ready to rise to the next level.

"Yeah, he's def hip," said the artist, looking nervous. "He's helped me so much. Can't believe what just went down. Surreal, right?"

He was a painter. Because he wanted to elevate his craft as well as improve his personal life, he followed The Spellbinder's work. But, for whatever reason, the demons within him seemed to hold power over his greater nature. So, he'd inevitably sabotage his Herculean ambitions and wonderfully original ideas.

The artist was heavy. A goatee jutted out from under his chin. He wore a black t-shirt and long black shorts that fell below his knobby knees. Black boots with rubber soles, the kind you may have seen Australians wear, completed the creative uniform. A fascinating cascade of tattoos rolled down both arms and across his left leg. One said, "Rich People Are Fakers." Another stole a line from Salvador Dalí, the famed Spanish artist. It read simply, "I don't do drugs. I am drugs."

"Hi, guys," the homeless man spoke inappropriately loudly from a few rows behind the entrepreneur and the artist. The auditorium was still emptying, and the audiovisual crew was noisily tearing down the staging. Event staff swept the floor. A Nightmares on Wax song played soothingly in the background.

The two new acquaintances turned around to see a tangled mess of wild-person hair, a face that looked like it hadn't been shaved in decades and a tattered arrangement of terrifically stained clothing.

"Yes?" asked the entrepreneur in a tone as cold as an ice cube in the Arctic. "Can I help you?"

"Hey, brother, what's up?" offered the artist, more compassionately.

The homeless man got up, shuffled over and sat next to the two.

"Do you think the guru's croaked?" he asked as he picked at a scab on one of his wrists.

"Not sure," the artist replied as he twirled another dreadlock. "Hope not."

"Did you guys like the seminar? You into what the old-timer said?" continued the scruffy stranger.

"Def," said the artist. "I love his work. I have a hard time living it all, but what he says is profound. And powerful."

"I'm not so sure," the entrepreneur said cynically. "I like a lot of what I heard today, but I'm still not convinced on some other things. I'll need some time to process it all."

"Well, I think he's numero uno," stated the homeless man with a burp. "I made my fortune thanks to the teachings of The Spellbinder. And have enjoyed a pretty world-class life because of him, too. Most people wish for phenomenal things to happen to them. He taught me that exceptional performers *make* phenomenal things happen to them. And the great thing is, he not only gave me a secret philosophy to get my big dreams done but he taught me the technology—the tactics and tools—to translate the information into results. His revolutionary insights on how to install a fiercely productive morning routine alone transformed the impact I've had on my marketplace."

A jagged scar ran along the homeless man's forehead, just above his right eye. His threatening beard was gray. Around his neck he sported a beaded necklace, like the ones Indian holy men wear at their temples. Though his hyperbole made him sound unstable and his visage made it appear that he'd lived on the streets for many years, his voice displayed an irregular sense of authority. And his eyes revealed the confidence of a lion.

"Total crackpot," the entrepreneur whispered to the artist. "If he's got a fortune, I'm Mother Teresa."

"Got you. He seems insane," the artist replied. "But check out his humungous watch."

On the left wrist of the homeless man, who seemed to be in his late sixties, was one of those massive timepieces that British hedge fund managers are prone to wear when they go out to dinner in Mayfair. It had a dial the color of a revolver surrounded by a stainless-steel rim, a red needle-thin hour hand and a sunset orange minute hand. This noteworthy badge of honor was united with a wide black rubber strap, lending a diver-like feel to the whole luxurious look.

"A hundred grand, easily," said the entrepreneur discreetly. "Some of the people at my shop bought watches like that the day after our IPO. Unfortunately, our share price plummeted. But they kept their damn timepieces."

"So, what part of The Spellbinder's talk did you cats like best?" the vagabond asked, still scratching his wrist. "Was it all the stuff about the psychology of genius that he started out with? Or maybe those incredible models he taught on the productivity hacks of billionaires that he jammed on in the middle? Maybe you were stoked by all the neurobiology that creates top performance. Or did you vibe with his theory on our responsibility to reach legendary while serving as an instrument for the benefit of humanity that he walked us through before that dramatic finish?" The homeless man then winked. And glanced at his big watch.

"Hey, dudes, this has been fun. But time is one of the most precious commodities I've learned to bulletproof. Warren Buffett, the brilliant investor, said the rich invest in time. The poor invest in money. So I can't hang with you humans too long. Got a meeting with a jet and a runway. Know what I mean?"

"He seems to be delusional," thought the entrepreneur.

"Buffett also said, 'I buy expensive suits. They just look cheap on me.' Maybe you'll remember that quote, too. And," she continued, "I really don't mean to be rude, but I'm not sure how you got in here. And I have no idea where you got that fat watch from or what jet you're talking about. And please stop speaking the way you do about what happened at the presentation. Nothing funny about it. Seriously, I'm not sure the gentleman's still breathing."

"Def true," the artist agreed as he stroked his goatee. "Not cool. And why do you talk like a surfer?"

"Hey guys, chill," said the homeless man. "First, I *am* a surfer. I spent my teenage years on a board in Malibu. Used to ride near a point where the rad breaks are. Now I surf the smaller waves in Tamarin Bay, a spot you cats have probably never been to."

"Never heard of the place. You're fairly outrageous," the entrepreneur said frostily.

The homeless man was unstoppable.

"And second, I *have* been very successful in the business world. I've built a bunch of companies that are extremely profitable in this age of firms making billions in income yet nothing on their bottom line. What a joke. The world's going a little berserk. Too much greed and not enough good sense. And third, if I may," he added as his gravelly voice grew stronger, "there *is* a plane waiting for me. On a tarmac not so far from here. So, before I go, I'll ask you again—because I want to know. What part of The Spellbinder's presentation did you two like best?"

"Pretty much the whole thing," the artist answered. "Loved it all so much, I recorded every word the old legend said."

"That's illegal," cautioned the homeless man, crossing his arms firmly. "You could get into serious lawyer trouble doing that."

"It is against the law," confirmed the entrepreneur. "Why would you do that?"

"Because I wanted to. Just felt like it. I do what I want to do. Rules are made for destruction, you know? Picasso said you should learn the rules like a pro so you can break them like an artist. Need to be myself and not some sheep with no balls, blindly following the flock down a path that leads to nowhere. Most people, especially people with cash, are nothing but a bunch of frauds," declared the artist. "It's like The Spellbinder sometimes says: 'You can fit in. Or you can change the world. You don't get to do both.' So, I recorded the whole thing. Shoot me. And jail would be interesting. I'd probably meet some cool people in there."

"Um, okay," said the homeless man. "I don't like your decision. But I do love your passion. So, go ahead. Bring it on. Play the parts of the seminar that turned you on."

"Everything I recorded will blow your mind!" The artist raised his arm to reveal a detailed tattoo of guitar virtuoso Jimi Hendrix. The phrase "When the power of love overcomes the love of power, the world will know peace" appeared over the dead superstar's face. "You're about to hear something special," he added.

"Yes. Go ahead and play the parts you liked," encouraged the entrepreneur as she stood up. She wasn't quite sure why but, ever so slightly, something was beginning to shift deep within her core. "Maybe life has been breaking me down," she thought. "So I can make some sort of a breakthrough."

Being at this event, meeting the artist, hearing The Spellbinder's words, even if she didn't agree with all he said, was giving her the feeling that what she was experiencing at her firm just might be some form of preparation demanded by her greatness. The entrepreneur was still skeptical. But she sensed she was opening. And possibly growing. So, she promised herself she'd keep following this process instead of retreating. Her former way of existing no longer served her. It was time for a change.

The entrepreneur thought about a quote she loved from Theodore Roosevelt: "It's not the critic who counts; not the man who points out how the strong man stumbles, or where the doer of deeds could have done them better. The credit belongs to the man who is actually in the arena, whose face is marred by dust and sweat and blood; who strives valiantly; who errs, who comes up short again and again because there is no effort without error and shortcoming; but who does actually strive to do the deeds; who knows great enthusiasms, the great devotions; who spends himself in a worthy cause; who at the best knows in the end the triumph of high achievement, and who at the worst, if he fails, at least fails while daring greatly, so that his place shall never be with those cold and timid souls who neither know victory nor defeat."

She also recalled the phrase she'd learned from The Spellbinder's address—something like "The moment when you most feel like giving up is the instant when you must find it in you to press ahead." And so, the businesswoman reached deep within herself and made a vow to continue her quest to find her answers, solve her problems and experience vastly better days. Her hope was gradually expanding, and her worries were slowly shrinking. And the small, still voice of her finest self was beginning to whisper that a very special adventure was about to begin.

CHAPTER 4

Letting Go of Mediocrity and All That's Ordinary

"Why, sometimes I've believed as many as six impossible things before breakfast." —**Lewis Carroll**, *Alice in Wonderland*

"You're a painter, right?" the homeless man asked as he toyed with a loose button on his shabby shirt.

"Yeah," mumbled the artist. "Sort of a frustrated one. I'm good. But not great."

"I have a lot of art at my flat in Zurich," said the homeless man, smiling indulgently. "Bought a place right on the Bahnhofstrasse just before the prices skyrocketed. I've learned the importance of being around only the highest quality, wherever I go. That's one of the best winning moves I've made to create the life I've crafted. In my businesses, I only allow in top players, because you can't have an A-level company with C-level performers. We only release products that totally disrupt our market and then absolutely change the field by how valuable they are. My enterprises only offer services that ethically enrich our clients, deliver a breathtaking user experience and breed fanatical followers who couldn't imagine doing business with anyone else. And in my personal life, it's the same thing: I only eat the best food, though I don't eat a lot of it. I only read the most original and thoughtful books, spend my time in the most light-filled and inspiring of spaces and visit the most enchanting of places. And when it comes to relationships, I only surround myself with human beings who fuel my joy, stoke my peace and excite me to become a better man. Life's way too valuable to hang with people who don't get you. Who you just don't vibe with. Who have different values and lower standards than you do. Who have different Mindsets, Heartsets, Healthsets and Soulsets. It's a little miracle how powerfully and profoundly our influences and environments shape our productivity as well as our impact."

"Interesting," noted the entrepreneur as she stared at her phone. "He does seem to know what he's talking about," she muttered softly to the artist, her eyes still down on the screen.

The spider's web of wrinkles on her face relaxed further. On one wrist dangled two immaculate silver bracelets. One bore the phrase "Turn I cant's into I cans," while the other was engraved with "Done Is Better Than Perfect." The entrepreneur had purchased these presents for herself when her company was in its startup phase and she'd been in a highly confident mood.

"I know about Mindsets," said the artist. "Never heard of Heartsets, Healthsets and Soulsets, man."

"You will," suggested the homeless man. "And once you do, the way you create, produce and show up in your world will never be the same. Seriously revolutionary concepts for any empire-maker and world-builder. And so few businesspeople and other human beings on the planet currently know about them. If they did, every important element of their lives would increase rapidly. For now, I just wanted to keep jamming on my personal commitment to ultra-high quality, in everything around me. Your surroundings really do shape your perceptions, your inspirations and your implementations. Art feeds my soul. Great books battleproof my hope. Rich conversations magnify my creativity. Wonderful music uplifts my heart. Beautiful sights fortify my spirit. And all it takes is a single morning filled with positivity to deliver a monumental download of inventive ideas that elevate an entire generation, you know. And I need to say that uplifting human-kind is the master sport of business that The Top 5% play. The real purpose of commerce is not only to make your personal fortune. The true reason to be in the game is to be helpful to society. My main focus in business is to serve. Money, power and prestige are just the inevitable by-products that have shown up for me along the way. An old and remarkable friend taught me this way of operating when I was a young man. It totally transformed the state of my prosperity and the magnitude of my private freedom. And this contrarian business philosophy has dominated my way of doing things ever since. Who knows, maybe I'll introduce my mentor to you sometime."

The vagrant paused. He studied his large watch. Next he closed his eyes and said these words: "Own your morning. Elevate your life." As if by magic, a fairly small and quite thick piece of white paper appeared in the palm of his outstretched left hand. It was quite a trick. You would have been exceedingly impressed if you were standing there with these three souls.

Here's what the image on the paper looked like:

The entrepreneur and the artist both had their mouths open at this point, appearing to be both confused and mesmerized.

"You two each have a hero inside of you. You knew this as a child before adults told you to limit your powers, shackle your genius and betray the truths of your heart," the homeless man told them, sounding a lot like The Spellbinder.

"Adults are deteriorated children," he went on. "When you were much younger, you understood how to live. Staring at stars filled you with delight. Running in a park made you feel alive. And chasing butterflies flooded you with joy. Oh, how I adore butterflies. Then, as you grew up, you forgot how to be human. You forgot how to be bold and enthusiastic and loving and wildly alive. Your precious reservoirs of hope faded. Being ordinary became acceptable. The lamp of your creativity, your positivity and your intimacy with your greatness grew dim as you began to worry about fitting in, having more than others and being popular. Well, here's what I say: participate not in the world of numbed-out grownups, with its scarcity, apathy and limitation. I'm inviting you to enter a secret reality known only to the true masters, great geniuses and genuine legends of history. And to discover primal powers within you that you never knew were there. You can create magic in your work and personal lives. I sure have. And I'm here to help you do so."

Before the entrepreneur and the artist could utter even a word, the homeless man continued his discourse. "Oh, I was jamming on the importance of art. And the ecosystem that your life is built within. Makes me think of the awesome words of the Portuguese writer Fernando Pessoa: 'Art frees us, through illusion, from the squalor of being. While feeling the wrongs and sufferings endured by Hamlet, Prince of Denmark, we don't feel our own, which are vile because they're ours and vile because they're vile.' Also reminds me of what Vincent van Gogh said: 'For my part I know nothing with any certainty, but the sight of the stars makes me dream.'"

The homeless man swallowed hard. His eyes darted away. He cleared his throat nervously.

"Guys, I've been through a lot. Been knocked down and kicked around a ton by life. Been sick. Been attacked. Been abused. Been misused. Hey, I'm sounding like a country song. If my gal cheated on me and my dog died, I'd have a hit single."

The homeless man laughed. An odd, guttural, circus clown on acid sort of laugh. He carried on. "Anyway, it's all good. Pain is the doorway into deep. Know what I mean? And tragedy is nature's great purifier. It burns away the fakeness, fear and arrogance that is of the ego. Returns us to our brilliance and genius, if you have the courage to go into that which wounds you. Suffering yields many rewards, including empathy, originality, relatability and authenticity. Jonas Salk said, 'I have had dreams and I've had nightmares, but I have conquered my nightmares because of my dreams,'" the uninvited vagabond added wistfully.

"He's super-weird. Incredibly eccentric. But there's something special to him," admitted the entrepreneur quietly to the artist, removing just a little more of the armor of cynicism that had protected her over her stellar career. "What he just said is exactly what I've needed to hear. I get that he looks like he lives in a cardboard box on the streets. But listen to his words. Sometimes he speaks like a poet. How could he be so articulate? Where did his depth come from? And who is this 'old friend' he says has taught him so much? He also has a warmth that reminds me of my dad. I still miss him. He was my confidant. My top supporter. And my best friend. I think of him every day."

"Okay," said the artist to the quirky stranger. "You asked me what I liked best from the talk. I def liked the part where The Spellbinder talked about the Spartan warrior credo that says, 'one who sweats more in training bleeds less in war.' And I liked his line 'high victory is made in those early morning hours when no one's watching and while everyone else is sleeping.' His teachings on the value of a world-class morning routine were great."

The entrepreneur glanced down at her device. "I've taken some good notes. But I didn't pick up those gems," she said as she captured what she had just heard.

"We only hear what we're ready to hear," observed the homeless man sagely. "All learning meets us exactly where we're at. And as we grow greater, we understand better."

The voice of The Spellbinder suddenly rang out. The homeless man's eyes looked as huge as the Taj Mahal. One could see he was terrifically surprised to hear that famous tone. He spun around—seeking the source. Quickly, all became clear.

The artist was playing his illicit recording from the seminar.

"Here's the part I liked most, to fully answer your question, brother," he stated, staring directly into the eyes of the shabby tramp.

In a culture of cyber-zombies, addicted to distraction and afflicted with interruption, the wisest way to guarantee that you consistently produce mastery-level results in the most important areas of your professional and personal life is to install a world-class morning routine. Winning starts at your beginning. And your first hours are when heroes are made.

Wage a war against weakness and launch a campaign against fearfulness. You truly can get up early. And doing so is a necessity in your awesome pursuit toward legendary.

Take excellent care of the front end of your day, and the rest of your day will pretty much take care of itself. Own your morning. Elevate your life.

The Spellbinder could be heard wheezing like a novice swimmer who went too far, too fast. The artist continued presenting his recording, turning up the volume so the sound was blaring.

Here's the precious little secret that the titans of industry, the standout performers of artistry and the ultra-achievers of humanity will never share with you: gargantuan results are much less about your inherited genetics and far more about your daily habits. And your morning ritual is by far the most essential one to calibrate. And then automate.

When we see the icons in action, the forceful seduction sold to us by our civilization is to believe they were always that great. That they were born into their exceptionalism. That they won the fortunate DNA lottery. That their genius was inherited. Yet the truth is that we are watching them in their full blazing glory after years of following a process, one that involved ceaseless hours of practice. When we observe magnificent players in business, sport, science and the arts we are observing the earned results of a monomaniacal concentration around a single pursuit, astronomical focus on one skill, intensity of sacrifice applied to one aim, unusual levels of deep preparation and extreme amounts of solid patience. Remember, every professional was once an amateur, and every master started as a beginner. Ordinary people can accomplish extraordinary feats, once they've routinized the right habits.

"This cat is so solid," said the homeless man. He clapped his dirty hands like a kid at a carnival. He checked his watch yet again. Then he began to shuffle his feet while swaying his hips forward then backward. His hands were now waving in the air and he was snapping his fingers, with closed eyes again. Sounds like the early rappers used to make without their boom boxes emerged from his cracked lips. You would have been astonished to watch him in action.

"What the hell are you doing?" shouted the artist.

"Dancing," replied the homeless man, moving gloriously. "Keep bringing me this beautiful knowledge. Socrates said, 'Education is the kindling of a flame.' And Isaac Asimov wrote 'Self-education is, I believe, the only kind of education there is.' So, keep playing the old guru's words, dude. It's all so gnarly."

The artist resumed the recording:

Heavily resist all piracy of your mastery from this world tempting you into distractibility and causing digital dementia. Force your attention back to the Everests of potential aching for fuller expression and, today, release all reasons that feed any stagnation of your strengths. Start being an imaginationalist—one of those rare individuals who leads from the nobility of your future versus via the prison bars of your past. Each of us thirsts for days filled with tiny bursts of the miraculous. Every one of us wishes to own our pure heroism and step into unchained exceptionalism. All human beings alive at this moment have a primitive psychological need to produce masterworks that wow, live daily amidst uncommon awe and know that we are somehow spending our hours in a way that enriches the lives of others. The poet Thomas Campbell said it beautifully when he observed, "To live in hearts we leave behind is not to die."

Each of us—truly—has been built to make history, in our own authentic way. For one, this might mean being an excellent coder or a fine teacher who lifts young minds. For another, this opportunity could mean becoming a tremendous mother or a magnificent manager. To yet another, this good fortune may mean growing a great business or being a fantastic salesperson who serves customers superbly. This chance to be remembered by future generations and lead a life that truly matters is not some platitude. This is, in fact, a truth. Yet, so few of us have discovered, and then installed, the very mentalities, morning practices and consistent conditions that will guarantee these results appear for us. We all want to reaccess our birthright of towering talent, limitless joy and freedom from fear, but few of us are willing to do the very things that would cause our hidden genius to present itself. Strange, right? And it's very sad. The majority of us have been hypnotized out of the luminosity that is our essence. Most of us in this age spend our most valuable hours being busy being busy.

Chasing trivial pursuits and artificial amusements while neglecting living a real life. This is a formula for heartbreak at the end. What's the point of spending your best mornings and potentially productive days climbing mountains that you realize were the wrong ones when you are frail and wrinkled? Very sad.

"That part really resonated with me," interjected the entrepreneur, slightly emotionally. "I'm definitely addicted to my technology. Can't stop checking everything. First thing in the morning and last thing at night. It's draining my concentration. I can hardly focus on the important deliverables my team and I have committed to. And all the noise in my life is taking my energy. It all feels so complicated. I just don't feel I have any time for myself anymore. It's fairly overwhelming, all the messages and notifications and ads and diversions. And what The Spellbinder said is also so helpful to me as I raise my standards as a leader. I've sort of hit a wall. My company has grown faster than I ever expected. I've become more successful than I ever imagined. But there are some things causing me a ton of stress." She looked away and crossed her arms again.

"I can't tell them what I'm really dealing with," thought the entrepreneur.

Then she continued: "I've had to let go of people I really liked because I've learned people who fit at one stage of a business's lifecycle may not work as the firm evolves. That's been hard. They were the right employees for an earlier time but they don't belong now. And some things are unfolding at my shop that have turned my life upside down. I don't really want to get into it. It's just a very shaky time for me."

"Well, on your point about elevating your leadership game," responded the homeless man, "please remember that the job of the leader is to help disbelievers embrace your vision, the powerless to overcome their weaknesses and the hopeless to develop faith. And what you said on letting go of employees you liked but who no longer fit where your business is now at—that's a normal part of growing a business. And it happened because they failed to grow as your enterprise rose. They started coasting. They stopped learning, inventing and making everything they touched better than they found it. And as a result they stopped being awesome value incubators for your venture. They likely blamed you. But they did it to themselves," the uninvited stranger indicated, surprising his listeners by the sophistication of his insights on team-building and winning in commerce.

"Uh. Exactly," replied the entrepreneur. "So we had to leave them behind since they no longer delivered the results we were paying them for. A lot of nights I wake up at 2 AM soaked in steamy sweat. Maybe it's like what F1 racer Mario Andretti said: 'If everything seems under control you're not going fast enough.' That's how I seem to feel most days. We're blowing past our key performance indicators so quickly it makes my head spin. New teammates to mentor, new brands to manage, new markets to penetrate, new suppliers to watch, new products to refine, new investors and shareholders to impress and a thousand new responsibilities to handle. It really does feel like it's a lot. I have a huge capacity to get big things done. But there's a lot on my shoulders."

The entrepreneur tightened her arms and scrunched her forehead together absentmindedly. Her thin lips pulled together like a sea anemone shutting on sensing a fatal predator. And her eyes suggested she was suffering. Intensely.

"And, about your point about being addicted to technology, just remember that *intelligently* used, it advances human progress. Through using technology wisely our lives become better, our knowledge becomes richer and our wonderful world becomes smaller. It's the *misuse* of technology that's ruining people's minds, damaging their productivity and destroying the very fabric of our society. Your phone is costing you your fortune, you know? If you're playing with it all day long. And what you just said about all the pressure on you, how fantastic. 'Pressure is a privilege,' said tennis legend Billie Jean King," the homeless man shared. "You get to grow. And ascending as a person is one of the smart-est ways to spend the rest of your life. With every challenge comes the gorgeous opportunity to rise into your next level as a leader, performer and human being. Obstacles are nothing more than tests designed to measure how seriously you want the rewards that your ambitions seek. They show up to determine how willing you are to improve into the kind of person who can hold that amount of success. Failure's just growth in wolf's clothing. And pretty much nothing else is as important in life as personal expansion, the unfoldment of your potential. Tolstoy wrote, 'Everyone thinks of changing the world but no one thinks of changing himself.' Become a bigger person and you'll also automatically become a better leader—and a greater producer. And yes, I agree that growth can be scary. But my mentor once taught me that 'the part of you that clings to fear must experience a sort of crucifixion so that the portion of you that deserves high honor undergoes a kind of reincarnation.' Those are the exact words he shared with me. Freaky and deep, right?" said the hobo as he rubbed the holy-man beads he was wearing.

He kept going without waiting for an answer.

"My special teacher also told me that 'to find your best self you must lose your weak self.' And that only happens through relentless improvement, continuous reflection and ongoing self-excavation. If you don't keep rising daily you'll get stuck in your life, for the rest of your life. Makes me consider what the journalist Norman Cousins said: 'The tragedy of life is not death but what we let die inside of us while we live.'"

The homeless man raised his raspy voice and observed, "My special teacher taught me that once we transform the primary relationship with ourselves, we'll find that our relationships with other people, our work, our income and our impact transform. Most people can't stand them-selves. So, they can never be alone. And silent. They need to constantly be with other people to escape their feelings of self-hatred over all their wasted potential, missing the wonders and wisdom that solitude and quiet bring. Or they watch TV endlessly, not realizing it's eroding their imagination as well as bankrupting their bank account."

"My life feels so complicated. I feel so overwhelmed. I don't have any time for myself," the entrepreneur repeated. "Not sure what's happened to my life. Things have just become hard."

"I understand you," the artist said as he placed an arm over his new friend's shoulder. "My intuition tells me that you're going through a lot more than you're sharing. And that's okay. You know, some days life seems so messy that I can't get out of bed. I just lie there, man. I close my eyes and wish the fog in my head would just go away. Even for a day. I can't think straight some of the time. And on those days, my heart has no hope in it at all. It sucks. And a lot of people suck, too, man. I'm not anti-social. I'm just anti-moron. Too many dumb people around these days. Taking stupid fashion pictures of themselves with pouty lips in clothes they can't afford. Hanging with people they don't even like. I'd rather live a thoughtful life. A risky life. A real life. An artist's life. Drives me crazy how superficial people have become."

The artist then punched one fist into his other hand. Unyielding creases appeared along his jawline and a blue vein twitched in his thick neck.

"Sure. I got you," said the homeless man. "Life isn't easy, people. Tough slog a lot of the time. But like John Lennon said: 'Everything will be okay in the end. And if it's not okay, it's not the end,'" he offered kindly, spouting yet another quote from what seemed to be an unlimited supply in his brain.

The artist softened instantly, smiling in a way that looked almost sweet. He exhaled mightily. He liked what he'd just heard.

"And," the vagrant continued, "this climb up into the rare-air of personal and professional mastery that the three of us have obviously signed up for is not for the weak. Upgrading your life so you know real joy and optimizing your skills so you own your field can be uncomfortable a lot of the time. I need to be honest. But here's one key thing I've learned: the soreness of growth is so much less expensive than the devastating costs of regret."

"Where'd you learn that?" questioned the artist, as he scrawled the words into his notebook.

"Can't tell you. Yet," the homeless man responded, heightening the mystery of where he'd discovered much of his insight.

The entrepreneur turned away from the artist and jotted down some of her thoughts into her device. The homeless man then reached into a pocket of his hole-ridden plaid shirt and produced a heavily used index card. He held it up like a kindergarten student at show-and-tell.

"A distinguished person gave this to me when I was a lot younger, as I was starting my first company. I was a lot like you cats: dripping with dreams and set to make my mark on the world. Hungry to prove myself. Amped to dominate the game. The first fifty years of our lives are a lot about seeking legitimacy, you know. We crave social approval. We want our peers to respect us. We hope our neighbors will like us. We buy all sorts of things we really don't need and obsess about making money we really don't enjoy."

"Totally right," muttered the artist, nodding his head aggressively and shifting his posture noticeably as his dreadlocks dangled over his shoulders.

The event venue was now empty.

"If we have the courage to look within, we discover that we do this because we have a series of holes within us. We falsely believe that material from the outside will fill what's empty within ourselves. Yet it never will. Never will. Anyhoo, when many of us reach the half-time point of our lives, we make a right-angle turn. We begin to realize that we're not going to live forever and that our days are numbered. And so, we connect with our mortality. Big point here. We realize we are going to die. What's truly important comes into much sharper focus. We become more contemplative. We start to wonder if we've been true to our talents,

31

loyal to our values and successful on the terms that feel right to us. And we think about what those we most love will say about us when we're gone. That's when many of us make a giant shift: from seeking legitimacy in society to constructing a meaningful legacy. The last fifty years then become less about *me* and more about *we*. Less about selfishness and more about service. We stop adding more things into our lives and begin to subtract—and simplify. We learn to savor simple beauty, experience gratitude for small miracles, appreciate the priceless value of peace of mind, spend more time cultivating human connections and come to understand that the one who gives the most is victorious. And what's left of your life then becomes a phenomenal dedication to loving life itself as well as a ministry of kindness to the many. And this becomes, potentially, your gateway into immortality."

"He's really special," whispered the entrepreneur. "I haven't felt this hopeful, energized and grounded in months. My father used to help me navigate difficult times," she told the artist. "Ever since he passed away I don't have anyone to lean on."

"What happened to him?" quizzed the artist.

"I'm a little fragile right now, even though I feel stronger now than I did when I walked in here this morning, that's for sure. But I'll simply say that he took his own life. Dad was a remarkable man—a tremendously successful business pioneer. He flew airplanes, raced fast cars and loved superb wine. He was so *alive*. Then his business partner took everything away from him, not so different from the horrible scenario I'm living right now. Anyway, the stress and shock of his world collapsing pushed him to do what we could never have imagined. He just couldn't see any way out, I guess," the entrepreneur revealed as her voice broke.

"You can lean on me," the artist said tenderly. He placed a hand with a hippie ring on a pinky finger onto his heart as he spoke these words, looking both chivalrous and bohemian.

The homeless man interrupted the intimate moment the two were sharing.

"Here, read this," he instructed as he handed over his index card. "It'll be useful as you both rise to your next performance levels and experience everything that comes with this adventure into human leadership, personal mastery and creating a career of uncommon productivity."

In red lettering over the paper that had yellowed by the advances of time, it read: "*All change is hard at first, messy in the middle and gorgeous at the end.*"

"That's very good," noted the entrepreneur. "A valuable piece of information for me. Thank you."

The artist then resumed playing his illegal copy of The Spellbinder's presentation:

Each one of you carries a quiet genius and a triumphant hero within your hearts. Dismiss these as idealistic words of an elderly inspirationalist if you wish. But I'm proud to be an idealist. Our world needs more of us. And yet, I am also a realist. And here's the truth: Most people on the planet today don't think much of themselves, unfortunately. They secure their identity by who they are externally. They evaluate their achievement by what they've collected versus by the character they've cultivated. They compare themselves to the orchestrated— and fake—highlight reels presented by the people they follow. They measure their self-worth by their net worth. And they get kidnapped by the false thought that because something has never been done it can't be done—depleting the grand and electrifying possibilities their lives are meant to become. This explains why the majority is sinking in the quicksand of uncertainty, boredom, distraction and complexity.

"Drama mamas," the homeless man interrupted again. "That's what I call men and women who've caught the virus of victimitis excusitis. All they do is complain about how bad things are for them instead of applying their primal power to make things better. They take instead of give, criticize instead of create and worry instead of work. Build antibodies to combat any form of average from getting anywhere near your professional days at the office and your private life at home. Never be a drama mama."

The entrepreneur and the artist peeked at each other. Then they giggled, both at the terms the quirky stranger was using and at the way he'd raised an arm and made the fingers of one hand into a peace sign as he spoke the words he'd just shared. If you were standing there with them, you would think he was weird too.

The Spellbinder could then be heard speaking the following words on the recording with dramatic flair:

To be clear, every day—for the rest of your life—you'll be faced with the chance of showing leadership, wherever you are and in all that you do. Leadership isn't just for global icons and marketplace titans. It's an arena everyone gets to play in. Because leadership is a lot less about having a formal title, a large office and money in the bank. And a lot more about committing to mastery over all you do—and in who you are. It's about resisting the tyranny of the ordinary, refusing to allow negativity to hijack your sense of awe and preventing any form of slavery to mediocrity from infesting your life. Leadership is about making a difference, right where you're planted. Real leadership is about sending out brave work that exemplifies genius, turns your whole field on its head by its scope, innovation and execution, and is so staggeringly sublime that it stands the test of time.

And never work only for the income. Labor for the impact. Make your dominant pursuit the heartfelt release of value that represents an uncommon magic that borders on the poetic. Demonstrate the full-on expression of what's possible for a human being to create. Develop the patience to stick with your dedication to absolute world-class output, even if over a lifetime you only generate a single masterpiece. To achieve this feat alone will have made your life's journey a worthy trek.

Be a virtuoso. A standout. An exceptionalist. The Top 5% are a lot less concerned with fame, cash and approval and a lot more invested in punching above their weight class within their craft, playing above their pay grade around their talents and creating the kind of productivity that inspires—and serves—millions. That's often why they make millions. So never mail it in. *Always bring it on.*

The homeless man now had his eyes closed. And was down on the floor doing a series of one-armed push-ups. All the while he was chanting, "Own your morning. Elevate your life."

The entrepreneur and the artist shook their heads.

"One of my favorite books is *The Prophet,*" mused the artist. "It's one of the bestselling works of poetry ever written. I read that Khalil Gibran carried the manuscript around with him for four long years and refined it constantly before giving it to his publisher, just so it was pure art. I still remember the exact words he spoke when he was interviewed by a journalist about his creative process because they guide me a lot when I'm in the studio. His words keep me reaching for a greater power as an artist, even though I battle procrastination a lot. Like I said, I'm pretty good. But I know I can be great. If I could just beat my self-sabotage. And my demons."

"What did he say?" asked the homeless man, now standing and twiddling with his big watch. Beads of perspiration meandered down his angular face.

"Here's exactly what he said," mentioned the artist: "'I wanted to be sure, very sure, that every word of it was the very best I had to offer.'"

"Gnarly," replied the homeless man. "That's the standard that the best ones always hold themselves to."

Abruptly, The Spellbinder could be heard coughing in the audio. His comments that followed seemed to struggle out of him, like an unborn child fiercely reluctant to leave the security of its loving mother's warm and safe womb.

> Anyone can become an everyday leader by showing up as I'm encouraging. When it's easy and especially when it's difficult. Starting today. And if you do so, a guaranteed victory is in your future. And I need to add that there's not one person alive today who cannot lift their thinking, performance, vitality, prosperity and lifetime happiness magnificently by wiring in a series of profound daily rituals and then practicing them until they become your second nature. And this brings me to the single most important principle of my talk: The greatest starting point for winning in your work and making a splendid life is joining what I call The 5 AM Club. How can you ever be world-class if you don't carve out some time each morning to make yourself world-class?

The entrepreneur was now taking notes with a ferocious intensity not previously seen. The artist's face had a "this makes me feel strong" smile on it. The homeless man burped, then got down to the floor and held a plank, the kind fitness pros at the gym love to do to build a strong core.

You could hear The Spellbinder begin to cough even more fiercely. A brutal—and sustained—pause followed.

Next, he uttered these words, haltingly. He was wheezing audibly. His voice began to quiver like a novice telemarketer on her very first sales call.

> Rising at 5 AM truly is The Mother of All Routines. Joining The 5 AM Club is the one behavior that raises every other human behavior. This regimen is the ultimate needle mover to turn you into an undefeatable model of possibility. The way you begin your day really does determine the extent of focus, energy, excitement and excellence you bring to it. Each early morning is a page in the story that becomes

your legacy. Each new dawn is a fresh chance to unleash your brilliance, unprison your potency and play in the big leagues of iconic results. You have such power within you and it reveals itself most with the first rays of daybreak. Please do not allow past pains and present frustrations to diminish your glory, stifle your invincibility and choke the unlimited possibilitarian that lurks within the supreme part of you. In a world that seeks to keep you down, build yourself up. In an epoch that wishes you would stay in the dark, step into your light. At a time that mesmerizes you to forget your gifts, reclaim your genius. Our world requires this of each of us. To be champions of our crafts, warriors for our growth and guardians of unconditional love—for all of humankind.

Display respect and compassion for all other people who occupy this tiny planet, regardless of their creed, color or caste. Lift them up in a civilization where many get energy tearing others down. Help others sense the marvels that sleep within them. Show us the virtues we all wish more would practice. Everything I'm saying will speak to the unspoiled part of you, that side of yourself that was ferociously alive before you were taught to fear, hoard, contract and distrust. It's your job as a hero of your life, as a creative achiever set to change the culture and as a citizen of Earth to find this dimension within you. And, once done, to spend the rest of your days reconnected with it.

Accept this opportunity to human mastery and I promise you that a synchronicity of success as well as an orchestrated magic well beyond the boundaries of logic will infuse the remainder of your days. And the larger angels of your grandest potential will begin to visit you regularly. Actually, an orderly series of seemingly impossible miracles will descend onto your most genuine of dreams, causing the best of them to come true. And you will evolve into one of those rare and great spirits who upgrade the whole world by the simple act of walking amongst us.

The conference hall was now dark. The entrepreneur let out a sigh the size of Mexico City. The artist was motionless. The homeless man began to cry.

He then stood on a chair, raised his arms like a preacher and boomed these words of Irish playwright George Bernard Shaw:

This is the true joy in life, the being used for a purpose recognized by yourself as a mighty one; the being a force of nature instead of a feverish little clod of ailments and grievances complaining that the world will not devote itself to making you happy.

I am of the opinion that my life belongs to the whole community, and as long as I live it is my privilege to do for it whatever I can.

I want to be thoroughly used up when I die, for the harder I work the more I live. I rejoice in life for its own sake. Life is no 'brief candle' for me. It is a sort of splendid torch which I have got hold of for the moment, and I want to make it burn as brightly as possible before handing it on to future generations.

The homeless man then fell to his knees. Kissed his holy beads. And continued to weep.

CHAPTER 5

A Bizarre Adventure into Morning Mastery

"Everyone holds his fortune in his own hands, like a sculptor the raw material he will fashion into a figure. . . . The skill to mold the material into what we want must be learned and attentively cultivated." —Johann Wolfgang von Goethe

"If you two are interested," said the homeless man, "I'd be happy to spend a few mornings coaching you at my oceanside compound. I'll show you my private morning routine and explain why dialing in the way you run your first hour to the highest degree is essential for personal mastery and exceptional business performance. Let me do this for you cats. Your lives will start to look glorious—within a fairly short time. And the ride with me will be fun. Not always easy, as we heard from the old guy on the stage. But valuable and prolific and beautiful. Maybe even as wonderful as the ceiling of the Sistine Chapel."

"First time I saw it I cried," the artist said, stroking the hairs of his goatee.

"Michelangelo was a bad dude. And I mean that in a good way," the homeless man offered as he, too, played with his beard, which was soiled. He then raised his shirt to show Greek god abdominal muscles. A long finger of a grimy hand moved along the contours, the way a raindrop zigzags down the stem of a rose after a May shower.

"Hit me with a stick," shouted the artist with the enthusiasm of a cat let loose in a parrot shop. "How the heck did you get those?"

"Not from some plastic ab machine I bought from a late-night TV show, that's for sure. Work is how I got all lean and chiseled up like this. Plenty of push-ups, pull-ups, planks, sit-ups and seriously sweaty cardio sessions, often on my special beach." The homeless man pulled out an obviously expensive leather wallet, then carefully removed from it a piece of plastic with a drawing on it. Here's what it looked like, so you see exactly what the entrepreneur and the artist saw in that moment:

Without allowing for any responses from his two listeners, the disheveled drifter kept on speaking. "Commitment, discipline, patience and work. Values few believe in these days, where so many have an entitlement mentality, expecting a rich, productive and fulfilling life to just show up one day like a sparrow at the beginning of spring. And expecting everyone around them to invest the effort they are responsible for inputting. Where's the leadership in this way of operating?

"A society of adults behaving like spoiled little children is how I sometimes see our world right now. Not judging, just saying. Not complaining, just reporting. Hey, cats, here's the point I'm trying to make by letting you have a peek at my sculpted abs: *Nothing works for those who don't do the work*. Less talk and more do is what I say. Oh, and check this out."

The hobo spun around and unbuttoned his hole-ridden shirt. On his firm, striated back was a tattoo with the words "Victims love entertainment. Victors adore education."

"Come hang with me at my place on a magical little island in the middle of a fantastic ocean, five hours from the coast of Cape Town." He handed the entrepreneur the plastic card with the seaside scene etched on it. "Those are my dolphins," he said, happily pointing to the hand-drawn image.

"The trip will be so worth it," he continued. "The adventure of a lifetime, for sure. Some of your most valuable and sensational moments ever will unfold there. You need to take a trust walk with me, people. I'll teach you everything I know about a world-class morning ritual. I'll help you both become members of The 5 AM Club. You'll learn to rise early, regularly—so you'll get more done by noon than most people get done in a week, and so you'll optimize your health, happiness and peacefulness. There's a reason so many of the great achievers of the world get up before the sun—*it's the most special part of the day*. I'll explain how I used this revolutionary method to build my empire. And, to be clear, empires arrive in many forms—economic is just one of them. You can also create empires of artistry, productivity, humanity, philanthropy, personal freedom and even spirituality. I'll download pretty much everything I've been blessed to have been taught by the mentor who transformed my life. You'll discover so much. You'll be moved at the deepest level. You'll see the world through an all-new set of lenses. You'll also eat the finest food and watch the most spectacular sunsets. You guys can swim in the sea, go snorkeling with the dolphins and fly over the sugar cane stalks that dance in the wind in the helicopter I own. And should you both accept my heartfelt invitation to visit me, I insist you stay at my home."

"My God, you're kidding me, right?" boomed the artist. It was becoming increasingly evident that, like many in his field, he was acutely emotional, vigilant to the infinitesimal and carried a sensitivity born of latent pain. Those who feel more than most people sometimes believe they have been cursed. In fact, they have been granted a gift: one that allows them to sense what others miss, experience the delights that most neglect and notice the majesty in ordinary moments. Yes, such people get hurt more easily, yet they are also the ones who create great symphonies, architect dazzling buildings and find cures for the sick. Tolstoy once noted that "only people who are capable of loving strongly can suffer great sorrow," while the Sufi poet Rumi wrote, "You have to keep breaking your heart until it opens." The artist seemed to personify these insights.

"Nope. Totally serious, dudes," the homeless man said enthusiastically. "I have a house not far from a village called Solitude. And believe me, they named it accurately. It's only when you get away from the noise and nuisance and be in quiet and tranquility that you remember who—and all—you're truly meant to be. Just say yes to life. And let's do this! Like the guru on the platform said, a magic will show up for you the more you start exploiting the terrific opportunities that appear along your path, seemingly by accident. You can't win a game you don't play, right? The reality is that life has got your back, even when it doesn't look like it does. But you need to do your part and go all in when windows of opportunity appear. Oh—and if you come to my home on the island, the only thing I ask is that you stay long enough for me to teach you the philosophy and methodology that my secret adviser shared with me. Joining The 5 AM Club requires a little time."

The homeless man paused before adding, "I'm also going to take care of all your expenses. Everything's covered. I'll even send my private jet to pick you guys up, if that's cool."

The entrepreneur and the artist glanced at each other, amused, confounded and entirely uncertain.

"Mind if my friend and I have a few moments alone, brother?" requested the artist, notebook still in hand.

42

"No sweat. Sure. Take all the time you need. I'll just go back to my seat over there and make some calls to my executive team," mentioned the homeless man as he paced away.

"This is absurd. Just asinine," the artist said to the entrepreneur. "I def agree with you that there's something special about him. Maybe even something magical. I know how insane that sounds. And I *am* fascinated by this mentor he keeps talking about, this teacher who sort of sounds like a modern-day master. I'll admit that this street person has got some great insights, for sure. And he obviously seems to have a lot of experience. But just look at him! Man, the guy looks completely down and out—a complete mess. I don't think he's had a shower in weeks. His clothes are all ripped. He's beyond freaky. And sometimes he talks total crazy talk. We have no idea who he is. This could be dangerous. He could be dangerous."

"Yes. Definitely super-weird. *Everything* that's happened here today is super-weird," confirmed his companion. The entrepreneur's lean face then softened. Her eyes still seemed melancholic, though. "I'm at a place in my life where I need to make some big changes," she confided. "I just can't keep going on like this. I hear what you're saying. I've been suspicious of pretty much everyone and everything ever since I lost my dad when I was eleven. A daughter growing up without a father is incredibly scary. To be honest, I still carry a lot of the emotional trauma with me. I think of him every day. I've had some bad intimate relationships. I've struggled a lot with low self-worth and made some horrible choices in the relationships I've had.

"About a year ago I started seeing a therapist who made me aware of why I was behaving the way I was behaving," the entrepreneur continued. "Psychologists call it 'fatherless daughter syndrome.' Deep within, I had a huge fear of abandonment and all the strong insecurities that come with that wound. Yes, this made me extraordinarily tough on the outside. And ruthless in some ways. The chip on my shoulder over the loss of my father gave me my drive and my ambition. Yet the loss also left me empty within. I'm learning that I've been trying to fill the void that he left, when he left, by pushing myself to exhaustion in my work with the belief that when I'm even more successful I'll get the love I lost. I've been attempting to fill my emotional holes by chasing more money like a heroin addict needing a fix. I've been starving for social status and hungry for industry approval—escaping online for quick pleasure hits of entertainment when I could be doing things that matter. As I said, I'm realizing a lot of my behavior has been pushed from the fear created by my early challenges as a young woman. I felt inspired when The Spellbinder spoke about never doing something for the money but, instead, reaching for world-class as a leader and a person for the meaning it provides, for the opportunity to grow it provokes and for a shot at changing the world. His words made me feel so hopeful. I want to live in the way he spoke of, but I'm nowhere near that place now. And recently, what's happened at my company pushed me to the edge. I'm really not doing well at life right now. I only came to this meeting because my mom gave me a free ticket. And I'm so desperate for a change."

The entrepreneur took a deep breath. "Sorry," she apologized, looking embarrassed. "I hardly know you so I'm not sure why I'm revealing all this to you. I guess I just feel safe with you. I'm not sure why. I'm so sorry if I'm oversharing."

"No problem," said the artist. His body language showed he was engaged. He no longer anxiously played with his goatee and dreadlocks.

"We're so honest when we chat with taxi drivers and other people we don't really know, right?" the entrepreneur went on. "All I'm trying to say is that I'm ready for a transformation. And my gut tells me this down-and-out man who wants to teach us how an excellent morning routine can build creative, productive, financial and happiness empires really can help me. And help *us*.

"And," she added, "remember his watch."

"I like him," said the artist. "He's a character. I love that he expresses himself so poetically sometimes and so passionately at others. He thinks so vividly and quotes George Bernard Shaw like his life depended on it. Really cool. But I still don't really trust him," the artist expressed as he punched a fist into an open palm again. "Probably ripped the watch off some rich idiot."

"Look, I understand how you're feeling," responded the entrepreneur. "A lot of me feels the same way. And you and I just met as well. I'm not sure what it would be like to go on this trip with you. I hope you don't mind me saying that. You seem like such a nice person. A few rough edges maybe. I think I understand where those come from. But you're good deep down. I know it."

The artist looked mildly pleased. He glanced at the homeless man, who was eating slices of avocado from a plastic bag.

"I'll have to see if I can arrange my schedule to be away from the office so we can spend time with *him*," shared the entrepreneur as she pointed to the homeless man. While he was munching on his snack he was also talking on a relic of a mobile phone and staring at the ceiling. "I'm starting to like the idea of spending some time near a village called Solitude on some tiny island, eating fabulous food and swimming with wild dolphins. I'm beginning to feel this will be a phenomenal adventure. I'm starting to feel more alive again."

"Well, now that you say it that way, I'm liking the sound of this, too," said the artist. "I'm beginning to think there's a delicious insanity to all of this. A special opportunity to access a whole new universe of originality. This might be the best thing yet for my art. It makes me think of what the writer Charles Bukowski said: 'Some people never go crazy. What truly horrible lives they must lead.' And The Spellbinder did encourage us to leave the boundaries of our normal lives we grow into our gifts, talents and strengths. Some instinct is also telling me to do this. So, if you go, I'll go."

"Well, you know what? I'll take the leap. It's done. I'm all in. Let's go!" pronounced the entrepreneur.

"All in," agreed the artist.

They both stood up and made their way to the homeless man, who was now sitting with his eyes closed.

"What are you doing now?" quizzed the artist.

"Intense visualization of all I want to be and the higher order life I wish to create. A Turkish fighter pilot once told me that before every flight, he'd 'fly before we'd fly.' He was suggesting that meticulously rehearsing the way he and his team wanted the mission to unfold in the theater of his imagination set them up to execute that vision of mastery in reality, flawlessly. Your Mindset is an enormously potent tool for private greatness, prodigious productivity and creative victory—along with your Heartset, Healthset and Soulset. I'll teach you all about these remarkable concepts if you accept my invitation. Anyhoo, back to why I closed my eyes. Nearly every morning, I envision my ideal performance for the day ahead. I also reach deep into my emotions so I feel what it will feel like when I achieve the wins I've planned to accomplish. I lock myself into an extremely confident state where any form of failure isn't within the realm of possibility. Then I go out and do my finest to live out that perfect day."

"Interesting." The entrepreneur was fascinated.

"This is just one of the SOPs I run daily to stay on peak. Good science is confirming that this practice helps me upregulate my genome by turning on genes that were previously asleep. Your DNA isn't your destiny, you know. Not to worry, cats. You'll learn about the breakthrough field of epigenetics when you're on the island. You'll also learn some beautiful neuroscience on multiplying your success in this age of scattered attention, so the weapons of mass distraction don't destroy your amazingness. I'll reveal everything I've discovered about creating projects that are so masterfully done they endure for generations. You'll hear about fabulous ways to armor-plate your mental focus and fireproof your physical energy. You'll discover how the best businesspeople in the world build dominant enterprises and learn a calibrated system that the most joyful human beings on the planet apply each morning to create a life that borders on the magical. Oh, in case you were wondering, an SOP is a standard operating procedure. It's a term my special adviser used when he'd speak about the daily structures needed to find triumph at the game of life. I assume you two are coming?"

"Yes. We're coming," confirmed the entrepreneur in an upbeat tone. "Thank you for your offer."

"Yeah, thanks, man," added the artist, now looking more composed.

"Please," the entrepreneur said earnestly, "teach us *everything* you know about creating the morning routine of a high-impact leader and a supremely successful businessperson. I desperately want to improve my performance and my daily productivity. I'll also need your help to restructure my life. To be honest, I'm feeling more inspired today than I've felt in a long time. But I'm not in the best place."

"Yeah, brother," said the artist. "Tell us your secrets for an epic morning routine that helps me become the best painter—and man—I can become." He waved his notebook in the air as he spoke. "Send us your plane. Take us to your village. Give us some coconuts. Let us ride your dolphins. And improve our lives. We're all in."

"None of what you'll discover will be motivation," noted the scraggly soul with a degree of seriousness he hadn't shown before. "All of this will definitely be about *transformation*. And it will be supported by strong data, the latest research and immensely practical tactics that have been battle-tested in the tough trenches of industry. Get ready for the greatest adventure you cats will ever experience!"

"Excellent," declared the entrepreneur as she reached out to shake the weather-beaten stranger's hand. "I need to admit that this entire scenario has been extremely odd for both of us but, for whatever reason, we now trust you. And, yes, we're totally open to this new experience."

"You're very kind to do this for us. Thank you," blurted out the artist. He looked somewhat surprised by the extent of his graciousness.

"Awesome. Smart decision, guys," came the warm response. "Please be outside this conference center tomorrow morning. Bring at least a few days' worth of clothes. That's all. Like I said, I'm stoked to take care of everything else. All expenses are on me. I thank you."

"Why are you thanking us?" wondered the entrepreneur.

The homeless man smiled tenderly and scratched his beard thoughtfully. "In his final sermon before he was assassinated, Martin Luther King, Jr., said, 'Everybody can be great because anybody can serve. You don't have to have a college degree to serve. You don't have to make your subject and verb agree to serve. You don't have to know about Plato and Aristotle to serve. You don't have to know Einstein's Theory of Relativity to serve. You don't have to know the Second Theory of Thermodynamics and Physics to serve. You only need a heart full of grace. A soul generated by love.'"

The tramp wiped a morsel of avocado from the edge of his mouth and then carried on what he was saying.

"One of the big lessons I've learned over the years is that giving to other people is a gift you give to yourself. Raise the joy of others and you'll get even more joy. Increase the state of your fellow human beings and, naturally, your own state of being ascends. Success is cool. But significance is rad. Generosity—not scarcity—is the trait of all of the great men and women who have upgraded our world. And we need leaders, pure leaders and not narcissists obsessed with their own self-interests, as never before."

The homeless man looked down at his large watch one last time. "You can't take your title, net worth and fancy toys with you when you die, you know? I've yet to see a moving truck following a hearse on its way to a funeral." He chuckled. The two listeners grinned.

"He's a treasure," whispered the entrepreneur.

"Def is," acknowledged the artist.

"Stop saying 'def' so much," said the entrepreneur. "It's getting irritating."

The artist looked a little shocked. "Okay."

"All that matters on your last day on Earth is the potential you've leveraged, the heroism you've demonstrated and the human lives you've graced," the homeless man said eloquently. He then grew quiet. And let out a deep breath. "Anyhoo. Incredible that you're coming. We'll have a cool hang."

"May I bring my paintbrushes?" the artist asked politely.

"Only if you want to paint in paradise," came the homeless man's reply with a wink.

"And what time should we meet you outside this place tomorrow morning?" asked the entrepreneur, placing her handbag onto a thin, bony shoulder.

"5 AM," instructed the homeless man. "Own your morning. Elevate your life."

Then, he disappeared.

CHAPTER 6

A Flight to Peak Productivity, Virtuosity and Undefeatability

"Your time is limited, so don't waste it living someone else's life. Don't be trapped by dogma—which is living with the results of other people's thinking. Don't let the noise of others' opinions drown out your own inner voice. And most important, have the courage to follow your heart and intuition. They somehow already know what you truly want to become." —**Steve Jobs**

"I'm so tired," the entrepreneur muttered with the energy of an ancient turtle on a vacation day, while holding a monstrous cup of coffee. "This journey might be harder than I thought. I'm starting to feel like I'm walking into a whole new world. Like I told you yesterday after the seminar, I'm definitely ready to change. Set for a new beginning. But I'm also feeling uneasy about all this. I didn't sleep much last night. Such eerie—and sometimes violent—dreams. And, yes, this experience we've agreed to might be dangerous."

"Well, I feel like death, man," said the artist. "I hate being up this early. This was a terrible idea."

The two brave souls were standing on the sidewalk outside the hall where The Spellbinder had worked his legendary skills—and broken many hearts with his collapse—the day before.

It was 4:49 AM.

"He won't show up," barked the artist roughly. He was dressed in black with a ruby red polka-dotted bandana on his left wrist. Same boots as yesterday. Those Australian ones. He hurled a mouthful of spit into the desolate street. He squinted at the sky. And then he folded his tattooed arms.

The entrepreneur had a nylon duffle bag over her shoulder. She styled a silk blouse with bohemian sleeves, designer blue jeans and a pair of sandals with high heels—the kind you see off-duty supermodels with sunglasses the size of Greek island sunsets wearing. Her lips were scrunched together and the lines on her face were arrayed in a series of interesting intersections.

"I'd bet the homeless man's a no-show," she said with a sneer. "I don't care about his watch. It doesn't matter that he could be so articulate. It means nothing to me now that he reminded me of my dad. God, I'm exhausted. He was probably at the seminar because he needed a place to rest for a few hours. He probably knew about the whole 5 AM Club morning routine because he heard—and stole—that bit of The Spellbinder's presentation. And the private plane he talked about was probably part of his favorite hallucination."

The entrepreneur had returned to her familiar skepticism and hiding within her fortress of protection. The hopefulness of the day before had clearly dissolved.

Just then, a pair of strikingly powerful halogen headlights pierced the wall of darkness.

The two companions looked at each other. The entrepreneur managed a smile. "Okay. Maybe instinct really is much smarter than reason," she muttered to herself.

A gleaming Rolls-Royce, the color of coal, pulled up to the curb. With swift efficiency, a man in a crisp white uniform leapt out of the sedan and greeted the two with old-school civility.

"Good morning to you, Madam. And to you as well, Sir," he enunciated in a British accent as he placed their bags into the vehicle with one skillful swoop.

THE 5 AM CLUB

"Where's the derelict?" asked the artist with the tact of a hillbilly who'd never left the woods.

The driver couldn't help but laugh. Quickly, he regained his composure.

"So sorry, Sir. Yes, Mr. Riley dresses in very unassuming attire, shall we say. He does that when he feels the need to 'get gritty,' as he classifies the practice. He leads a remarkably exclusive life most of the time and is a man accustomed to getting anything he wants. Everything he wants, to be more precise. So, once in a while, he does things to ensure his modesty and humility remain in check. That's part of his quirky charm, I might add. Mr. Riley asked me to give these to you."

The driver pulled out two envelopes, made of the highest quality paper. On opening them, the entrepreneur and the artist saw these words:

Hey, cats! Hope you're awesome. Didn't mean to spook you both yesterday. I just needed to keep my boots on the ground. Epictetus, one of my favorite philosophers, wrote: "But neither a bull nor a noble-spirited man comes to be what he is all at once; he must undertake hard winter training and prepare himself and not propel himself rashly into what is not appropriate to him."

Voluntary discomfort, whether by dressing as I did or by fasting once a week or by sleeping on the floor once a month, keeps me strong, disciplined and focused on the central few priorities my life's built around. Anyhoo, have a tremendous flight, and I'll see you in Paradise soon. Big hug.

The driver continued, "Please remember that appearances can be misleading and clothing doesn't convey one's character. Yesterday you met a great man. Looks really do not reveal the quality of a person."

"I guess neither does shaving," proclaimed the artist, kicking a black boot against the shiny Rolls-Royce symbol at the center of one of the wheels.

"Mr. Riley would never tell you what I'm about to tell you as he's far too courteous and decent. But the gentleman you refer to as a 'derelict' happens to be one of the wealthiest people in the world."

"Are you serious?" asked the entrepreneur, her eyes widening.

"I most certainly am." The driver smiled politely as he opened a door, waving a white-gloved hand to welcome both passengers into the vehicle.

The seats had that marvelously musky smell of new leather. The wood paneling seemed like it had been prepared by hand, by a small family of finicky craftspeople who'd built their reputations around this singular obsession.

"Mr. Riley made his fortune many years ago, in various commercial ventures. He was also an early investor in what has now become an internationally admired company. Discretion prevents me from mentioning the name and, if Mr. Riley found out I was speaking of financial matters with you, he'd be exceedingly disappointed. His instructions were simply to treat you with the utmost of care along with assuring you of his sincerity and reliability. And to deliver you safely to Hangar 21."

"Hangar 21?" the artist asked as he eased languidly into the opulent vehicle like a rock star accustomed to this method of transport or a hip-hop artist ready for a weekend roll.

"That's where Mr. Riley's fleet of jets are kept," stated the driver succinctly.

"Fleet?" questioned the entrepreneur, her beautiful brown eyes alive with an immensely curious look.

"Yes," was all the chauffeur would allow.

There was silence as the driver sped through the early morning streets. The artist looked out the window while rolling a bottle of water in one hand absentmindedly. He hadn't seen the sun rising in many years. "Very special. Truly beautiful," he admitted. "Everything's so peaceful at this time of the day. No noise. Such peace. Even though I feel tired right now, I can really think. Things seem clearer. My attention isn't a mess. It feels like the rest of the world is asleep. What tranquility."

A cavalry of wispy amber rays, the ethereal palette of the daybreak and the quietude of this moment left him encouraged. And awestruck.

The entrepreneur studied the driver. "So, tell me more about your boss," she requested, restlessly toying with her device as she spoke.

"I can't tell you much more. He's worth multiple billions of dollars. He's given most of his money to charity. Mr. Riley's the most fascinating, generous and compassionate person I know. He also has incredible willpower, along with having ironclad values, such as honesty, empathy, integrity and loyalty. And, of course, he's also a real oddball, if I may be so bold as to say so. Like a lot of the very, very, very rich."

"We've noticed," agreed the entrepreneur. "I'm interested, though. What makes you say he's odd?"

"You'll see," was the stark response.

The Rolls soon arrived at a private airport. No sign of Mr. Riley. The driver accelerated up to an ivory jet that looked immaculately kept. The only color it bore appeared on the tail. In the hue of a mandarin orange, three characters read "5AC."

"What does '5AC' stand for?" asked the entrepreneur tensely, gripping her gadget tightly.

"The 5 AM Club. 'Own your morning. Elevate your life.' It's one of the maxims Mr. Riley has conducted his many business interests under. And now, with regret, this is where I must bid you adieu. Au revoir," he said before carrying the luggage over to the sparkling aircraft.

Two handsome crew members chatted near the metal stairway that led up to the cabin. A tastefully refined blonde flight attendant handed the entrepreneur and the artist hot towels and offered them coffee from a silver tray. "Dobroe utro," she said, greeting them in Russian.

"It has been a great pleasure to meet you," the driver called up to the jet, as he got back into the car. "Kindly convey my best wishes to Mr. Riley once you see him. And do have fun in Mauritius."

"Mauritius?" the companions exclaimed, as surprised as a vampire waking up to a garlic clove.

"This is all unbelievable," the artist said as he climbed into the cabin. "Mauritius! I've always wanted to go to that island, and I've read a bit about it. It's a high-frequency place. French flavor. Tremendous beauty. And, from what they say, many of the warmest and happiest people on Earth live there."

"I'm blown away, too," the entrepreneur said as she sipped her coffee and peeked into the cockpit. She studied the pilots as they performed their pre-flight preparation. "I've also heard Mauritius is splendid, and that the people are super-friendly, helpful and spiritually advanced."

After a perfect takeoff, the first-class plane floated high into the clouds. Once at cruising altitude, premium champagne was served, caviar was recommended and an array of fabulous main courses were suggested. The entrepreneur was feeling fairly content and far less incited by the cruel attempt of her investors to take her company away from her. True, this might not be the ideal time to take a vacation to learn about The 5 AM Club philosophy and its underlying methodology that had served Mr. Riley's ascent to business titan and global philanthropist like rocket fuel. Or perhaps this was the perfect time to get away from her usual reality to discover how the most successful, influential and joyful people on the planet start their days.

After sipping on some champagne, the entrepreneur watched a movie. She then fell into a deep sleep. The artist had a book called *Michelangelo Fiorentino et Rafael da Urbino: Masters of Art in the Vatican*. He read it for hours. You can just imagine how happy he felt.

The jet made its trajectory over a number of vast continents and above varied terrain. The flight was meticulously conducted, and the landing was as fluid as the overall experience was fine.

"Bienvenue au Île Maurice," announced the captain over the public address system as the aircraft taxied along the freshly paved runway. "Merci beaucoup. Welcome to Mauritius and Sir Seewoosagur Ramgoolam International Airport," he continued, speaking his words with the well-earned confidence of someone who had spent most of his life in the sky. "It's been a privilege having you two VIPs with us. We'll see you again in several days, from what Mr. Riley's personal assistant has informed us of your itinerary. Thank you once again for flying with us, and we trust that the journey was elegant, excellent and above all else, safe."

A polished black SUV glittered on the tarmac as the flight attendant escorted her special passengers off the plane and into the humming vehicle.

"Your luggage will follow shortly. Not to worry—it shall be delivered to your guest rooms at Mr. Riley's seaside estate. Spasiba," she added in a graceful tone and with an earnest wave.

"This is so A-list," observed the entrepreneur as she happily snapped some selfies, uncharacteristically pouting like a fashionista.

"Def," replied the artist, as he photobombed her, sticking out his tongue like Albert Einstein did in that famous photo that betrayed his seriousness as a scientist and revealed his undiminished childlike sense of wonder.

As the Range Rover rolled along the highway, tall stalks of sugar cane swayed in the fragrant breezes blown by the Indian Ocean. The quiet chauffeur wore a white cap, the kind you see bellmen at five-star hotels wearing, and a well-pressed dark gray uniform that hinted at an understated yet refined professionalism. He never missed slowing down when the speed limit descended and ensuring his signal light was on whenever a turn was to be made. Though it was evident that the man was older, he moved the vehicle along the roadway with the precision of a young apprentice dedicated to becoming the absolute best. Through the drive, his focus remained transfixed on the pavement ahead, in a sort of trance designed to keep his passengers secure yet deliver them to their destination with a smooth efficiency.

They passed through some tiny villages that had a timeless feel. Bougainvillea lined the streets, wild dogs with king-of-the-road demeanors stood at the meridian line, confronting the SUV in a deadly game of chicken, and children played on small grassy lawns with thoughtless abandon. Roosters could be heard shrieking from time to time, and old men in basic woolen hats with tooth-missing mouths and chestnut-colored skin sat on weather-beaten wooden chairs. They looked like they had too many hours to pass in the day, at once tired from life's hardships and yet wise from days fully lived. Choirs of upbeat birds sang melodically while colorful butterflies seemed to be fluttering everywhere.

In one tiny community the SUV snaked through, a skinny boy with legs that appeared too long for his body pedaled a banana bike with a seat that was set too high on its creaky metal frame. In another, a group of teenaged girls in tank tops, surf shorts and flip-flops shuffled along the narrow but attentively maintained road, following a man in army green cargo shorts wearing a t-shirt that had "The No.1 Flame-Grilled Chicken" printed on the back of it.

Everything seemed to move on island time. People looked cheerful. They beamed with a radiant vitality not so commonly seen in the over-scheduled, machine-dominated and sometimes soulless lives so many among us are experiencing. The beaches were unspeakably beautiful. The gardens were entirely glorious. And the entire Gauguin-looking scene was draped by a series of mountains that looked like they'd been carved by a sixteenth-century Florentine sculptor.

"See that structure up there?" the driver said, breaking his self-imposed silence and pointing to a rock formation at the top of one of the peaks that resembled a human figure. "That's called Pieter Both. It's the second-highest mountain in Mauritius. See the summit up there? It resembles a human head, right?" he noted with a finger pointed upward at the structure.

"It definitely does," responded the artist.

"When we were in elementary school," the chauffeur continued, "we were told the story of a man who fell asleep at the foot of the mountain. Hearing strange sounds, he woke up to see fairies and angels dancing all about him. These creatures instructed the man never to tell anyone what he had just seen or he would be turned to stone. He agreed but then, given his excitement over the mystical experience he'd witnessed, broke his commitment and told many of his good fortune. Upset, the fairies and angels turned him to rock. And his head swelled to such a degree it rose to sit at the peak of the majestic mountain you both are looking at now, reminding everyone who sees it to keep their promises. And honor their word."

The SUV meandered past another community. Music played from a small loudspeaker on a front porch as two teenaged boys and three teenaged girls with white and pink flowers in their hair danced gleefully. Another dog barked modestly in the background.

"Great story," noted the entrepreneur. Her window was open, and her wavy brown hair flitted in the wind. Her usually lined face now appeared completely smooth. She enunciated her words more slowly now. An unprecedented peacefulness emerged from her voice. One of her hands rested on the seat—not so far from where a hand of the artist, which bore finely etched tattoos on its middle and index fingers, lay.

"Mark Twain wrote, 'Mauritius was made first, and then heaven; and heaven copied Mauritius,'" the driver shared, now warming up after being somewhat steely. He beamed as proudly as a president on Inauguration Day after saying what he'd just said.

"Never seen anything like this," the artist said, his goth-meets-angry-man hostility now replaced with a more untroubled, carefree and relaxed demeanor. "And the vibe I feel here is stirring something deeply creative inside of me."

The entrepreneur glanced at the artist for a little longer than was politely acceptable. Then she looked away, out at the sea. Though reluctant, she couldn't help but smile gently.

The driver could be heard whispering into the SUV's speakerphone, "Five minutes away." Then he handed each of his passengers a handcrafted tablet that seemed made of gold. "Please study these," he told them.

Engraved, finely, in the apparently precious metal were five statements. Here's what the tablets looked like:

RULE #1

An addiction to distraction is the end of your creative production. Empire-makers and history-creators take one hour for themselves before dawn, in the serenity that lies beyond the clutches of complexity, to prepare themselves for a world-class day.

RULE #2

Excuses breed no genius. Just because you haven't installed the early-rising habit before doesn't mean you can't do it now. Release your rationalizations and remember that small daily improvements, when done consistently over time, lead to stunning results.

RULE #3

All change is hard at first, messy in the middle and gorgeous at the end. Everything you now find easy you first found difficult. With consistent practice, getting up with the sun will become your new normal. And automatic.

RULE #4

To have the results The Top 5% of producers have, you must start doing what 95% of people are unwilling to do. As you start to live like this, the majority will call you crazy. Remember that being labeled a freak is the price of greatness.

RULE #5

When you feel like surrendering, continue.
Triumph loves the relentless.

The vehicle slowed to a crawl as it passed an orderly row of faded white beach houses. A compact pickup truck was parked in the dusty driveway of one house. Dive gear was strewn across the front yard of another. In front of the last house, a gaggle of kids played in a yard, laughing hysterically as they enjoyed their game.

The ocean appeared, both greenish and bluish with foam-topped waves making *shaaaashing* sounds before colliding with the sandy shore. The air now smelled a marine life smell, yet sweet like nectar with unexpected cinnamon hints blended into it. On a wide-planked dock, a thin line of a man with a Santa Claus beard and rolled-up khakis fished barefoot for his family's dinner. A motorcycle helmet was perched on his old head.

The sun was beginning to set, a glamorous sphere of blinding radiance that cast liquid yellow streaks and reflections on the welcoming water that lay before it. Birds still chirped. Butterflies still flew. Quite magical, all of this.

"We're here," announced the chauffeur into an intercom perched beside a metal fence that seemed to have been erected more to keep wildlife out than to prevent interlopers from getting in.

The gate opened. Slowly.

The SUV rolled down a winding road teeming with bougainvillea, hibiscus, frangipani and Boucle d'Oreille, the national flower of Mauritius, along the sides. The driver opened his window, inviting in a sea breeze carrying a swirling scent that also included fresh jasmine mixed with rich roses. Gardeners in smart gardening attire waved sincere waves. One shouted "Bonjour" as the vehicle sailed by. Another said "Bonzour" as two fat doves the size of a trucker's fist hopped along a stone path.

The billionaire's house was low-key. The design was of the beachfront chic sort. Kind of a Martha's Vineyard cottage meets Swedish farmhouse feel. It was both sensationally beautiful and completely private.

A massive veranda at the back of the home extended over the ocean. A muddy mountain bike leaned against a wall. A surfboard rested near the end of the driveway. Massive floor-to-ceiling windows were the only extravagant architectural flourish. More precious flowers were meticulously arranged along a deck where a trolley supporting hors d'oeuvres, assorted cheeses and a service of fresh lemon tea with precisely cut slices of ginger waited. Sun-bleached gray steps wound down to a breathtakingly lovely beach, the type seen in the travel magazines the elite crowd like to read.

Amid all this exquisiteness, an isolated figure stood on the milk-colored sand. He made not one movement. Perfect stillness.

The man was Eiffel Tower tall, shirtless and bronzed, and sporting a pair of loose shorts with a camouflage pattern. Canary yellow sandals and uber-stylish sunglasses, the kind you might purchase on Via dei Condotti in Rome, completed the surfer Zen meets Soho swagger appearance. He peered out into the sea, remaining still as a star in the big African sky.

"There," said the entrepreneur, pointing. "We finally get to see our host. The illustrious Mr. Riley," she noted energetically, picking up her pace as she hustled down the wooden stairs that led to the seashore. "Look at him! He's just hanging out by the water, soaking up those rays and totally lovin' life. Told you he's special. So happy I trusted my gut and agreed to this wonderful escapade. He's been true to his word, in a world where too many people say things they never do and make promises they fail to keep. He's been super-consistent. He's treated us so well. He doesn't even know us, and yet he's really trying to help us. Zero doubt in my mind he's got our backs. Hurry up, will you," she urged her slow-moving companion as she waved an encouraging hand. "I feel like giving Mr. Riley a giant hug!"

The artist laughed as a baby gecko jaywalked across a broad plank. He took off his black shirt in the dazzling sunshine, exposing a Buddha-sized belly and man breasts the size of fleshy mangoes.

"Me, too. He does walk his preach. Man, I need to get some sun," the painter murmured as he sped up to stay close to the entrepreneur. He breathed hard.

As the two guests walked toward the man at the water's edge of this Nirvana of an ocean compound, they observed there were no other houses in sight. Not even one. Just a few wooden fishing boats with paint peeled off from the passage of years moored in the shallow waters near the shore. And aside from the sun worshipping empire-builder in Italian shades, there was no other human being in evidence. Anywhere.

"Mr. Riley," shouted the artist, now on the sand hungrily sucking air into his extraordinarily unfit lungs.

The slender figure remained as fixed as a palace guard awaiting the arrival of the royal motorcade.

"Mr. Riley," echoed the entrepreneur passionately.

No response. The man just kept looking out at the sea and at container ships the size of football stadiums that sat sprinkled across the horizon.

The artist soon stood behind the set of intensely tanned shoulders of the figure and tapped three times on the left one. Instantly, the figure spun around. The two visitors gasped. The entrepreneur put a slender hand over her mouth. The artist jerked backward, instinctively, before falling to the sand.

Both were stunned by what they saw.

It was The Spellbinder.

CHAPTER 7

Preparation for a Transformation Begins in Paradise

"A child has no trouble believing the unbelievable, nor does the genius or the madman. It's only you and I, with our big brains and our tiny hearts, who doubt and overthink and hesitate." —**Steven Pressfield**

"Um. Wow!" declared the entrepreneur with a crooked smile that displayed part surprise and part delight.

"We were at your seminar. Um. You were brilliant up on that stage," she finally managed to express, pivoting impressively from soft shock to the master-of-the-universe business bearing she was more accustomed to. "I lead a technology company. We're what pundits in our industry call 'a rocket ship' because of the exponential growth we've been experiencing. Things were going phenomenally well until a little while ago . . ." The entrepreneur's voice trailed off.

She looked away from The Spellbinder and stared at the artist. For a moment she played nervously with her bracelets. The lines along her face became more vivid. And her visage gave off a heavy, tired and injured look in that instant, on that spectacular beach.

"What happened?" asked The Spellbinder. "To your business?"

"Some of the people who invested in my enterprise felt I had too much equity in it. They wanted more for themselves. Super-greedy people. So, they manipulated my executive team, convinced key employees to rally against me and are now trying to throw me out of the firm. That place is my whole life." The entrepreneur choked up.

A school of luxuriously colored tropical fish swam through the shallow water at the edge of the sand.

"I was ready to take my life," she carried on. "Until I showed up at your seminar. Many of your nuggets of knowledge gave me hope. A lot of your words made me feel strong again. Not sure exactly what it was, but you pushed me to believe in myself and my future. I just want to thank you." She embraced The Spellbinder. "You've started me on the journey to optimizing my life."

"Thank you so much for your generous words," The Spellbinder replied, appearing dramatically different from the way he looked the last time the entrepreneur and the artist saw him. Not only did he have that healthy glow people get from time in the sun, he now stood steadily and had gained a little weight.

"I'm grateful for what you've said," The Spellbinder continued. "But the truth is that I didn't start you on the quest to improve your life. *You* are changing your life by starting the process of bringing application to my insights and methods—by *implementing* my teachings. So many people chat a good game. They tell you all the ambitions they're going to get done and all the aspirations they plan to deliver on. I'm not judging. I'm just reporting. I'm not complaining, I'm just saying: *most people stay the same their entire lives.* Too frightened to leave the way they operated yesterday. Married to the complacency of the ordinary and wedded to the shackles of conformity while resisting all opportunity for growth, evolution and personal elevation. So many good souls among us are just so scared they refuse the call on their lives to go out into the blue ocean of possibility where mastery, the dignity of bravery and the authenticity of audacity await them. You had the wisdom to act on some of the information I shared at my event. You're one in a tiny minority of people alive today willing to do what it takes to become a better leader, producer and human being. Good on you. And I know transformation isn't an easy play. Yet, the life of the caterpillar must end for the glory of the butterfly to shine. The old 'you' must die before the best 'you' can be born. You're so smart not to wait until you have ideal conditions to step up to a work world and private life of stainless excellence. Great power is unleashed with a simple start. When you begin to close the loop opened by your utmost aspirations by making them real, a secret heroic force within you makes itself known. Nature notices your effortful actions and then goes ahead and replies to your faithful commitment with a series of unanticipated wins. Your willpower heightens. Your confidence climbs. And your brilliance soars. A year from now, you'll be so happy you began today."

"Thank you," said the entrepreneur.

"I heard a man say he needed to lose weight before he could start running. Imagine that. Lose the weight so he could initiate the running habit. That's like a writer who waits for inspiration to begin the book, or the manager who waits for a promotion to lead the field, or a startup that waits for full funding before launching a status quo–disrupting product. The flow of life rewards positive action and punishes hesitation. Anyway, I'm thrilled I could contribute to your rise, in some small way. Sounds like you're at a difficult yet exciting time on your personal adventure. Please consider that a bad day for the ego is a great day for the soul. And what your voice of fear claims is a mean season the light of your wisdom knows is a splendid gift."

"We thought you were dead," the entrepreneur announced, unfiltered. "Thank God you're okay. And I appreciate how humble you are."

"I believe the humblest is the greatest. Pure leaders are so secure in their own skin their main mission is the elevation of others. They have such self-respect, joyfulness and peacefulness within themselves that they don't need to advertise their success to society in a feeble attempt to feel a little better. I should also say, if I may, that there's a big difference between real power and fake power," The Spellbinder explained, dropping even deeper into the guru mode that had made him so famous worldwide.

"Our culture tells us to pursue titles and trinkets, applause and acclaim, money and mansions. All that's fine—it truly is—so long as you don't get brainwashed into defining your worth as a human being by these things. Enjoy them, just don't get attached to them. Have them, just don't base your identity around them. Appreciate them, just don't *need* them. These are only forms of fake power our civilization programs us to believe we must pursue to be successful—and serene. The fact is that should you lose any one of these things, the substitute power you derived from them evaporates. Just vanishes in an instant, revealing itself as the illusion it was."

"Tell us more, please." The entrepreneur was absorbing every word.

"Real power never comes from anything external," The Spellbinder continued. "A lot of people with a lot of money aren't very wealthy. Take that line to the bank," stated The Spellbinder as he slipped off his bright yellow flip-flops and placed them neatly on the sugary sand. "Genuine power—the stuff legends are made of—doesn't arise from who you are outside and what you possess externally. The world is lost right now. True and enduring power expresses itself when you contact your original gifts and realize your most lavish talents as a human. I should also say real riches come from living by the noble virtues of productivity, self-discipline, courage, honesty, empathy and integrity as well as being able to lead your days on your own terms versus blindly following the sheep that so many in our sick society have been trained to become. 'Sheeple' is what too many people now are. The excellent news is that this kind of power I speak of is available to *anyone* alive on the planet today. We might have forgotten and disowned this form of potency we have as life has hurt, disappointed and confused us. But it's still there waiting for us to build a relationship with it. And develop it. All of the great teachers of history owned very few things, you know. When Mahatma Gandhi died he had about ten possessions, including his sandals, a watch, his eyeglasses and a simple bowl to eat from. Mother Teresa, so prosperous

THE 5 AM CLUB

of heart and rich with the authentic power to influence millions, died in a tiny room containing almost no worldly goods. When she'd travel, she'd carry all her things in a white cloth bag."

"Why do so many of the heroes of humanity have so little?" asked the artist, now relaxing on the sand.

"Because they've reached a level of individual maturity that allowed them to see the futility of spending their days chasing objects that count for nothing at the end. And they had cultivated their characters to such a degree that they no longer had the common need of most to fill the holes within themselves with distractions, attractions, escapes and luxuries. The more their appetite for superficial possessions demater-ialized, the more hungry they became for substantial pursuits like hon-oring their creative vision, expressing their inherent genius and living by a higher moral blueprint. They viscerally understood that being inspirational and masterful and fearless are all inside jobs. And once *true* power is accessed, external substitutes pale in comparison to the feelings of fulfillment this treasure provides. Oh, and these heavy-weights of history, as they discovered their supreme natures, also came to realize that one of the primary aims of a wonderfully crafted life is contribution. Impact. Usefulness. Helpfulness. What business-builders might call 'unlocking stakeholder value.' Like I suggested at my seminar before I fell, 'to lead is to serve.' The philosopher Rumi made the point much more brilliantly than I ever could when he observed, 'Give up the drop, become the ocean.'"

"Thanks for sharing," offered the entrepreneur sincerely, sitting down next to the artist on the sand and placing one of her hands carefully only a short distance away from one of his.

"It's good to see you're doing better," mentioned the artist, his boots now off. He was sockless. As he basked in the strong rays like a sunbathing cat he asked, "What the heck happened to you anyway?"

"Exhaustion," confided The Spellbinder. "Too many cities. Too many airplanes. Too many media appearances. Too many presentations. I just ground myself down in pursuit of my mission to help people accelerate their leadership, activate their gifts and become heroes of their lives. I know better."

The Spellbinder then pulled off his sleek sunglasses and extended a hand to his two students. "It's a great pleasure to meet you both."

"You too, brother," the artist replied. "Your work has helped me make it through some tough times."

As the artist spoke these words, he spotted a catamaran overflowing with festively dressed tourists whizzing along in the distance. Another school of fish, called capitaines, could be observed swimming busily in the clear water. The Spellbinder spied them, smiled broadly and then continued.

"You must be wondering why I'm here," he stated.

"True," said the entrepreneur as she took off her shoes and twisted her feet into the white sand alongside her companion.

"Well, I've been advising Mr. Riley since he was a thirty-three-year-old man. All pro athletes have peak performance coaches, and so do all extraordinary businesspeople. You just can't get to iconic alone. He was starting out when we met, but even then he understood that the more one learns, the more one can achieve. Growth is the real sport that the best play, every day. Education truly is inoculation against disruption. And as you become better you will have better, within all arenas of your life. I call this *The 2x3x Mindset*: to double your income and impact, triple your investment in two core areas—your personal mastery and your professional capability."

"Love it," the artist said as he scratched his flabby belly. Then he picked at a decrepit toenail.

"Mr. Riley understood, early on, that to rise to world-class, you need world-class support. We've become fantastic friends over the years. We've shared tremendous joys together, like five-hour-long lunches with palm heart salad, fresh grilled prawns and excellent French wine here on this private beach of his."

The Spellbinder stretched his arms into the air. He looked over at the mighty mountains. He remained silent for a few moments.

"And we've experienced deep sorrows together as well, like the time my buddy got sick with cancer just after his fiftieth birthday. He appeared to have everything a man could desire. But without his good health, he realized he had nothing. That one changed him. Health is the crown on the well person's head that only the ill person can see, you know? Or, as one tradition says, when we are young we sacrifice our health for wealth and when we grow old and wise we realize what's most important—and become willing to sacrifice all our wealth for even one day of good health. You never want to be the richest person in the graveyard, you know.

"He beat it, though," The Spellbinder quickly added, staring at the noisy tourists partying on the catamaran. "Just like he defends himself against everything that tries to defeat his dreams. Stone's an amazing guy. I love him like a brother.

"Well, look, it really has been good to meet you both," The Spellbinder continued. "I heard you were coming. Mr. Riley's tremendously excited to share what he promised he'd share with you about reaching maximum productivity, sustaining exceptional performance and creating a life you love by coding in a superior morning routine. I'm pleased he's paying it forward and sharing what I, as his mentor, taught him. You'll love all the insights and learning models that will soon be coming your way. The 5 AM Club will be *revolutionary* for you both. I know it sounds strange and unbelievable, but being exposed to the methodology Stone is about to teach you will cause outstanding shifts deep within you. Just being around the information will awaken something special in you."

The Spellbinder put on his chic sunglasses.

"Anyway, Mr. Riley asked me to tell you to make yourselves at home here over the next few days. You won't see a lot of me because I'll be snorkeling, sailing and fishing most of the time. Fishing is one of the things I most love to do in life. I come down to Mauritius not only to coach the great and kind soul you'll soon meet, I show up here to regenerate and get away from this overcomplicated world of ours, flush with so many difficulties, damaged economies, saturated industries and environmental decays, just to mention a few of the factors that threaten to bring down our creativity, energy, performance and happiness. I show up here to renew and refuel. Elite production without quiet vacation causes lasting depletion. Rest and recovery isn't a luxury for anyone committed to mastery—it's a necessity. I've taught that principle for many years—yet I forgot it myself, and paid the price at the event. I've also learned that inspiration gets fed by isolation, away from the ceaseless digital diversion and mindless overcommunication that dominates the hours of the majority these days. And, know too that your natural genius presents itself when you're most joyful. We get our ideas that change the world when we're rested, relaxed and filled with delight. This tiny spot in the Indian Ocean helps me reaccess my best. It's also a genuine sanctuary of safety, staggering beauty and awesome gastronomy, with affectionate people who still wear their hearts on their sleeves. I just adore the Mauritians. Most still have an appreciation for the wonders of life's simplest pleasures. Like family meals or swimming with friends, followed by sharing a roast chicken dinner purchased from the Super U, washed down with an ice cold can of Phoenix."

"Phoenix?" asked the artist.

"It's the beer of Mauritius," replied The Spellbinder. "And I must say that I always leave the island one hundred times stronger, faster, centered and fired up. I really work hard in my everyday life. I hope this doesn't sound like vanity, but I care so much about uplifting society and am so committed to doing my part to reduce the greed, hatred and conflict in it. Coming here remakes me. Reconnects me to what's important. So I can go back and work for the world. We all work for the world, you know? Anyway, you two have fun, okay? And thanks again for coming to my seminar and for your positive words. They mean more to me than you could ever know. Anyone can be a critic. Takes guts to be an encourager.

Being a high-impact leader never requires being a disrespectful person. I wish more leaders understood this principle.

"Oh, one last thing," The Spellbinder added as he flicked some sand off his camouflage-patterned surf shorts.

"What?" asked the entrepreneur in a respectful tone.

"Please be here on the beach tomorrow morning. Your training will begin then."

"Sure," agreed the entrepreneur. "What time?"

"5 AM," came the reply. "Own your morning. Elevate your life."

CHAPTER 8

The 5 AM Method: The Morning Routine of World-Builders

"It is well to be up before daybreak, for such habits contribute to health, wealth and wisdom." —Aristotle

"Welcome to The 5 AM Club!" the billionaire bellowed as he bounded down the steps from his seaside home. "Bonzour! That's Creole for 'good morning.' You're right on time! I love it! Punctuality is the trait of royalty. At least it is in my playbook. Stone Riley's my name," he declared as he graciously extended a hand to greet his two guests.

The tattered old clothes had been replaced with a black pair of trimly cut running shorts and a pristine white t-shirt with the line "No idea works until you do the work" emblazoned on it. He was barefoot and cleanly shaven, seemed extremely fit and sported a wonderful suntan, all of which made him look many years younger than he had appeared at the seminar. On his head he wore a black baseball cap, turned backward.

His green eyes were still uncommonly clear. And his smile was astonishingly radiant. Yes, there was something exceedingly special about this man, as the entrepreneur had sensed.

A white dove hovered over the tycoon, floating in the air for about ten seconds as if suspended by magic. Then it flew off. Can you imagine this? It was a miraculous thing to see.

"Let me give you two a hug, if you don't mind," the billionaire enthused, wrapping his long arms around the entrepreneur and the artist at the same time, without waiting for a reply.

"God, you have courage. Yes, you do," he mused. "You trusted a disheveled old man. A total stranger. I know I looked like a vagrant the other day. Hey, it's not that I don't care about how I look. I just don't care that much about how I look," he said as he laughed at his own lack of self-consciousness. "I just like to keep things real. Nice and simple. Completely authentic. Makes me think of that old insight: Having lots of money doesn't make you different. It just makes you more of who you were before you made the cash."

The billionaire peered out into the ocean and allowed the early rays of a fresh dawn to wash over him. He closed his eyes and inhaled deeply. The contours of his chiseled abdominal muscles were noticeable through his t-shirt. Next, he pulled a flower from the back pocket of his black shorts. Neither the entrepreneur nor the artist had ever seen a flower like this one. And it wasn't at all damaged from being in the billionaire's pocket. Strange.

"Flowers are very important to anyone serious about creating magic in their work and private lives," spoke the mogul as he sniffed the petals. "Anyhoo, I wanted to mention that my father was a farmer. I grew up on a farm, before we moved to southern California. We thought simple, spoke simple, ate simple and lived simple. You can take the boy out of the country, you know, but you can't take the country out of the boy," he added, expressing an enthusiasm that was contagious while his sights were riveted on the magnificent sea.

The entrepreneur and the artist thanked the billionaire profusely. They explained that their adventure so far had been phenomenal and mentioned sincerely that the island and his exclusive beach were more beautiful than anything they had previously seen.

"Utopia, isn't it?" said the billionaire as he put on his sunglasses. "I am blessed, that's for sure. I'm so glad you cats are here."

"So, was it your father who got you into the habit of getting up with the sun?" asked the artist as they strolled along the water's edge.

A tiny crab raced by while three butterflies ascended above.

Stunningly, the billionaire started twirling around like a whirling dervish. While he spun, he began to shout these words: "I would have it inscribed on the curtains of your chamber: 'If you do not rise early you can make progress in nothing!'"

"Um, what are you doing?" questioned the entrepreneur.

"It's an excellent quote from William Pitt, the Earl of Chatham. For some reason I just felt the need to share it right now. Anyhoo, let me answer the question about my father," the billionaire said awkwardly.

"Yes and no. I watched him rise early every morning of my child-hood. As with any good routine, he did it so many times that it became impossible for him *not* to do it. But like most kids, I resisted what my dad wanted me to do. I always had some form of rebel within me. I'm a bit of a pirate in a way. Rather than fight a small war with me every day, for whatever reason, he just let me do what I wanted to do. So, I'd sleep. Late."

"Cool father," spoke the entrepreneur, who was dressed in yoga gear this morning and carried her device with her to take careful notes.

"He was," affirmed the billionaire, warmly putting his arms around his students as they continued to walk slowly along the pristine beach.

Mr. Riley continued. "It was actually The Spellbinder who taught me The 5 AM Method. I was a young man when I first met him. I'd just launched my first company. I needed someone to guide me, challenge me and develop me as an entrepreneur, a peak achiever and as a leader. Everyone said he was the best executive coach in the world, by far. He had a three-year waiting list. So, I called him every day until he agreed to become my mentor. He was pretty young back then, too. But his teachings had a depth of wisdom, a purity of power and an ingenious impact that was remarkably advanced for his age."

"And the early-rising discipline helped?" the artist broke in.

The billionaire smiled at the artist. And stopped walking.

"*It was the one practice that changed—and elevated—every other practice.* Researchers now call this kind of a core behavior that multiplies all your other regular patterns of performing 'a keystone habit.' Wiring it in as a profound neural pathway took some effort, a little suffering along the way and the strongest commitment I had in me. I'll be honest with you, there were days during the process of automating this routine that I was cranky, days when my head pounded like a jackhammer and mornings when I just wanted to keep sleeping. But once I locked and loaded getting up at 5 AM regularly, my days grew consistently—and vastly— better than anything I've ever experienced."

"How?" both listeners wondered aloud, in unison.

The entrepreneur touched one of her fingers on the artist's arm affectionately, as if to suggest they were together in this experience, that they were now a team and that she had his best interests at heart. The artist locked his eyes onto hers. A gentle grin emerged.

The billionaire went on: "In this time of exponential change, overwhelming distractions and overflowing schedules, getting up at 5 AM and running the morning regime The Spellbinder taught me was my antidote to average. No more rushing in my morning! Imagine what that alone does for the quality of your day. Starting your day luxuriating in the quietude only the early morning provides. Beginning your day feeling strong and centered and free. I found that my mind became dramatically more focused as the days progressed. Every great performer, whether we're talking about a championship athlete, a top-tier executive, a celebrated architect or a revered cellist, has developed the ability to concentrate on optimizing their particular skill for long, uninterrupted periods of time. This capability is one of the special factors that allows them to generate such high-quality results in a world where too many people dilute their cognitive bandwidth and fragment their attention, accepting poor performances and ordinary achievements while leading lives of disappointing mediocrity."

"I definitely agree," indicated the artist. "It's rare to see someone focus on their art for many, many hours in a row these days. The Spellbinder was right when at his session he called people addicted to their devices 'cyber zombies.' I see them every day. It's like they're not real human beings anymore. More like robots, glued to their screens. Not present. And half-alive to life."

"I hear you," said the billionaire. "Protection from distraction is precisely how you need to work if you're serious about dominating your field and winning at your craft. Neuroscientists call this peak mental state we're speaking of, where our perception becomes heightened and our availability to original ideas rises and we access an all-new level of processing power, 'Flow.' And rising at 5 AM promotes The Flow State gorgeously. Oh—and by getting up at before daybreak, while almost everyone around you is asleep—my creativity also soared, my energy definitely doubled, my productivity surely tripled, my . . ."

"You're serious?" the entrepreneur interrupted, unable to contain her fascination with the idea that a simple shift toward a bespoke morning routine could reorder a human life so completely.

"Absolutely. Honesty has been one of my core convictions for all my years in business. Nothing beats going to sleep early each night with an unspoiled conscience and a mess-free heart. That's part of my farm boy nature, I guess," observed the billionaire.

Abruptly, the entrepreneur's phone signaled the arrival of an urgent incoming message. "So sorry. I told my team not to call me here. I was clear with them. I can't imagine why they're bothering me now," she said as she looked down at the screen.

In all caps, the following stark words appeared:

LEAVE THE COMPANY. OR ELSE YOU DIE.

The entrepreneur fumbled with her phone. Then she accidentally dropped it into the sand. Soon she was gasping for air.

"What happened?" the artist asked quickly, sensing trouble.

Seeing the blood wash out of his friend's face and her hands trembling, he repeated with greater intensity and even higher empathy, "What happened?"

The billionaire also appeared concerned. "Are you okay? Do you need some water or something?"

"I just received a death threat. From . . . um . . . my . . . investors. They want my firm. They are . . . um . . . trying to kick me out because they think I have too big a share. They just told me that if I don't walk away they'll—um—kill me."

Instantly, the billionaire ripped off the sunglasses he was sporting and held them in the air, making a circling movement. Seconds later, from behind a flourish of palm trees, two large men with earpieces and rifles sprinted down to the beachfront as fast as a cyclist on steroids.

"Boss, you all right?" the tallest of the two big men asked tensely.

"Yes," came the confident and calm reply to his security detail. "But I need you two to check this out immediately—if it's cool for me to do this for you," he said as he looked at the entrepreneur. "I can help you make this go away."

The billionaire then muttered something to himself. And a flight of doves soared by.

"Sure. Yes. I'd appreciate some help," the businesswoman replied, her voice still shaking and pearls of perspiration appearing on her forehead, in the area where all those creases were.

"Leave this with us," declared the billionaire. He then spoke to his protection people, politely yet with an undeniable air of authority. "Seems my guest here is being seriously harassed by some thugs hoping to take over her enterprise. Please figure out exactly what they're up to and then present me with your solution.

"Don't worry," he told the entrepreneur. "My guys are the best in the business. *This won't be a problem.*" Mr. Riley articulated this last sentence in a fashion that emphasized each word, for powerful effect.

"Thank you very much," the entrepreneur responded, looking enormously relieved.

The artist held her hand tenderly.

"Okay if I continue?" the billionaire requested as the sun rose higher into the glamorous tropical sky.

His guests nodded.

An attendant, impeccably attired, emerged from a hut that sat higher up on the beach. It was painted green with white trim. Soon, the aide was serving the richest, most delicious coffee the entrepreneur and the artist had enjoyed in their lives.

"Fantastic cognitive enhancer when consumed in moderation each morning," expounded the billionaire as he sipped away. "And it's packed with antioxidants, so coffee also slows aging.

"Anyhoo—where were we? I was telling you about the awesome benefit that flowed to me after I joined The 5 AM Club and ran the morning methodology The Spellbinder revealed to me. It's called *The 20/20/20 Formula* and, trust me, once you learn this concept alone and then apply it with persistency, your productivity, prosperity, performance and impact will increase exponentially. I can't think of another ritual that has contributed to my success and well-being as much. I'm exceedingly low-key about what I've been able to accomplish in my business career. I've always viewed bragging as a major defect of character. The more powerful a person truly is, the less they need to promote it. And the stronger a leader is, the less they need to announce it."

"The Spellbinder spoke a bit about what you've been able to achieve," offered the entrepreneur, now looking even more relaxed.

"And the wild way you dressed at the conference definitely confirmed it!" interjected the artist, flashing a sensational smile that showcased a few broken teeth.

"Rising at 5 AM every morning was the main personal practice that made most of that happen. Allowed me to become a visionary thinker.

Gave me a reflective space to develop a formidable inner life. The discipline helped me to become ultra-fit, with all the beautiful income advancements as well as lifestyle enhancements that come with superior health. Early rising also made me a pretty amazing leader. And it helped me grow myself into a much better person. Even when the prostate cancer tried to devastate me, it was my morning routine that insulated me. It really was. I'll go into *The 20/20/20 Formula* in an upcoming lesson so you'll know exactly what to do to get amazing results from the first moment you wake up. You cats won't believe the power and value of the information that's coming. I'm so excited for you two. Welcome to Paradise. And welcome to the first day of a substantially better life."

———

The entrepreneur slept more soundly that night in Mauritius than she had in years. Despite the threat she had received, the combination of the billionaire's brief instruction, the magnificence of the natural setting, the purity of the clean ocean air and her growing fondness for the artist caused her to let go of many of her concerns. And rediscover a state of calm she'd long since forgotten.

Then, at precisely 3:33 AM, she heard a thunderous bang on her door.

She knew it was this time because she glanced at the alarm clock on the wooden night table in the stylish guesthouse her host had arranged for her to stay in. The entrepreneur assumed it was the artist, perhaps dealing with jet lag or sleepless after the excellent yet large dinner they had enjoyed together. Without asking who it was, she opened the door.

No one was there.

"Hello?" she announced to a star-filled sky.

Waves softly collided with the seashore near her cottage, and the scents of roses, incense and sandalwood could be detected in the breeze.

"Anyone here?"

Silence.

The entrepreneur carefully shut the door. This time, she bolted the lock. As she shuffled back to her bed that was covered with Egyptian cottons and English linens, three mighty knocks pounded on the door.

"Yes?" cried the entrepreneur, now alarmed. "Yes?"

"We have the morning coffee you ordered, Madam," a husky voice replied.

The entrepreneur's face was crowded by crevices again. Her heart began to thump vigorously. She grew deeply distressed, and her stomach filled with knots as humungous as the Alps. "They're bringing me coffee at this nutso hour? Unbelievable."

She returned to the front of the guest house, undid the lock and opened the front door, haltingly.

A stocky man with a disagreeable bald head and one eye that seemed out of joint stood there, smirking. He wore a red windbreaker and denim shorts that dropped just below his knees. Around his neck was a thin piece of blue string. Dangling from it was a plastic-laminated photo of a person's face.

The entrepreneur squinted to see the face more clearly in the darkness. And as she did, she saw the image of an older man. One she knew very well. One she loved very much. One she missed considerably.

The picture in the plastic she was studying was of her dead father.

"Who are you?" screamed the terrified entrepreneur. "How did you get this photo?"

"I've been sent by your business partners. We know everything there is to know about you. Everything. We've tracked all your personal data. We've hacked all your files. We've investigated your entire history." The bald man in the windbreaker reached under the front of his belt—and pulled out a knife, bringing it to within a few inches of the entrepreneur's thin and particularly veiny throat.

"No one can protect you now. We have an entire team focused on you. I'm not going to hurt you . . . yet. This time's just about me making a point. Giving you an in-person message . . . Leave your company. Give up your equity. And say bye-bye. Or you get this blade in your neck. When you least expect it . . . when you think you're safe. Maybe with that chubby painter friend of yours . . ."

The man pulled the knife away and replaced it under his belt. "Have a good night, Madam. It's been a pleasure meeting you. I know we'll see each other soon." Then he reached forward and pulled the door shut with a slam.

The entrepreneur, badly shaken, fell to her knees.

"Please, God. Help me. I can't take this anymore! I don't want to die."

Three more strikes came to the door. These ones were gentler.

"Hey, it's me. Please open the door."

The knocking startled the entrepreneur. And woke her up. The tapping continued. She opened her eyes, peered around the lightless room—and realized she'd been caught in a bad dream.

The businesswoman rose from her bed, shuffled across the wide-planked oak floor and opened the front door, knowing it was the artist after hearing his familiar voice.

"I just had the most insane dream," said the entrepreneur. "A brutal man showed up here, had a piece of plastic hanging from his neck with a photo of my dad in it and threatened to stab me with a knife if I didn't give my firm over to the investors."

"You okay now?" the artist asked softly.

"I'll be fine."

"I had an unusual dream, too," the artist explained. "I couldn't sleep after it. It's got me thinking about so many things. The quality of my art. The depth of my belief system. The foolishness of my excuses. My cynical attitude. My aggressiveness. My self-sabotage and my endless procrastination. I'm analyzing my daily routines. And how I'll spend the rest of my life. Hey, you sure you're okay?" the artist questioned, realizing he was talking a little too much about himself and not empathizing with his alarmed companion.

"I'm fine. Better now that you're here."

"You sure?"

"Yes."

"I missed you," the artist said. "Do you mind if I tell you more about my dream?"

"Go ahead," encouraged the entrepreneur.

"Well, I was a little kid, at school. And every day, I'd pretend I was two things: a giant and a pirate. All day long, I believed I had the strength of a giant and the rule-breaking swagger of a pirate. I told my teachers I was these two characters. And at home, I told my parents the same thing. My teachers laughed at me—and put me down, telling me to be more realistic, to behave more like the other kids and to stop all my ridiculous dreaming."

"What did your parents say? Were they kinder to you?" asked the entrepreneur, now sitting on the sofa with her legs crossed in a yoga posture.

"Same as my teachers. They told me I wasn't a giant. And that I definitely was no pirate. They reminded me that I was a little boy. And told me that if I didn't limit my imagination, stifle my creativity and put an end to my fantasies, they'd punish me."

"So, what happened?"

"I did what I was told to do. I caved in. I bought into the attitudes of the adults. I made myself tinier instead of grander, so I'd be a good boy. I suffocated my hopes, gifts and powers in an effort to conform—like most people do every single day of their lives. I'm starting to realize how much we've been hypnotized away from our brilliance and brainwashed out of our genius. The Spellbinder and the billionaire are right."

"Tell me more about your dream," the entrepreneur urged.

"I began to mold myself to the system. I started to become a follower. I no longer believed I was as powerful as a giant and as swashbuckling as a pirate. I sheepwalked with the flock, becoming like everybody else. Eventually I grew into a man who spent money I didn't have, buying things I didn't need to impress people I didn't like. What a poor way to live."

"I do some of that behavior too," admitted the entrepreneur. "I'm learning so much about myself, thanks to this very weird and hugely useful voyage. I'm starting to realize how superficial I've been, how selfish I am and how many good things I actually have going for me in my life. Many people in the world couldn't even imagine experiencing all the blessings I have."

"Got you," said the artist. "So, in my dream, I became a bookkeeper. I married and had a family. I lived in a subdivision. And drove a good car. I had a fairly nice life. A few true friends. Work that paid my mortgage, and a salary that handled my bills. But each day looked the same. Gray versus vivid. Boring instead of enchanting. As I got older, the children left home to live lives of their own. My body aged, and my energy fell. And, unfortunately, my wife in my dream passed away. As I grew even older, my eyesight began to fail, my hearing began to fade and my memory became extremely weak."

"This is making me feel sad," voiced the entrepreneur, sounding vulnerable.

"And when I got really old, I actually forgot where I lived, couldn't remember my name and lost all sense of who I was in the community. But—get this—I began to remember who I *truly* was again."

"A giant. And a pirate. Right?"

"Exactly!" replied the artist. "The dream made me understand that I can't postpone doing amazing work anymore. That I can't put off improving my health, my happiness, my confidence and even my love life."

"Really?" wondered the entrepreneur wistfully.

"Really," responded the artist.

He then reached forward. And kissed her on the forehead.

CHAPTER 9

A Framework for
the Expression of Greatness

"The men who are great live with that which is substantial, they do not stay
with that which is superficial; they abide with realities, they remain not with
what is showy. The one they discard, the other they hold." —**Lao Tzu**

"Hey, cats," boomed the billionaire. "You're right on time, as usual.
Nice work!"

It was 5 AM and, while the retreating outline of the moon remained
in the sky, the rays of a new dawn greeted the three human beings standing on the perfect beach.

The perfumed ocean breeze swirled with notes of red hibiscus, clove
and tuberose. A Mauritius kestrel, the rarest falcon in the world, flew
overhead, and a pink pigeon—the scarcest on the planet—minded its
business near a lush cluster of palm trees. A family of geckos shot by on
their way to someplace important and a giant Aldabra tortoise crawled
along a grassy bank above the shore. All this natural splendor elevated
the joy and electrified the spirits of the three members of The 5 AM Club
who stood on the sand.

The billionaire pointed to a bottle floating in the ocean. As he
waved his finger from side to side, the bottle moved from side to side.
When he twirled a digit, the bottle in the water swirled with it. And

when he lifted a hand slowly, the bottle appeared to rise above the surface of the ocean.

Soon the container washed up onto the wet sand and it became clear that a swatch of silk had been rolled up inside of it. Picture how mysterious all this seemed.

"A message in a bottle," declared the billionaire happily. He started clapping his hands like a little tyke. He sure was an abnormal and totally wonderful character. "This conveniently sets the tone for my mentoring session with you this morning," he added.

The industrialist then lifted the vessel, unscrewed the cap and pulled out the fabric, which had the framework below stitched onto it:

THE 3 STEP SUCCESS FORMULA

"This is one of the simplest yet gnarliest of the teaching models The Spellbinder shared when he started coaching me as a young man," explained the billionaire, using more of his surfer slang. "And it'll provide the context for all the teachings that will follow. So, I really want you both to understand it intimately. At first glance, it seems like a really basic model. But as you integrate it over time, you'll see how profound it is."

Mr. Riley then closed his eyes, covered his ears with his hands and recited these words:

The beginning of transformation is the increase of perception. As you see more you can materialize more. And once you know better you can achieve bigger. The great women and men of the world— the ones responsible for the magical symphonies, the beautiful movements, the advancements of science and the progress of technology—started by reengineering their thinking and reinventing their awareness. In so doing, they entered a secret universe that the majority could not perceive. And this, in turn, allowed them to make the daily choices few choose to make. Which, automatically, delivered the daily results few get to experience.

The tycoon reopened his eyes. He raised an index finger to his lips, as if immersed in some splendidly weighty insight. Looking intently at the framework embedded into the silk, he continued, "Heroes, titans and icons all have a personal trait that average performers just don't show, you know."

"Which is?" asked the artist, who was dressed goofily in a muscle shirt and a Speedo swimsuit.

"Rigor," replied the billionaire. "The best in the world have depth. Members of the majority often get stuck in a mindset of superficiality in their work. Their whole *approach* is light. No real preparation. Very little contemplation and then the setting of a towering vision for the desired outcome along with patiently considering the sequencing of executions that will result in an awesome result. The 95% of performers don't invest *painstaking* attention into the tiniest of details and fail to refine the smallest of finishes like the great masters do. For most people the truth is that it's all about the path of least resistance. Getting what they need to get done fast and just sneaking by. *Mailing it in instead of bringing it on.* The minority of exceptional creative achievers operate under a completely different philosophy."

"Tell me," appealed the artist, intrigued.

"They apply a mentality of granularity instead of a mindset of superficiality. They have encoded depth as a lifetime value and exist under a profound insistence on greatness in all that they do. Exceptionalists fully understand that their creative output—no matter if they are bricklayers or bakers, chief executive officers or dairy farmers, astronauts or cashiers—represents their reputation. The best, in any endeavor, appreciate the fact that your good name is branded onto every piece of work that you release. And they get that you can't put a price tag on people saying superb things about you."

The billionaire rubbed the bottle. Then he held it up and viewed the last evidence of the disappearing moon through its glass before continuing his discourse.

"But it goes deeper than social approval," the industrialist indicated. "The grade of work you offer to the world reflects the strength of the respect you have for yourself. Those with unfathomable personal esteem wouldn't dare send out anything average. It would diminish them too much.

"If you want to lead your field," Mr. Riley went on, "become a performer and person of depth," he reinforced. "Commit to being a highly unusual human being instead of one of those timid souls who behave like everyone else, living a sloppy life instead of a magnificent one, a derivative life instead of an original one."

"Profound," the artist contributed, showing great exuberance while taking off his muscle shirt to get some sun.

90

"In their work, the maestros of mastery are extraordinarily thoughtful. They think precisely about what they are doing. They hold their labor to the highest of standards and sweat the smallest of strokes, like master sculptor Gian Lorenzo Bernini did as he crafted *Fontana dei Quattro Fiumi*—Fountain of the Four Rivers—his masterpiece that sits gloriously in the center of Piazza Navona in Rome. Such producers are meticulous and craft at near-flawless. And, as obvious as this sounds, they just really, really, really care."

"But people have a lot to do in their days, these days," interjected the entrepreneur. "This isn't the 1600s. My inbox is full. My schedule is packed. I have back-to-back meetings most days. I need to do pitches. I feel like I can never keep up with all that's coming at me. Shooting for mastery isn't easy."

"I understand," the billionaire replied kindly. "Less is more, you know? You're attempting too much. Geniuses understand that it's smarter to create one masterwork than one thousand ordinary pieces. One of the reasons I love being around the finest art is that the belief systems, emotional inspiration and ways of working of those great virtuosos rub off on me. And I can tell you with absolute certainty, these epic performers inhabited an entirely different universe than most people in business and society populate today, as I've suggested."

Just then, a brilliantly colored butterfly perched on the very tip of Stone Riley's left ear. He smiled and said, "Hey, little buddy—nice to see you again." The magnate then added, "When you deconstruct how the superstars, virtuosos and geniuses achieved what they did, you'll realize that it was their heightened *awareness* of the opportunities for daily greatness that inspired them to make the better daily choices that yielded better daily results."

Mr. Riley pointed to the learning model.

"That's the power of self-education," he went on. "As you become aware of new ideas, you'll grow as a producer and as a person. As you escalate your personal and professional development, the level at which you implement and execute around your gorgeous ambitions will rise. And, of course, as your ability to make your dreams and visions into reality increases, you'll be rewarded with greater income and higher impact," the magnate spoke as he tapped a finger onto step three of the diagram. "This is why agreeing to this training with me was such a smart move. And this is what this framework here is designed to teach you."

The billionaire scratched his lean abs. And inhaled a deep breath of ocean air.

"And may I say that because of the way the remarkable ones saw the world and how they behaved when it came to their crafts, and because they showed up in their lives so very differently from the way the mass of humanity operates, they were called kooks. Misfits. Weirdos. They weren't!" exclaimed the billionaire, exuberantly.

"They just played at a much higher level—in rare-air. They brought *rigor* to what they did. They'd spend weeks, months, sometimes years getting the finishing touches perfect. They forced themselves to stay with the work when they felt alone or scared or bored. They persisted in the translation of their heroic visions into everyday reality when they were misunderstood, ridiculed and even attacked. God, I admire the great geniuses of the world. I really do."

"'The further a society drifts from the truth, the more it will hate those that speak it,'" offered the artist succinctly.

The entrepreneur looked at him as she began to rub a bracelet on her wrist.

"George Orwell said that," he pronounced. "And 'Whenever you are creating beauty around you, you are restoring your own soul,'" the artist carried on. "Alice Walker said that."

"The masters produce in a way that ordinary workers would label as 'obsessive,'" expounded the industrialist. "But the reality of remarkability is that what The 95% of performers call 'picky behavior' surrounding an important project, The Top 5% of creators know is simply the price of admission for world-class. Here, look at the model again so we can bring even more precision to your understanding around it," instructed the billionaire as he touched the diagram on the piece of silk.

"The majority of people on the planet today really are trapped in superficiality," he confirmed. "Superficial understanding of their power to rise. Superficial intimacy with the possibilities of their potential. Superficial knowledge of the neurobiology of mastery, the daily routines of the world-builders and the very ambitions they wish to prioritize the remainder of their lives around. The majority is stuck in vague, imprecise thinking. And vague, imprecise thinking yields vague, imprecise results. A quick example: ask the average person for directions and most of the time, you'll discover, their instructions are unclear. That's because the way they think is unclear," said the billionaire as he picked up a stick from the beach and pointed it toward the word "granularity" on the framework.

"Legendary achievers are vastly different. They get that amateur levels of awareness will never lead to the highest grade of professional results. Another example that I hope will dial in this important insight for you two. I'm a huge fan of Formula One racing. I was invited to hang out with my favorite team in the pit area recently. Their attention to the slightest of particulars, their dedication to the demonstration of extreme excellence and their willingness to do whatever it took to make things great was not only validating but tremendously inspiring. Again, to the ordinary person, the suggestion of the need for an obsessive attention to the most minor of details and the importance of a ridiculously rigorous approach in their pro and private lives seems odd. But that F1 crew! Their flawless calibration of the race car, their superhuman speed in executing pit stops and even the way they cleaned the pit area with an industrial vacuum cleaner after the car roared away so there wasn't even a hint of dirt anywhere was fantastic. This is my point. The Top 5% go granular versus applying a superficial mindset to their daily attitudes, behaviors and activities."

"They really sweat the fine points so much they removed the dirt from the pit area after the race car left?" questioned the artist, fascinated.

"Yep," remarked the billionaire. "They swept and vacuumed the whole bay. And when I asked them why, they told me that if even a molecule of sediment got into the race machine's engine it could cost them a win. Or even worse—it could result in the loss of a life. Actually, any small failure of even one team member to act with precision could create a tragedy. One loose screw left by an unfocused crew member could lead to a calamity. One checklist item missed by a distracted associate might cause a catastrophe. Or one missing measurement overlooked by a squad partner leaving some of his precious attention on the phone he was playing with prior to the pit stop could cost a victory."

"I'm beginning to agree with you that the approach you are speaking of is important," admitted the entrepreneur. "Very few businesspeople and those in other fields like the arts, sciences and sports think and behave like this anymore. It used to be normal, I guess. Developing high awareness around the things that we do and having a painstaking approach to making our work perfect. Refining the details. Sweating the little points. Producing with precision rather than being unprofessional and careless. Underpromising and overdelivering. Taking immense pride in our craft. Going deep and embracing—to use your words—granularity versus superficiality."

"I must give credit where it's due," said the billionaire humbly. "This languaging and this model was taught to me by The Spellbinder. But, yes. Small things matter when it comes to mastery. I read somewhere that the space shuttle *Challenger* disaster, which broke so many hearts, was caused by the failure of a single O-ring seal that some experts valued at seventy cents. A horrific ending of lives was caused by a flaw around what appeared to be an insignificant detail."

"This all makes me think of the Dutch genius Vermeer," the artist contributed. "He was a painter who pursued work of the highest quality. He experimented with different techniques that would allow natural light to fall in a way that made his art look three-dimensional. There was such a depth to what he created. Such attractiveness to each stroke and such refinement in every move. So, I agree too: The average artist has a really light, basic, impatient approach to their painting. Their focus is more on the cash than on the craft. Their attention is on the fame, not the finesse. I guess that because of this, they never build the higher awareness and acumen that will help them make the better choices that will give them the better results that will make them the legends of their fields. I'm starting to get how powerful this simple model is."

"I love Vermeer's *Woman in Blue Reading a Letter* and, of course, *Girl with a Pearl Earring*," said the billionaire, cementing the fact that he appreciated great art.

"I love this insight that you're sharing with us," observed the entrepreneur as her eyes widened. She then grasped the artist's hand. Mr. Riley winked.

"I knew this was coming," he muttered with obvious happiness on seeing their growing romantic connection. He closed his eyes, once again. The butterfly was still sitting on the ear of the eccentric tycoon. As it flapped its exotic-colored wings, Mr. Riley spoke these words from the mighty poet Rumi:

Gamble everything for love, if you are a true human being. If not, leave this gathering. Half-heartedness doesn't reach into majesty.

"Can I ask you a question?" wondered the entrepreneur.

"Absolutely," replied the billionaire.

"How does this philosophy of rigor and granularity play out in personal relationships?"

"Not well," was the candid reply of the shirtless baron. "The Spellbinder schooled me on a concept called 'The Dark Side of Genius.' Basically, the idea is that every human gift comes with a downside. And the very quality that makes you special in one area is the same one that makes you a misfit in another. The reality is that many of the great virtuosos of the world had messy private lives. The very gifts of seeing a

95

vision few else could see, holding themselves to the absolute highest of standards, being content alone for long stretches of time as they worked monomaniacally detailing the most minor points on their projects, behaving relentlessly in following through on their masterpieces, acting with rarely seen self-discipline and listening to their hearts while ignoring their critics made personal relationships hard. They were misunderstood and seen as 'difficult' and 'different,' 'rigid' and 'unbalanced.'"

The billionaire then fell to the sand and started doing more push-ups at a ferocious pace. Next, while staring at a white dove that glided over the roof of his oceanside home, he did twenty burpees. Then he carried on.

"And many of these legends of creativity, productivity and world-class performance *were* out of balance," the magnate stated. "They were perfectionists, mavericks and fanatics. This is The Dark Side of Genius. The very things that make you amazing at your craft can devastate your home life. Just telling you cats the truth," observed the billionaire as he sipped from a water bottle that had tiny lettering on it. If you looked at it closely and carefully, here's what you'd read:

Philip of Macedonia in a message to Sparta: "You are advised to submit without further delay, for if I bring my army into your land, I will destroy your farms, slay your people and raze your city."

Sparta's reply: "If."

"But just because your gifts have downsides to them doesn't mean you shouldn't express them!" expounded the billionaire energetically. "You just need to develop awareness around where they can lead you into trouble in your personal life and then manage those traps. And this brings me beautifully back to this morning's learning model that really does set the stage for everything you'll learn about the transformational value of The 5 AM Club—and how to lock it in as an enduring habit."

The industrialist bent down, picked up a sea-worn stick and touched it to the silk swatch.

"Please always remember the core maxim for elite performance that this framework for personal greatness has been built around: with better daily awareness you can make better daily choices, and with better daily choices you'll start seeing better daily results. The Spellbinder calls this *The 3 Step Success Formula*. See, with better awareness of your natural ability to achieve great things, for example, or on how installing The 5 AM Method into your morning routine will upgrade your productivity, you'll rise from the community of superficiality that currently dominates the Earth up into the society of granularity. This heightened level of insight and consciousness will then optimize your daily decisions. And, logically, once you get your daily choices right, you'll accelerate your leadership, accomplishment and impact dramatically. Because it's your decisions that make your results."

"For one of our coaching sessions," the billionaire continued, "The Spellbinder and I met in Lucerne, Switzerland. Such a pretty city set on a magnificent lake surrounded by breathtaking mountains. Sort of a fairy-tale kind of a place. Anyhoo, one morning he ordered a pot of hot water, along with some lemon wedges so he could have the fresh lemon tea he enjoys sipping most mornings. Here's the thing . . ."

"This should be interesting," the artist interrupted as he scratched an arm with a tattoo built around an Andy Warhol quote that said: "I never think that people die. They just go to department stores."

"The tray arrived," the billionaire went on. "Perfect silverware. Excellent china. Everything calibrated to the highest order. And get this: whoever cut the lemons in the kitchen exercised the deep-craft rigor essential to sustained mastery by actually going the extra mile—and carving the seeds out of the wedges. Amazing, right?"

The billionaire began to do the same quirky dance that he did at the conference center. Then he stopped. The entrepreneur and the artist shook their heads.

"A pretty uncommon level of care and attention to detail in a world of such superficiality and performers stuck in apathy," said the entrepreneur, pretending not to be distracted by the mogul's dancing.

"The Spellbinder calls the phenomenon pervading commerce these days 'The Collective De-Professionalization of Business,'" noted the billionaire. "People who should be working, delighting customers, showcasing extraordinary skills, unlocking otherworldly value for their organizations so both they and their firms experience success are watching inane videos on their phones, shopping online for shoes or scrolling through their social feeds. I've never seen people so disengaged at work, so checked out and so exhausted. And I've never seen people making so many mistakes."

The billionaire pointed the crooked stick at *The 3 Step Success Formula* again.

"Deseeding the lemon wedges is a fine metaphor to challenge you to consistently make the shift from superficiality to granularity. Real rigor in terms of your approach to not only what you do at work but how you operate in your private life. True depth as it relates to how you think, behave and deliver. Healthy perfectionism—and an unyielding quest to be the best that you are capable of becoming is what I'm suggesting to you two good folks here on this awesome beach. This will give you what The Spellbinder calls a 'GCA: Gargantuan Competitive Advantage.' It's never been so easy to own the sport in business today because so few performers are doing the things required to reach industry dominance. Mastery is a rarity, and people who play at a brilliant level are a scarcity. So, the field is yours! If you show up the way I'm encouraging you to show up. Here's the powerful insight: There's a ton of competition at ordinary, but there's almost none at extraordinary. There's never been such a glamorous opportunity to become peerless because so few people are dedicated to world-class in this age of such scattered focus, eroded values and deteriorated faith in ourselves along with the inherent primal power we hold. How often do you meet someone at a store or in a restaurant who is fully present, astoundingly polite, un-usually knowledgeable, full of enthusiasm, incredibly hardworking, intensely imaginative, noticeably inventive and gaspworthily great at what they do? Almost never, right?"

"Yes," acknowledged the entrepreneur. "I'd have to interview thou-sands of people to find one treasure like this."

"So, you cats have a GCA! Lucky you," shouted the billionaire. "You can pretty much dominate your fields because so few are like this now. Raise your commitment. Step up your standards. And then get busy on hardwiring in this way of being as your default. And that's really important: you have to optimize *daily*. Consistency really is the DNA of mastery. And small, daily, seemingly insignificant improvements when done consistently over time yield staggering results. Please remember that great companies and wonderful lives don't happen by sudden revo-lution. Nope. They materialize via incremental evolution. Tiny, daily wins and iterations stack into outcomes of excellence, over the long-term. But few of us have the patience these days to endure the long game. As a result, not many of us ever become legends."

"All this information is fantastic. And so valuable for my art," the artist said gratefully as he put his shirt back on.

"Wonderful to hear," acknowledged the billionaire. "Look, I know that you both have experienced a ton of learning in a very short time. I understand that getting up early is a new skill you're installing and everything you've heard about chasing greatness, leaving the crowd, relinquishing average and renouncing ordinary is probably over-whelming. So just breathe—and relax, please. Exceptionalism is a journey. Virtuosity is a voyage. Rome wasn't built in a day, right?"

"Right," agreed the artist.

"Definitely," accepted the entrepreneur.

"And I also get that rising into the more pure reaches of your superior strengths and most sovereign human gifts is an uncomfortable and scary process. I've been through it and the rewards that are on their way to you as you remain dedicated to learning The 5 AM Method are worth more than any amount of money, fame and worldly power you'll ever have. And what I've taught you today is a necessary component to the system for waking before daybreak and preparing yourself to be an elite achiever and luminous human being that we'll go much deeper into in our upcoming sessions together. I guess what I really want to say before I let you cats go for this morning, so you can go have some fun, is that while growth as a producer and as a person can be hard—it truly is the finest work a human being can ever do. And fully remember that you are most alive when your heart beats quickest. And we are most awake when our fears scream loudest."

"So, we need to keep going ahead, right?" confirmed the entrepreneur as a lovely ocean breeze washed through her brown hair.

"Absolutely," said the tycoon. "All shadows of insecurity dissolve in the warm glow of persistency.

"Okay. One last example about assuming a rigorous approach in your professional and home life and gaining a GCA by going all granular on important projects, around essential skills and during meaningful activities. After that, I'd love for you two to go swimming, snorkeling and sunbathing. You should see the spectacular lunch my team has prepared for you! I need to head into Port Louis for a meeting, but I really hope you both will make yourselves at home. So . . ."

Mr. Riley stopped for a moment, reached down and touched his toes four times while muttering the following mantra: "Today is a glorious day and I'll live it at excellence, with boundless enthusiasm and limitless integrity, true to my visions and with a heart full of love.

"I remember reading an article," the billionaire continued, "where the CEO of Moncler, the Italian fashion company, was asked what his favorite food was. He replied it was spaghetti pomodoro. Then he shared that while this dish seems strikingly simple to prepare as it's only pasta, fresh tomatoes, olive oil and basil, the executive remarked that to get the 'calibration' correct takes unusual expertise and uncommon prowess. That's an important word for all three of us to keep top of mind as we tighten up our A-games, elevate our performance and accelerate our contribution to the world: *calibration*. Dialing in the finest of attitudes and refining the littlest of details is what granularity and ascension into the orbit of your inherent genius—and a life magically lived—is all about."

The eccentric magnate then placed the piece of silk from the bottle into a pocket of his shorts. And vanished.

CHAPTER 10

The 4 Focuses of History-Makers

"The life given us, by nature is short, but
the memory of a well-spent life is eternal." —Cicero

The sunrise was dazzling as the entrepreneur and the artist walked hand-in-hand along the seashore to meet the billionaire at the designated meeting spot for the next morning's mentoring class.

Mr. Riley was already there when they arrived, sitting on the sand, eyes closed in a deep meditation.

He was shirtless, wearing camouflage-patterned shorts similar to the ones The Spellbinder styled the day he appeared on the beach and a pair of rubber diving booties with smiley face emojis scattered over them. You would have been more than amused if you saw him in them.

An assistant rushed out of the billionaire's home the instant he raised a hand toward the heavens, displaying the universal victory sign. Three crisp pages of paper were efficiently extracted from a shiny black leather satchel and handed to the titan of industry without a word being exchanged. Stone Riley simply offered a slight bow of appreciation. In turn, he gave a sheet to each of his two students.

It was exactly 5 AM.

The billionaire then picked up a seashell and skipped it across the water. It appeared as if he had something profound on his mind this morning. Gone were the usual lightheartedness, festivity and awkward antics.

"You okay?" inquired the entrepreneur as she touched a bracelet engraved with the words "Straight on hustle. Rise and grind. I'll sleep when I'm dead."

The tycoon read the words on the bangle. He placed a finger onto his lips.

"Who will cry when you die?" he asked.

"What?" exclaimed the artist.

"What will those who know you whisper about how you lived once you're no longer here?" The billionaire articulated the question in the manner of a skilled actor. "You live as if you were destined to live forever, no thought of your frailty ever enters your head, of how much time has already gone by you take no heed. You squander time as if you drew from a full and abundant supply, though all the while that day which you bestow on some person or thing is perhaps your last."

"Those are your thoughts? Brilliant," stated the artist.

The billionaire looked mildly embarrassed. "I wish! No, they belong to the stoic philosopher Seneca. They came from his treatise *On the Shortness of Life.*"

"So why are we talking about death on this beautiful morning exactly?" queried the entrepreneur, appearing a little uncomfortable.

"Because most of us alive today wish we had more time. Yet we waste the time we have. Thinking about dying brings what matters most into much sharper focus. You'll stop allowing digital distraction, cyber diversions and online nuisances to steal the irreplaceable hours of the blessing called your life. You never get your days back, you know?" said the billionaire in a friendly but firm fashion. "I reread *Chasing Daylight* yesterday after my meeting in town. It's the true story of high-powered CEO Eugene O'Kelly, who was informed he had only a few months left to live when his doctor discovered he had three brain tumors."

"So, what did he do?" asked the artist softly.

"He organized his last days with the same commitment to orderliness he ran his business life by. O'Kelly tried to make up for the school concerts he'd missed, the family outings he'd passed up and the friendships he'd forgotten. In one part of the book he shared how he'd ask a friend out for a walk in nature and that this 'was sometimes not only the final time we would take such a leisurely walk together but also the first time.'"

"Sad," was the contribution of the entrepreneur as she nervously played with her bracelet. The worry lines on her forehead reappeared in full blazing glory.

"Then last night I watched *The Diving Bell and the Butterfly*, one of my favorite movies," the billionaire continued. "It's also a true story, about a man who was also atop the world, an editor-in-chief of French *Elle* magazine. Jean-Dominique Bauby had it all and then suffered a stroke that left him unable to move any muscle in his body—except for his left eyelid. The condition's called 'locked-in syndrome.' His mind still worked perfectly. But it was as if his body was encased in a diving bell, totally paralyzed."

"Sad," said the artist, echoing his companion.

"Get this," added Mr. Riley. "His rehabilitation therapists taught him a communication method called 'silent alphabet' which allowed him to form letters of words by blinking. And with their help, he wrote a book about his experience—and the essential meaning of life. It took him two hundred thousand blinks, but he completed the book."

"I have nothing to complain about," the entrepreneur said quietly.

"He passed away shortly after the book was published," the billionaire kept on. "But the point I'm trying to offer with all this is that life is very, very fragile. There are people who will wake up today, take a shower, put on their clothes, drink their coffee, eat their oatmeal—and then be killed in a motor vehicle collision on their way to the office. That's just life happening. So, my advice to you two special human beings is not to put off doing whatever it takes to express your natural genius. Live in a way that feels true to you and pay attention to the small miracles every day brings."

"I hear you," commented the artist as he tugged a dreadlock and fidgeted with the Panama hat he'd chosen to wear for this morning's coaching session.

"I do, too," stated the entrepreneur somberly.

"Enjoy every sandwich," added the artist.

"Very wise insight," said Mr. Riley.

"It's not mine," the artist replied sheepishly. "They are the words of songwriter Warren Zevon. He spoke them after he discovered he was terminally ill."

"Be grateful for every moment. Don't be timid when it comes to your ambitions. Stop wasting time on insanely trivial things. And make it a priority to reclaim the creativity, fire and potential that is dormant within you. It's so important to do so. Why do you think Plato encouraged us to 'know thyself'? He understood intimately that we have vast reservoirs of ability that absolutely must be accessed and then *applied* in order for us to lead energetic, joyful, peaceful and meaningful lives. To neglect this hidden force inside of us is to create a breeding ground for the pain of potential unused, the frustration of fearlessness unembraced and the lethargy of mastery unexplored."

A kite surfer whizzed by. And a school of crown squirrelfish sailed through the water that was as clear as Abe Lincoln's conscience.

"This brings us beautifully to what I wanted to walk you through this morning. Please look carefully at your sheet of paper," the billionaire instructed.

Here is the learning model that the two students saw:

THE 4 FOCUSES OF
HISTORY-MAKERS

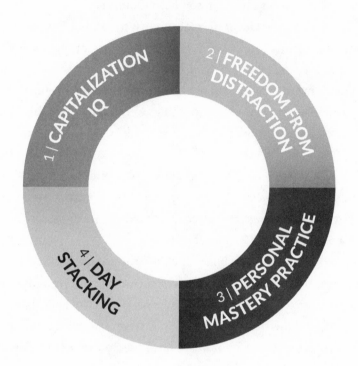

History-Maker Focus #1: Capitalization IQ

The mogul explained the concept of capitalization developed by eminent psychologist James Flynn. The valuable insight he conceived is that what makes a legendary performer so good isn't the amount of natural talent they are born into but the extent of that potential they actualize—and capitalize. "Many of the finest athletes in the world," Mr. Riley observed, "had less innate skill than their competition. But it was their exceptional dedication, commitment and drive to maximize whatever strengths they had that made them iconic.

"It's the old 'It's not the size of the dog in the fight, it's the size of the fight in the dog' insight," declared the billionaire as he rubbed his chiseled abdominals absentmindedly and put on a new pair of sunglasses, the kind you'd see on a surfer in southern California.

"The Spellbinder taught me early on that by joining The 5 AM Club, I'd have a gorgeous window of opportunity every morning to cultivate my highest assets, take some time for myself and do the preparation needed for me to make each day a tiny gem. He helped me understand that successful people use their mornings well and that by rising before daybreak, I'd win a primary victory that would set me up for a triumphant day."

"I never seem to have any 'me time,'" interjected the entrepreneur. "My schedule's always so full," she repeated. "I'd love to have a block in the morning to recharge my batteries—and do some things that would make me a happier and better person."

"Exactly," remarked the billionaire. "So many of us lead time-starved lives. We absolutely need to have at least an hour first thing in the morning to refuel, grow and become healthier, more peaceful people. Getting up at 5 AM and then running *The 20/20/20 Formula*, which you'll soon learn will give you an extraordinary head start on your days. You'll be able to concentrate on high-value activities instead of letting your day control you. You'll experience energy you never knew you had. The joyfulness you'll reclaim will blow you away. And your sense of personal freedom will totally soar."

Mr. Riley then turned around to display a temporary tattoo on his muscled back. It bore a quote by French philosopher Albert Camus that read: "The only way to deal with an unfree world is to become so absolutely free that your very existence is an act of rebellion."

Below these words, on the industrialist's back, was an image of a phoenix rising from the flames. It looked exactly like this:

"I so need this," the entrepreneur said. "I know my productivity, gratefulness and calmness would improve so much if I had some personal time every morning before it all gets so hectic."

"Me, too," said the artist. "An hour to myself every morning to reflect and prepare would be a game-changer for my art. And for my life."

"The Spellbinder taught me early on that investing sixty minutes in developing my best self and my greatest skills during what he called 'The Victory Hour' would transform the way the rest of my life unfolded mentally, emotionally, physically and spiritually. He promised it would give me one of those Gargantuan Competitive Advantages we discussed yesterday. And lead to the formation of absolute *empires* of creativity, money, joy and helpfulness to humanity. And I need to say he was completely right.

"Anyhoo," chirped the billionaire. "Back to the concept of capitalization and the importance of intelligently exploiting whatever primal gifts you've been given. Too many among us have bought into the collective hypnosis that those with extraordinary skill are cut from a different cloth and have been divinely blessed by The Gods of Exceptional Talent. But that just ain't so," observed the billionaire, a wisp of his farm boy manner emerging.

"Dedication and discipline beats brilliance and giftedness every day of the week. And A-Players don't get lucky. They make lucky. Each time you resist a temptation and pursue an optimization you invigorate your heroism. Every instant you do that which you know to be right over the thing that you feel would be easy, you facilitate your entry into the hall of fame of epic achievers."

The billionaire stared at a gigantic seagull clutching its slimy breakfast. He then released a loud burp. "Oops. So sorry," he spoke in the tone of apology.

"As I mentioned earlier, a lot of the latest research emerging on successful people is confirming that our private story about our potential is the key performance indicator on whether we actually exploit that potential."

"What do you mean?" requested the entrepreneur as she stopped taking notes on her device to look into the eyes of the billionaire, who had now put on a tight t-shirt that read, "Victims have big TVs. Leaders own large libraries."

"Well, if you're running a mental narrative that says that you don't have what it takes to be a superb leader in business or an acclaimed expert of your craft, then you won't even start the adventure of getting there, will you? *And world-class is a process, not an event.* Running a limiting psychological program that says 'everyday people can't become great' or 'genius is born, not developed' will cause you to think it would be a complete waste of time to do the studying, put in the practice hours and prioritize your days around your heartfelt desires. What would be the point of investing all that labor, vigor and time and making all those sacrifices when virtuoso-level results are impossible for someone like you, under your belief system? And then, because your daily behavior is always a function of your deepest beliefs, that very perception of your inability to realize victory becomes real," noted the billionaire. "Human beings are hardwired to act in alignment with our self-identity, always. You'll never rise higher than your personal story. Important insight there."

He then peered out into the ocean at a small fishing boat with a net strewn across the end of it. A fisherman in a red shirt was smoking a cigarette as he navigated the vessel away from some dangerous coral reef. The billionaire mumbled another mantra to himself.

"I am grateful. And I am forgiving. I am giving. My life is beautiful, creative, productive, prosperous and magical."

Then he continued the discussion around capitalization.

"The positive psychologists call the way we embrace a story about who we are and what we can achieve and then behave in a way that makes that fantasy actually come true 'The Self-Fulfilling Prophecy.' We subconciously adopt a thinking pattern by learning it from the people who most influence us at an early age. Our parents, our teachers and our friends. Then we act according to it. And since what we do creates the results we see, this generally faulty personal story becomes a reality of our very own causing. Amazing, right? But that's how most of us operate through the best years of our lives. The world is a mirror. And we get from life not what we want, but that which we are."

"And I guess that the more we accept that core belief about our inability to produce excellent results in whatever it is we hope to do, the more we not only reinforce it so it becomes a trusted conviction but we also deepen the behavior that's associated with it so it becomes a daily habit," recited the artist, sounding professorish instead of bohemian in the pure morning air.

"Wonderfully said!" replied the billionaire excitedly. "I love the 'trusted conviction' idea. That's good. You should share that phrase with The Spellbinder if you see him today. I think he's out fishing but, knowing him, he'll be getting some sun here on this beach later in the morning."

The billionaire continued. "Every human being has an instinct for greatness, a hunger for the heroic and a psychic need to rise toward the heavens of their finest capability, whether we remember this consciously or not. A lot of us have been minimized and pushed down so much by the dark and toxic influences around us we've forgotten all we truly are. We've become masters of compromise, slowly and steadily allowing in more aspects of mediocrity until a point arrives where it's our standard operating system. Real leaders never negotiate their standards. They know there's always room to improve. They understand that we are most connected to our sovereign nature when we are reaching for our best. Alexander the Great once said: 'I am not afraid of an army of lions led by a sheep; I am afraid of an army of sheep led by a lion.'"

The billionaire inhaled audibly. A butterfly fluttered by. And a crab scampered past him.

"I'm here to remind you," he carried on, "that each one of us holds a profound capacity for leadership within us. And as you now know, I'm not speaking of leadership in the sense of having a title, a lofty position or needing some formal authority. What I'm referring to is so much more weighty and exquisite than that. It's the *true* power inside a human heart versus the transitory power delivered by a big office, a fast car and a large bank balance. What I'm speaking of is the potency to do work that is so great we just can't take our eyes off you. The capability to create massive value in your marketplace. The capacity to impact— and disrupt—an entire industry. And the power to live with honor, nobility, audacity and integrity. So that you fulfill your opportunity to make history, in your own original way. Doesn't matter if you're a CEO or a janitor. A billionaire or a ditch digger. A movie star or a student. If you are alive today, you have the ability to lead without a title and make your mark on the world, even if you don't currently believe you can due to the limits of your current perception. Your perception isn't reality. It just isn't. It's just your current perception on reality, kindly remember that. It's simply the lens you happen to be looking at reality through at this moment of your ascent toward world-class. Makes me think of the words of the German philosopher Arthur Schopenhauer, who wrote, 'Most people take the limits of their vision to be the limits of the world. A few do not. Join them.'"

"So, there's a large difference between reality and our perception of reality, right?" inquired the entrepreneur. "It seems from what you're saying that it's almost as if we see the world through a filter that's made up of all our personal programming. And we run the program so much we get brainwashed into believing that the way we are seeing the world is real, right? You've got me rethinking the way I see everything now," she admitted as the skin on her forehead scrunched together like a rose contracting in the cold.

"I'm beginning to question so much," she went on. "Why I started my business in the first place. Why social status is so important to me. Why I have such urges to eat in the sleekest restaurants, live in the best neighborhoods and drive the most stylish cars. I think part of the reason I've been so crushed by the takeover attempt at my company is because I get my identity as a human being from being the founder. Honestly, I've been so busy driving my career, I haven't stopped for gas in terms of really thinking things through—and living intentionally. And it's like *The 3 Step Success Formula* you taught us yesterday. As I develop better daily awareness around myself and why it is that I do what I do, I'll make the better daily choices that will give me better daily results."

The entrepreneur was unstoppable.

"I have no clue what my authentic values are, what I want to represent as a leader, why I'm building what I'm building, what really makes me happy and how I want to be remembered when I'm no longer here. The story of that CEO and the stroke of that editor really spoke to me. Life really is super-fragile. And—now that I'm speaking so openly—I think I've been spending many days chasing the wrong things. Stuck in the noise of complexity instead of hearing the signal of those top-value pursuits in my career and in my private life that would really make a difference. And I think about the past a lot. What happened to me in my childhood. I also haven't had any time for any friendships. I have no real passions. I've never watched the sun rise, until now. And I've never found true love," said the entrepreneur as she anxiously rubbed her bracelet.

The entrepreneur looked over to the artist. "Until now."

Tears filled his eyes.

"Trillions of planets in this universe," he pronounced, "billions of people on our planet and I was fortunate enough to meet you."

The entrepreneur smiled and then proceeded to respond in a gentle tone. "I hope I never lose you."

"Don't be too hard on yourself," interjected the billionaire. "We're all on our paths, know what I mean? We're all exactly where we need to be to receive the growth lessons we're meant to learn. And a problem will persist until you get the education it showed up to bring. And I do agree with you that human beings have a tragic habit of remembering the things that would be smart to forget and forgetting the wonderful things it would be wise to remember. Anyhoo, I do understand you. Please just trust that the highest and wisest part of you is leading you. There are no accidents on this path to legendary and the making of a life that matters. And, if you ask me, there's *nothing* wrong with magnificent homes, fast cars and lots of money. I really, really need you to hear me on that. Please. We are spiritual beings having a human experience—as the old saying goes. Having plenty of money is what life wants for you. Abundance is nature's way. There's no scarcity of flowers, lemon trees and stars in the sky. Money allows you to do superb things for yourself—and for the people you care most about. And it offers you the chance to help those in need."

A tourist waterskiing behind a speedboat zoomed by. You could hear him laughing with glee.

"I'll let you in on a little secret," the magnate continued. "I've given away most of my vast liquid fortune. Yes, I still have the jets and the Zurich flat and this oceanside place. And though my business interests are still valued at an amount that makes me a billionaire, I need none of it. I'm not attached to any of this."

"I read a story that I think you'll like," shared the artist. "Kurt Vonnegut, the writer, and Joseph Heller, the author of *Catch-22*, were at a party hosted by a renowned financier on Long Island. Vonnegut asked his companion how it felt to know that their host made more money in the day before the gala than he had made from all royalties of his bestselling book. Heller replied, 'I've got something he can never have.' Vonnegut asked, 'What on Earth could that be, Joe?' Heller's reply was priceless: 'The knowledge that I've got enough.'"

"Brilliant!" enthused the billionaire. "Love it!" he shouted inappropriately loudly as he high-fived the artist. He then performed the little dance he loved to do when he was happy yet again before launching into a series of jumping jacks. His eyes were closed as he did them. Such an oddball.

The artist went on talking. "Anyway, I understand what you're teaching us on this point about capitalization and The Self-Fulfilling Prophecy. No one will believe in our ability to do great things until we first believe in our greatness and then put in the sincere and rigorous effort to realize it. You know what Pablo Picasso once said?"

"Tell us, please," implored the entrepreneur, her stance showing that she was very open in this instant.

"Picasso announced, 'My mother said to me, if you are a soldier, you will become a general. If you are a monk, you will become the pope. Instead, I was a painter. And became Picasso.'"

"Gnarly, man," the billionaire remarked. "Now that's faith and confidence in one's potential."

The billionaire ran a fist along his tanned chin, looking down at the white sand for a moment.

"And it's not only our parents who are responsible for the limited programs most people are running through their minds during the finest hours of their greatest days. Like I suggested, many well-meaning yet unaware teachers reinforce the idea that the heroic geniuses of the arts, sciences, sports and humanities are 'special' and that we need to accept that we are 'ordinary,' incapable of producing towering work that leaves people breathless by its excellence and generating a life that is matchless. And then we have the association of our friends and relentless messaging of the media supporting the same 'facts.' Essentially it all becomes this consistent hypnotization where, without us even knowing it, the once-blazing fire of genius within us grows dimmer. And the once-passionate voices of possibility get quieter. We minimize our abilities and begin a lifelong process of playing small with our powers and constructing prisons around our strengths. We stop behaving as leaders, creative producers and possibilitarians. And we start acting as victims."

"Disappointing what happens to so many good people. And most of us can't see this brainwashing away from our best selves happening," reflected the entrepreneur.

"Yup," responded the billionaire. "Even worse, the potential unexpressed turns to pain, I need to emphasize."

"What do you mean by that?" wondered the artist, turning his eyes away and shifting his posture somewhat nervously. "Maybe I'm sabotaging creating art as original and exceptional as the great masters did because I've avoided capitalizing on my potential for so long that I'm hurting deep inside," the artist thought to himself.

"Well, our noblest selves know the truth: each of us are built to do astonishing things with our human gifts and materialize astounding feats with our productive talents. The word 'astonish' is actually derived from the Latin word 'extonare,' which means 'to leave someone thunderstruck.' Every single person alive today carries the capacity deep within their hearts—and spirits—to do this. The more we decrease the volume of our unhealthy narrative which, neurobiologically speaking, is a creation of our limbic system, the more we will hear this sublime call on ourselves to rise up to the blatant expression of our greatest genius. This is true whether you're a supervisor within a large organization, a programmer in a small cubicle, a teacher in a school or a chef in a restaurant. You absolutely have the capacity to lift your work to the level of artistry and have an impact for the betterment of humanity. And yet we resign our lives to apathy because of this faulty perception of who we truly are and what we can really accomplish, staying violently stuck in half-alive lives. And here's the really big idea: as we betray our true power, a part of us starts to die," noted the billionaire.

"Dramatic insight," acknowledged the artist. "I seriously need to make some massive changes. I'm tired of feeling tired. And neglecting my creative abilities. I'm beginning to get that I'm special."

"You are," affirmed the entrepreneur. "You are," she repeated, in a voice of tenderness.

"I'm also starting to see that I care too much about what others think. Some of my friends make fun of my paintings. And they say I'm a screwball behind my back. I'm realizing they just don't understand me. And my vision for my art."

"Many of the great geniuses of the world were not appreciated until decades after they died, you know," the billionaire offered, in a murmur.

"And on your point about your friends, I'm not so sure you're surrounding yourself with the right ones. And maybe now it's time to do you rather than limiting your talent and aliveness because you are seduced by the opinions of others. Kurt Cobain said it better than I ever could: 'I was tired of pretending that I was someone else just to get along with people, just for the sake of having friendships.'"

"Hmm," was the artist's only response.

"What I'm sharing is accurate. We become our associations. And you'll never have a positive influence in your field and make a beautiful life if you hang with negative people," continued the billionaire. "Oh—and that pain I was just speaking of—if not attended to and released—starts to form a deep reservoir of fear and self-hatred within us. Most of us don't have the awareness or possess the tools to process through this well of suppressed anguish. Most of us are unconscious to this quiet torment created by the disrespect we have shown to our promise. And so, we deny it if someone even suggests it. We flee from it when presented with an opportunity to manifest it. And we subconsciously develop a series of soul-crushing escape routes to avoid feeling this pain generated by our talents denied."

"Like what?" quizzed the entrepreneur.

"Addictions. Like constantly checking for messages or scanning for 'likes.' Or spending vast chunks of our daily lives watching too much television. TV shows have become so superb these days, it's so easy to get hooked. And when one episode ends, on some viewing platforms, the next one begins automatically. Many among us also make flights from their greatness by chatting and gossiping endlessly, not really understanding that *there's a staggering difference between being busy and being productive.*

"High-impact performers and genuine world-builders aren't very available to whoever seeks their attention and demands their time. They're hard to reach, waste few moments and are far more focused on doing real work versus artificial work—so they deliver the breathtaking results that advance our world. Other avoidance tactics from the pain of potential unexpressed are hours mindlessly surfing online, electronic shopping, working too much, drinking too much, eating too much, complaining too much and sleeping too much."

The tycoon sipped from his water bottle. Another fishing boat motored by. The woman who captained it waved to Mr. Riley, who bowed mightily in reply.

"The Spellbinder calls this whole phenomenon 'Learned Victimhood,'" the billionaire carried on in a wonderfully exuberant way. "As we leave our youth, there's a pull toward complacency. We can start to coast, settle for what's familiar and lose the juicy desire to expand our frontiers. We adopt the paradigm of a victim. We make excuses and then recite them so many times we train our subconscious mind to think they are true. We blame other people and outer conditions for our struggles, and we condemn past events for our private wars. We grow cynical and lose the curiosity, wonder, compassion and innocence we knew as kids. We become apathetic. Critical. Hardened. Within this personal ecosystem the majority of us create for ourselves, mediocrity then becomes acceptable. And because this mindset is running within us each day, the viewpoint seems so very real to us. We truly believe that the story we are running reveals the truth—because we're so close to it. So, rather than showing leadership in our fields, owning our crafts by producing dazzling work and handcrafting delicious lives, we resign ourselves to average. See how it all happens?"

"Yes. At least it's all becoming clearer. So, the key is to rescript our personal story, right?" inquired the entrepreneur.

"Absolutely," confirmed the billionaire. "Every time you become aware of yourself dropping into victim mode and make a more courage-ous choice, you rewrite the narrative. You raise your self-identity, elevate your self-respect and enrich your self-confidence. Each time you vote for your superior self you starve your weaker side—and feed your inherent power. And as you do this with the consistency demanded by mastery, your 'Capitalization IQ,' that is your ability to materialize whatever gifts you've been born with, will only grow."

The billionaire invited his two students to move to the terrace of his home to continue the morning's lesson on The 4 Focuses of History-Makers.

History-Maker Focus #2: Freedom from Distraction

The billionaire pointed to the model with a pinky finger.

"Remember that important brain tattoo of successful people? '*An addiction to distraction is the death of your creative production.*' It will guide us through this section of today's mentoring session. And I've decided to go deep into the importance of winning the war against diversion and cyber nuisances because it's an extremely serious issue in our culture. In some ways, the new technologies and social media are not only eroding the Everests of our glorious productive potential, they are also training us to be less human. We have fewer real conversations, fewer true con-nections and fewer meaningful interactions."

"Um. Yes, I'm realizing this more and more as the mornings pass on this beach," admitted the entrepreneur.

119

"Filling valuable hours with meaningless moves is the drug of choice for most people," the billionaire continued. "Intellectually we know we shouldn't be wasting time on zero-value activities, but emotionally we just can't beat the temptation. We just can't fight the hook. This behavior is costing organizations billions of dollars in lost productivity and deficient quality. And as I suggested earlier, people are making more mistakes in their work than ever before because they aren't present to what they're doing. Their precious concentration has been hijacked by a foolish use of technology and their priceless focus has been kidnapped, costing them their chance to create their best work and calibrate their finest lives."

The stillness and quietude that only the day's earliest hours provide was still evident.

The industrialist paused. He scanned the entire scene, gazing at the flowers neatly ordered around his home, then at the cargo ships on the horizon that looked like they hadn't moved and finally at the ocean.

"Look, cats," he said at last. "I *love* the modern world—I really do. Without all the technology we have available to us life would be a lot harder. My businesses wouldn't be as successful as they are, I wouldn't be as efficient as I am and I possibly wouldn't be here with you two."

"Why?" wondered the artist as a single dolphin swam by gracefully. Astoundingly, it then soared high out of the ocean and spun in the air four times before returning to the water with a lavish splash.

Mr. Riley looked delighted. "I'm so happy I discovered how to become a magnet for miracles," he whispered to himself. "And I can't wait to teach these good folks how to do the same for themselves." He then kept on with his discourse.

"All the innovations in healthcare tech saved my life when I was sick," the billionaire explained. "Anyhoo, technology well used is a phenomenal thing. It's all the silly ways people apply it now that really concerns me. So many potentially outstanding people are suffering from 'broken focus syndrome' because they've filled their professional and personal lives with so many gadgets, interruptions and cybernoise. If you're in the sport of winning, please model all of the great masters of history and strip away all the layers of complexity from your days. Simplify. Streamline everything. *Become a purist.* Less really is more. Concentrate on just a few work projects so you make them amazing versus diluting your attention on too many. And socially, have fewer friends but go deep with them so the relationship is rich. Accept fewer invitations, major in fewer leisure activities and study, then master, a smaller number of books versus skimming many. An intense concentration only on what matters most is how the pros realize victory. Simplify. Simplify. Simplify.

"Stop managing your time and start managing your focus," added the billionaire. "Now there's a principle for greatness in this overstimulated society we live in."

"Thanks to your teaching so far," said the artist, "I now understand that being busy doesn't mean you're being productive. I've also come to see that when I work on a new painting, the closer I get to great art, the more some darker part of me wants to get me distracted so that I avoid doing something mind-blowing. It happens fairly often now that I think about it. I'll get nearer to fantastic work and I then begin to break my work routine. I'll go online and just surf. I'll sleep later and watch entire seasons of my favorite shows or play video games with my virtual friends all night. Sometimes I'll just drink too much cheap red wine."

"The closer you get to your genius, the more you'll face the sabotage of your fears," agreed the billionaire powerfully. "You'll become scared of leaving the majority and having to deal with the by-products of mastery, like being different from most people, jealousy from competitors and the pressure to make your next project even better. As you rise toward virtuosity, you'll become anxious about failure, threatened by a concern of not being good enough and insecure about blazing new paths. So, your amygdala—an almond-shaped mass of gray matter in the brain that detects fear—gets all fired up. And you begin to tear down the productivity you've built up. We all have a subconcious saboteur that lurks within our weakest selves, you know? The good news is that once you become aware of this condition . . ."

"I can make the better daily choices that will give me better daily results," the artist interrupted with all the energy of a puppy seeing its owner after a long day alone.

"Exactly," said the billionaire. "Once you are aware of the fact that, as you near your highest talents and most luminous gifts, the scared side of you will rear its ugly head and try to mess up the masterpieces you've been creating by pursuing every distraction and escape route possible to avoid finishing, you can manage that self-destructive behavior. You can step outside of it. You can disempower it, simply by watching its attempts to denounce your mastery."

"Really profound insights here," contributed the entrepreneur. "This explains so much about why I'm limiting my productivity, performance and influence at my company. I'll set an important target. I get the team enrolled in it. We sequence the key deliverables. Then I get distracted. I'll say 'yes' to another opportunity that adds more complexity to our business. I'll fill my days with useless meetings with people who love to hear the sound of their own voice. I'll check my notifications obsessively and watch 'breaking news' reports religiously. This morning it's become super-clear how I'm totally sabotaging my effectiveness. It's also pretty obvious that I am addicted to the digital nonsense you're speaking about. I'll be honest, I haven't gotten over some of my exes because it's so easy to watch their lives on social media. I'm understanding now that a lot of the hours I could be super-creative I trade for online recreation. Like you said, Mr. Riley, it's a form of escape. I can't seem to stop shopping on my devices. It's just too easy. And it makes me feel happy, for a few minutes. I'm getting why Steve Jobs didn't give his kids the very things he sold to the world. He understood how addictive they could be, if improperly used. And how they could make us less human and less *alive*."

The billionaire raised a hand. Another assistant sprinted from the beach hut up to the now sun-soaked terrace. He wore a crisp white shirt, charcoal gray sailing shorts and well-cared-for black leather sandals.

"Here you are, sir," the young man said with a French accent as he handed the mogul a tray with mysterious markings on it. In the center was a model of the human brain.

It looked exactly like this:

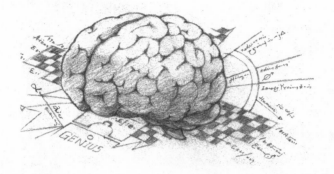

"Merci beaucoup, Pierre. Now let's explore the neuroscience of self-sabotage so you cats can understand it better—and then beat it. Remember, each of us has what The Spellbinder calls 'The Ancient Brain.' This is made up of the limbic system—a set of brain structures that sit on both sides of the thalamus, right under the cerebrum. The amygdala that I mentioned a few moments ago is part of this. This basic and lower-functioning brain served to keep us safe thousands of years ago in a primitive world of relentless threats like starvation, temperature extremes, warring tribes and saber-toothed tigers. It functions to do one main thing: maintain a steady state while warning us against dangers so we survive and propagate our species.

"With me so far?" asked the billionaire politely.

"Understood." The entrepreneur and the artist responded in unison as a housekeeper served fresh lemon tea with some chunks of ginger in it.

"Excellent. One of the fascinating traits of our ancient brain is its negativity bias. To keep us safe, it's far less interested in what's positive in our environment and significantly more invested in letting us know what's bad.

123

"This brain's default is to hunt for danger," the billionaire continued happily. "So back when life was much more brutal, we could respond swiftly and stay alive. That mechanism served our ancestors exceedingly well. But in today's world, most of us don't face death daily. The reality is that the ordinary person lives a higher quality life than most members of royalty did even just a few hundred years ago. Please think about this blessing."

The tycoon slurped some tea.

"And yet, because of this built-in negativity bias within our ancient brains, we're constantly scanning for breaches against our security. We're in hypervigilance mode, mostly anxious and uptight, even when everything's going great. Fascinating, right?"

"Explains a lot of why we think the way we do," noted the entrepreneur as she, too, enjoyed the tea. "Now I see why I always seem to feel I've never achieved enough, even though I've accomplished more than anyone I know," the entrepreneur carried on. "I have such a successful business, a robust net worth and before my investors got greedy—a fairly wonderful life. Yet despite everything I have, my brain seems to always focus on what I'm missing, where I don't have enough and how I'm falling short of expectations around winning. Drives me crazy. I hardly feel any peace. Ever."

The entrepreneur crossed her arms. The artist blew her a kiss as his dreadlocks dangled in the fragrant breeze.

"Theodore Roosevelt said something I think it's important you hear," expounded the billionaire.

"What did he say?" inquired the entrepreneur, her arms clenched tightly.

"'Comparison is the thief of joy,'" responded the billionaire. "Someone will always have more fortune, fame and stuff than you do. Think about my earlier point about detachment and embracing the wisdom of knowing when enough is enough."

"Yes. I remember," said the entrepreneur courteously.

"More and more of this hunger you have comes from deeper feelings of scarcity. And a lot of this is stemming from the workings of your ancient brain. It's scanning your environment and the negativity bias is being activated, preventing you from enjoying all the good you have. Okay," said the billionaire. "Let's go even more granular. As time advanced, our brains evolved. And the prefrontal cortex developed. This is the part of our brain responsible for higher thinking. Neuroscientists consider it the crown jewel of advanced reasoning. The Spellbinder calls it 'The Mastery Brain.' But here's the thing: As we began to dream bigger, learn quicker and raise our levels of creativity, productivity and performance, the ancient brain and the mastery brain began a conflict. They went to war. The primitive brain senses our growth, knows we're leaving our safe harbor of the known and gets fired up because we're leaving our traditional ways of being. It senses the threat—even though the threat is essential to our personal ascension and professional advancement. We absolutely must venture into those unexplored places where possibility lives to become more intimate with our primal genius and to become all we are meant to be. Knowing we have higher reaches of talent and courage left to visit floods a human heart with immense excitement. This knowledge is one of the vast treasures that make life worth living. The celebrated psychologist Abraham Maslow once stated, 'If you plan on being anything less than who you are capable of being, you will probably be unhappy all the days of your life.' But the amygdala kicks into high gear as we exit what's familiar and try something new. The vagus nerve gets provoked, the fear hormone cortisol gets released. And we begin to destroy the very intentions and implementations that our mastery brain so intelligently wants us to realize."

"This explains why so few people are highly creative and extremely productive," the artist observed. "As we leave our comfort zones, the ancient brain gets triggered. As we raise our expertise and lift our influence, it gets frightened by the change."

"Exactly," applauded Mr. Riley. "Then cortisol is released, our perception narrows, our breathing grows shallow and we drop into fight-or-flight mode. Actually, the three options of fear are flight, fight or freeze."

The artist added, "Our higher thinking wants us to grow, evolve, do more masterful work, lead better lives and inspire the world," continued the artist. "But there's a battle of our brains going on. And the ancient, lower—more primitive—brain inside all of us wants to stop our evolution."

"Exactly," said the billionaire as he fist-bumped the painter.

"And so, speaking to the second focus of history-makers on the model you're walking us through—freedom from distraction—I guess it's because of this fear we face that we embrace as many diversions as possible to make us feel better, even if only for a minute?" questioned the entrepreneur.

"Truth," confirmed the billionaire. "And to escape the discomfort that comes with us becoming more intimate with our inherent genius."

"This is such a big piece for me." The artist couldn't contain his enthusiasm. "You've just walked us through why our culture is so addicted to distractions. And why the majority don't experience their greatness. And I guess that's why creative and productive people are the real warriors of our society. We not only have to face the insults of our naysayers and the arrows of those critics who don't understand our art, we also need to have the guts to push past the alarm bells of our ancient brains pleading with us not to reach for our brilliance."

"Poetically said, my friend!" exclaimed the billionaire gleefully. He did that little dance again. The housekeeper, who was sweeping the veranda, just shook her head.

"It takes an awesome amount of courage to feel the terror of true personal and professional growth—and to keep going—even when you sort of feel you're dying," taught the titan. "But continuing when you're frightened is how you become a legend. You two cats are makers, builders of great things. And all builders consistently break through their fear, daily, to find higher levels of prowess, impact and human freedom. Oh—and the fantastic reward you'll receive as you fully express your strengths and gifts isn't only the product of your heroic efforts. It's *who you'll become* by advancing through the fire of your fears and the heat of your trials along the process to mastery. You get to know who you are, you see your abilities more clearly, your confidence soars, you need the stroking of the crowd a lot less and you begin to live your authentic life versus a plastic one manufactured by a world that doesn't want you to be free."

The billionaire sipped from his water bottle before continuing to explain the importance of breaking free from the death grip of device distraction and digital diversions.

"And that's where being a member of The 5 AM Club can also work its magic for you," he told his audience of two. "One of the ways the great men and women of the world avoided complexity was by incorporating tranquility and serenity into the front part of their days. This beautiful discipline gave them absolutely essential time away from overstimulation to savor life itself, replenish their creative reservoirs, develop their supreme selves, count their blessings and ground the virtues that they would then live out their days under. Many of the people who fueled the progress of our civilization shared the habit of rising before daybreak."

"Could you name a few of those people?" quizzed the entrepreneur.

"John Grisham, the famous novelist, for one," replied the billionaire. "Other celebrated early risers include Wolfgang Amadeus Mozart, Georgia O'Keeffe, Frank Lloyd Wright and Ernest Hemingway, who said that early in the morning 'there is no one to disturb you and it is cool or cold and you come to your work and warm as you write.'"

"Beethoven rose at dawn," said the artist.

"The great ones all spent a lot of time alone," offered the billionaire. "Solitude—the kind that you can access before the sun comes up—is a force multiplier around your power, expertise and connection to being human. *And your escalation requires your isolation.* See, you can be in the world all day long chatting endlessly on your phone about one thousand senseless things or you can change the world by exploiting your talent, refining your skills and being a light of upliftment that raises us all. But you can't do both. Princeton psychologist Eldar Shafir has used the term 'cognitive bandwidth' to explain the point that we have a limited amount of mental capacity when we rise each morning. And as we give our attention to numerous influences—ranging from the news, messages and online platforms to our families, our work, our fitness and our spiritual lives—we leave bits of our focus on each activity we pursue. Massively important insight to consider. No wonder most of us have trouble concentrating on important tasks by noon. We've spent our bandwidth. Sophie Leroy, a business professor at the University of Minnesota, calls the concentration we deposit on distraction and other stimuli 'attention residue.' She's found that people are far less productive when they are constantly interrupting themselves by shifting from one task to another throughout the day because they leave valuable pieces of their attention on too many different pursuits. The solution is exactly what I'm suggesting: work on one high-value activity at a time instead of relentlessly multitasking—and do so in a quiet environment. Albert Einstein made the point exquisitely when he wrote, 'Only one who devotes himself to a cause with his whole strength and soul can be a true master. For this reason, mastery demands all of a person.' This really is one of the most closely guarded secrets of the virtuosos and history-makers. They don't diffuse their cognitive bandwidth. They don't dilute their creative gifts chasing every shiny diversion and every attractive opportunity that comes their way. No, instead they exercise the fierce discipline required to do only a few things—but at an absolutely world-class level. It's like I said before: the great ones understand that it's far smarter to create one piece of art—a genuine masterpiece—that endures for generations rather than thousands of projects that express no genius. And please also remember: *the hours that The 95% waste The Top 5% treasure.* 5 AM is the time of least distraction, highest human glory and greatest peace. So leverage The Victory Hour well. You'll make quantum leaps in your productivity as well as in your personal mastery. I don't want to get too much further into the neuroscience I've shared this morning, and I have an amazing surprise planned. But there is one more concept that I'd love to share with you two. It's called 'transient hypofrontality.'"

"Transient what a whatta?" queried the artist as he laughed.

The billionaire walked over to a towering palm tree with a thick trunk revealing its vast age. A sun-bleached wooden table with a wide circular top sat under it. A model had been meticulously carved into the wood. You would have been most impressed—and fascinated—if you saw it.

The magnate cleared his throat and chugged some of the lemon tea. After a few seconds, he began to gargle. Yes, gargle. Then he carried on his discourse. "When you're up early and all alone, away from the overstimulation and noise, your attention isn't being fragmented by technology, meetings and other forces that can limit maximum productivity," mused the billionaire. "And so the prefrontal cortex, that part of your brain responsible for rational thinking—as well as constant worrying—actually shuts off for a short time. Lovely information, right? That's the 'transient' part of transient hypofrontality. It happens only temporarily. Your nonstop analyzing, ruminating and stressful overthinking stops. You pause from trying to figure everything out and being so concerned about things that will probably never happen. Your brain waves actually shift from their usual beta to alpha, and sometimes even down into theta state. The solitude, silence and stillness of daybreak also triggers the production of neurotransmitters like dopamine, the inspirational fuel that serves superproducers so well, and serotonin, the beautiful pleasure drug of the brain. Automatically and naturally, you enter what I described earlier as 'The Flow State.'

Mr. Riley waved his left hand over the diagram on the table. It looked like this:

"The Flow State is the peak mindset that all exceptionalists like top violinists, iconic athletes, elite chefs, brilliant scientists, empire-building entrepreneurs and legendary leaders inhabit when they produce their finest product," the industrialist added enthusiastically.

"When you give yourself the gift of some morning peace away from your busyness, the hardwired capacity of *every* human brain to access the realm of pure genius becomes activated. The excellent news for you two cats is that with the right moves, you can habituate this state of awesome performance so it shows up with absolute predictability."

"Transient hypofrontality. A very helpful model," declared the entrepreneur as she gingerly placed her phone into her shorts.

"The entire world would transform if people knew this information," pronounced the artist.

"They should be teaching all this to kids in schools," the entrepreneur suggested.

"So true," agreed the billionaire. "But, again, I need to give all the credit for this philosophy I'm sharing with you—and the transformational methodology that I'll soon walk you through so you *implement* all this potent information—to The Spellbinder. He's been my greatest teacher. And with zero doubt, the finest human being I know. Ingenuity without integrity isn't so impressive to me. Unusual accomplishment free of uncommon compassion is senseless. And, yes, if every person on the planet was educated in this material and then they had the commitment to apply it, the entire world would be advanced. Because each of us would own and then live our latent power to realize extraordinary results. And rise into completely glorious people."

History-Maker Focus #3: Personal Mastery Practice

The billionaire walked his two students past the expansive terrace that offered delightful views of the ocean around to the front of his house. A black SUV shimmered in the driveway, as the rays of the morning sun washed over it.

"Where are we going?" asked the entrepreneur.

"Well, I promised you both at that dramatic meeting we had at the conference that you would swim with the dolphins if you came to visit me in Mauritius. So, I'm delivering on my promise. We're going to the western part of the island, to a small seaside village called Flic-en-Flac. Two young and delightful dudes are waiting there for us. They're skilled at finding where the dolphins are. Get ready to be blown away by what you're about to experience, my friends. This will be unforgettable for you."

The SUV was soon veering through the charming pocket-sized towns that surrounded the compound of the industrialist and rolling onto a perfectly kept highway. The billionaire sat in the front with his driver, asking about his children, his latest fascinations and his aspirations for the future. Throughout the journey, Mr. Riley would ask a thoughtful question, then lean back and listen carefully. One could see he was a man of towering depth. With a mammoth heart.

As the vehicle eased up to a lovely harbor, graced by a sandy beach, a few white cottages, a quaint fish restaurant and many aging boats moored in the water, a rooster proudly sang his morning anthem. And the miraculous sight of a double rainbow unfolded across the magnificent blue sky.

Two young fishermen greeted the billionaire with hugs. The group then set off into the vast Indian Ocean, searching for a school of dolphins they could swim and play with. The song "Strength of a Woman" by Jamaican singer Shaggy blasted from an inexpensive speaker roughly installed into the side of the boat with gray duct tape. The spray coming off the motorboat as it struck the waves soaked the faces of the billionaire, the entrepreneur and the artist, making them giggle like children dancing in puddles left after the rain.

After a few attempts, dolphins were spotted swimming jubilantly in a small cove surrounded by soaring cliffs, the kind you'd see along the Pacific Coast Highway in California. The way those creatures rejoiced as they glided through the ocean would make you feel as if there were a thousand of them in that little inlet. But there were only about eleven or so.

The billionaire threw on a diving mask and quickly slipped into the water from a platform at the back of the motor boat. "C'mon, cats," he said excitedly. "Let's go!"

The entrepreneur went in next, her eyes alive and her heart beating with an elation she hadn't accessed since her youth. Her breathing sounded shallow and rapid through her snorkel. It sounded like *hooosh, hooosh.*

The artist followed, doing a belly flop off the end of the boat.

Guided by one of the young fishermen, who was wearing surf shorts with a colorful tropical print and sporting rubber shoes, the three adventurers frolicked with the dolphins as they swam smoothly just below the water's surface. When the dolphins descended, so did their three euphoric companions. When they would twirl around, so would the members of The 5 AM Club. When they would flirt with one another, so would the entrepreneur and the artist.

The experience only lasted about fifteen minutes. But it was miraculous.

"That was unbelievable," exuded the artist breathlessly as he emerged from the water and struggled to get back into the boat from the small stage near the motor.

"One of the most amazing experiences of my life," gushed the entrepreneur, as she kissed him lavishly.

The billionaire soon surfaced. He was hooting with laughter. "Boy, that was a blast!"

On returning to the harbor, the morning mentoring class resumed on the beach, next to a pile of stones that locals used for barbecuing fish. The double rainbow remained extended across the sweeping sky.

The billionaire lifted a hand toward the heavens. Four white doves appeared abruptly, out of nowhere. Then a cluster of pink and yellowish butterflies sailed by.

"Good," announced the tycoon as he stared at them. After letting out a few throaty coughs that also seemed to come out of nowhere, he proceeded to point to the third area of *The 4 Focuses of History-Makers* model he'd been walking his two students through on this particular day. It had "Personal Mastery Practice" printed on it.

"What are we talking about here?" wondered the artist, his dreadlocks dripping and his thick tattooed arms around the entrepreneur to keep her warm. She was shivering.

"Training the best parts of you," was the straightforward reply. "Remember the Spartan warrior credo that The Spellbinder shared at the seminar? 'Sweat more in practice, bleed less in war.' Well, the quality of your morning practice determines the caliber of your daily performance. Battles are won in the early light of intense training—when no one's watching. Victories occur *before* warriors walk onto the field. Triumph belongs to the one who prepares the most. It's obvious that if you want to be the best in the world at business or art or chess or as a designer or as a mechanic or as a manager, you need to put in enormous amounts of practice time to advance your expertise. Specifically, a performer must invest at least two hours and forty-four minutes of daily improvement on their chosen skill for ten years, as preeminent psychologist Anders Ericsson of Florida State University has taught us through his groundbreaking research. This is the minimum viable amount of practice required for the *first* signs of genius to appear within any domain. Yet so few of us think of the importance of putting what amounts to ten thousand hours of training *into becoming better human beings*. And that's why so few among us unlock that code which, once cracked, liberates our sovereign selves with all the wisdom, creativity, bravery, love and inner peace that comes with that manifestation. It's only when we improve that our lives improve, know what I mean? What I'm suggesting to you two is that you need to practice advancing toward personal mastery daily, just as we must dedicate ourselves to any other skill we seek to be world-class at. Fortify and bulletproof and nourish the core dimensions of your inner life and, trust me, you'll x*100* your life. Everything you do in your outer world is an absolute consequence of what's happening within you. This is where you need to do the real morning preparation. Then you'll walk out into the world every day thinking, feeling and producing at levels that make you unconquerable. You owe this gift to yourself."

"I've never believed much in self-improvement before The Spellbinder's conference," stated the entrepreneur flatly. "It's never seemed real to me."

"Have you ever tried it? I mean seriously practiced it over an extended period of time?" asked the billionaire, firmly. Yet another dove flew overhead. And when the mogul glanced up at the sun, it almost appeared that the clouds parted.

"Not really," admitted the entrepreneur. "Until now. Until I joined The 5 AM Club."

"Okay. Good. So, let's keep going. Here's the key," said the billionaire. "During your Victory Hour, from 5 to 6 AM each morning, concentrate on upgrading what The Spellbinder calls *The 4 Interior Empires*. This will be the smartest, and sometimes the most difficult, work you will ever do in your life. Deeply working on you. Cultivating the four central inner arenas that I'll walk you through in a moment is your golden key to transformation. It won't be easy—I need to reinforce that. But it will be totally worth it."

"Why?" wondered the entrepreneur. She'd stopped shaking from the cold water of the Indian Ocean. But the artist still held her. His dreadlocks still dripped. And the renegade rooster still crowed.

"Because inner empires need to be unfolded up to world-class before you'll ever see outer ones. And your fortune always follows your fearlessness. Powerful insight, cats: *Your influence in the world mirrors the glory, nobility, vitality and luminosity you've accessed in yourself.* Very few people in this time of superficiality and human creatures behaving like artificial machines remember this essential life truth. External always expresses internal, without always reflects within. Your creativity, productivity, prosperity, performance and impact on the planet are always a sublime expression of what's going on inside of you. For example, if you lack faith in your ability to get your ambitions done, you'll never achieve them. If you don't feel deserving of abundance, you'll never do what's required to realize it. And if your drive to capitalize on your genius is weak, your fire to train is dim and your stamina to optimize is low, it's clear you'll never take flight into the rare-air of outright mastery. And realize domain dominance. External always expresses internal. And to experience empires in your outer life you need to develop your inner ones first," reinforced the billionaire.

He started to sip from a bottle of green-colored liquid that one of the fishermen had given him when he hopped out of the motor boat. If you looked very closely at the text printed on the glass, you'd read these words of Mahatma Gandhi: "The only devils in the world are those running in our own hearts. That is where the battle should be fought."

"As you consistently increase the inherent power inside you," Mr. Riley continued, "you'll actually begin to see an *alternate* reality flush with gorgeous opportunity and luxurious possibility. You'll play in a universe of the marvelous that members of the majority can't even perceive. Because their eyes are blinded by doubt, disbelief and fear. Greatness is an inside game," the billionaire affirmed as he drew yet another learning model into the sand. It looked like this:

THE 4 INTERIOR EMPIRES

"Okay, let's go granular on this framework so you cats have a high and ultra-clear *awareness* of what aspects of your inner life to improve during your Victory Hour. I'll provide you with the complete morning routine to run soon, when I teach *The 20/20/20 Formula*. For now, please just know that there are four interior empires to train, cultivate and iterate before the sun comes up: Mindset, Heartset, Healthset and Soulset. Together, these four private arenas form the foundation of the true primal power that rests inside every human being alive today. Most of us have disowned and discredited this formidable force as we've spent our days pursuing things outside ourselves. But we *all* have this profound and illustrious capacity within us. And the best time to optimize your four interior empires is from 5 to 6 AM. That's the most special time of the day. Own your morning, and you'll elevate your life," encouraged the tycoon.

"Oh, a question: What if I only want to do this five days a week and take weekends off? How strict is this whole 5 AM Method?" asked the entrepreneur. An ancient dog shuffled by and the song "Occhi," by Italian music legend Zucchero, could be heard playing from the fish restaurant. You would probably have found that part of this scene quite strange. But it really did happen this way.

"It's your life. Do what fits you best and feels right to you. What I'm revealing is the information The Spellbinder shared with me. It caused me to make my fortune. And helped me find a consummate sense of daily joy and ongoing peace. Really, all of this gave me personal freedom. Apply it all in whatever way works for your values, aspirations and lifestyle. Yet also know that *part-time commitment truly does deliver part-time results*," stated the billionaire as he turned to catch a fly with his fist.

"Could you please go deeper into *The 4 Interior Empires*?" the entrepreneur asked. "This piece you're teaching us will really help me become a lot stronger in my fight with those investors and get even more of my hope, happiness and confidence back. I haven't told you this, but over these past days since I met you, I've been applying so much of what you've been so generous to share with us. As I'm sure you saw, at first I resisted a lot of The Spellbinder's philosophies. I really didn't want to go to his seminar, you know. But at least I was open to his—and your—teachings. Desperately open. I love life, you know. And I now plan to live a long time."

"Good," the artist said as he picked up a heart-shaped seashell and placed it tenderly into a palm of the entrepreneur. He closed her fingers around it. And pressed her hand to his chest.

"I'm already noticing some significant improvements," the entrepreneur went on. "By rising at five, I feel more focused, less stressed, more secure and way more energetic. I have a larger sense of perspective over all the aspects of my life. I'm becoming more grateful for all the positive in my world, a lot less concerned with the attack on my company and a lot more excited about my future. Look, those investors are bad guys. And I'm not ready to handle them yet. I will, though. But the fear I felt around the whole thing, and the dark sense of hopelessness about it all, well, that's faded."

"Neato," said the billionaire using the vintage slang of hipsters of a bygone era. He then changed his t-shirt on the beach. The SUV had returned, and the driver was parked directly in front of the seafood restaurant.

"And you're wise," the billionaire added. "All this information is priceless. But—as you're finding—it's the ceaseless practice and daily application of it that will make you a heroic human being and an inspirational leader in business and a worldwide uplifter of many. And I congratulate you for letting go of your past. No one's suggesting you act irresponsibly and not deal with the issue you're facing at your firm. *But your past is a place to be learned from, not a home to be lived in."*

The three friends climbed into the waiting vehicle and it pushed ahead to return to the estate of the eclectic host.

"So, let's talk more about this learning model, because it is so crucial to your success and happiness," the billionaire commented as the SUV sailed along. "Many gurus speak of mindset. They teach the importance of installing the psychology of possibility, to use Harvard psychologist Ellen Langer's phrase. They coach you to think optimistic thoughts every day. These teachers tell you that your thinking forms your reality and that, by improving your mind, you'll improve your life. For sure, calibrating your mindset is an essential move to make toward the personal mastery that will then lead to a legendary outer reality.

"Yet," the billionaire continued, "and it's *incredibly* important that you two understand this because most people don't: The Spellbinder taught me that elevating your Mindset—the first of the four interior empires—is only 25% of the personal mastery equation."

"Seriously?" the artist asked. "I always thought that our thinking determines everything. That there wasn't much more to it than that. The whole 'change your thinking and you'll change your life' and your 'attitude determines your altitude' kind of thing."

"Look," said the billionaire. "It's definitely true that your deepest beliefs drive your daily behavior. You know I believe that. And you know I also agree that the way you perceive the world drives the way you perform in it. Yet, a superbly developed Mindset without a magnificently purified Heartset is a hollow triumph. Just working on your Mindset will never deliver the fullness of your sovereignty and fully express your resident genius," the industrialist said with great clarity.

"I think I'm getting you," noted the artist with a grin the size of Mount Kilimanjaro. "Charles Bukowski said, 'Stop insisting on clearing your head . . . Clear your heart instead.'"

"He was right," agreed the billionaire as he relaxed deeper into his rich leather seat in the SUV.

"So, help me understand exactly what 'Heartset' is?" asked the entrepreneur. She was watching a group of school kids running in a playground with unsparing exhilaration. Her thoughts drifted to her childhood.

"Heartset is your emotional life. Even with battleproofed beliefs and the distinguished thinking of a world-class Mindset, you won't win if your heart is full of anger, sadness, disappointment, resentment and fear. Just think about it: How can you produce amazing work and realize astonishing results if toxic feelings are weighing you down? It seems like everyone's talking about building a healthy and undefeatable Mindset these days. You hear it everywhere. But no one's speaking of Heartset—or Healthset and Soulset. *All four* of these interior empires must be polished beautifully through morning practice for you to know the awe-inspiring power that lurks within you. And it's only when you grow and deepen your relationship with this natural authority that exists at your core that you can ascend into the company of the virtuosos. And the gods. As you elevate your four interior empires, you'll begin to achieve success in the external world at a level you've never believed you could achieve. And more elegantly than you've ever imagined. It's as if you've developed the capabilities of a magic worker. You start to increase the power of others, by your very presence. An improbable yet consistently reliable stream of miracles will infuse your common hours. And a prolific joyfulness born of brilliant accomplishment and worldwide service will come to you, as life's reward for the admirable ways you've behaved." Mr. Riley looked out of the vehicle's window. He then continued his discourse.

"So many of us know what we should do mentally but nothing extraordinary ever happens because our emotional life remains a mess. We stay stuck in the past. We haven't forgiven the unforgiven. We've repressed all those unhealthy emotions from all that has hurt us. Sigmund Freud wrote that 'unexpressed emotions will never die. They are buried alive and they will come forth later in uglier ways.' And we wonder why our attempts at positive thinking aren't working! What I'm sharing with you explains why so many self-improvement books don't lead to lasting evolution. And why so few conferences make an enduring difference. Our intellectual intentions are good. We really wish to become brighter producers and better people. But we merely get the information at the level of thought. And then we sabotage our lofty aspirations with the residue of our broken hearts. So, nothing shifts. So, nothing increases.

So, nothing *transforms*. If you want to experience exponential growth and unparalleled performance you need to dial in a masterful Mindset but also repair, rebuild and reinforce a winning Heartset. So that all the dark and toxic emotion from your past pains are cleared out. Released and cleansed and purified. Forever. And so your heart, once hardened by life's trials, reopens in all its noble glory."

"Amazing insights," the entrepreneur acknowledged. "But how exactly do I do this during my Victory Hour from 5 to 6 AM?"

"You'll learn how to implement The 5 AM Method in the near future," the billionaire replied. "You two cats are becoming open enough and strong enough to embrace *The 20/20/20 Formula* soon. And like I've suggested since we've hung together, your lives will never be the same once you know and run it. *The 20/20/20 Formula* is an absolute game-changer. For now, please just understand that a great Mindset with a poor Heartset is a giant reason good people end up dissolving their attempts at greatness.

"Oh," added the billionaire. "I should also mention that working on your Heartset isn't only about removing negative emotions that have built up from life's frustrations, disappointments and burdens. It's also about amplifying the healthy ones. That's why part of your morning routine needs to have a gratitude practice as part of it. To feed your sense of awe and fuel your reservoirs of exuberance."

"Love it," said the artist. "Profound what you're sharing, brother. Revolutionary, I'll admit," he emphasized.

"Yes. Absolutely. And so The Spellbinder taught me to do some profound work on my Heartset each morning, during my Victory Hour. Yet here's the thing: even upgrading your Heartset along with growing your Mindset before the first rays of the sun display themselves still means you're only doing 50% of the personal mastery work required to materialize the interior empires that will yield the outer empires of your highest wishes. After Mindset and Heartset, you also need to fortify your Healthset each morning."

"New word for me," observed the entrepreneur. "Healthset. I like it."

"Well, this one speaks to your physical dimension," explained the billionaire as the SUV passed one of the many tea plantations in Mauritius. "One of the main elements of your rise to legendary is longevity. Here's a quick tip if you want to lead your field and experience continuous escalations of your eminence: *do not die.* You'll never become a titan of your industry and an icon who makes history if you're dead."

Both the entrepreneur and the artist grinned as the billionaire began to clap vigorously, apparently as happy as a family of squirrels playing in a forest, on hearing his own words.

"But I am being serious. Beautiful things happen once you commit seriously to peak fitness and go hard on cheating aging. Just imagine living an extra few decades—and staying ultra-healthy as you do so. That's another few decades to refine your craft, to grow into an even more influential leader, to produce work that's radical artistry, to compound your prosperity and to build a luminous legacy that will enrich all of humanity. Epic producers and great leaders understand that you just can't rise to mastery without leveraging—and then armor-plating—your vitality. Every day's just dramatically better with some exercise in it. I need to say that again because it's so essential to a life amazingly lived: *every day is just dramatically better with some exercise in it.* And few things feel as good as getting uber-fit. I guess what I'm offering to you is that Healthset is all about dialing in your physical dimension so your brain is operating at its highest level of cognition and so your energy is igniting and so your stress is dissolving and so your joy is expanding. Getting really healthy and ultra-fit worked wonders for my business, you know?"

The billionaire paused. He drew his hands together as is the custom in India, where people say "Namaste," which is Sanskrit for "I bow to the divine in you."

"And that brings me to Soulset, lady and gentleman. I have learned that every single one of us has an unstained spirit and spotless soulfulness that rests at our very center. Most of the world is uninterested in whispers from and the requirements of the soul. As a race, we've neglected that portion of ourselves that is most wise, wonderful and eternal. The majority, programmed by society, is all about getting the goods that will boost popularity, gaining validation and social currency from their selfies and accomplishing popular results that will give them legitimacy. However, feeding your spirit—daily—is the activity of genuine leadership royalty."

"And tell me, Mr. Riley, when you refer to Soulset, what exactly are you speaking of?" inquired the entrepreneur, clearly making steady progress as a student of The Spellbinder's teachings. She also appeared more present, strong and free than at any time since the artist had met her.

"Yeah—I'm not clear either, brother," mentioned the artist sincerely as he, too, reclined in his seat as the chauffeur navigated the vehicle up the winding driveway of the tycoon's home.

More butterflies floated by. The double rainbow remained transfixed in the sky. The billionaire peered at it and then went on.

"'There is no exquisite beauty without some strangeness in the proportions,'" observed the billionaire as he waved to his gardeners and stuck his tongue out at a frog. "The English poet Christopher Marlowe said that. And, dude, he was speaking some truth there. Anyhoo, to help you understand the fourth interior empire, please allow me to bring this learning all together by simply saying that since Mindset is all about your psychology and Heartset is all about your emotionality, and Healthset relates to your physiology, Soulset refers to your spirituality. That's it. Nothing mystical, really. Nothing religious. Nothing voodoo or freaky."

"Go deeper, please," pressed the entrepreneur. "You're reordering my perception with all of these points."

"Well, it's all The Spellbinder's work, not mine, kindly remember that. Anyhoo, my encouragement is to become a devout spiritualist. And just so that term doesn't spook you—and shut you down to this education—all I mean to say is spend some time in the quietude of the early morning to make the return to the courage, conviction and compassion within you. All I'm encouraging is that you soar with the angels of your highest nature and dance with the gods of your most precious talents for a little time before sunrise, as a tribute to what's most wise and true within you. Only then will you begin to know—and understand—the Shangri-las of greatness and Nirvanas of light that inhabit your sovereign self. Soulset is all about remembering who you truly are. The sages, saints and seers of history all rose at dawn to forge even weightier bonds with the hero we all have at our cores. Insecurity, scarcity, selfishness and unhappiness are all children of fear. These characteristics were taught to you. They sure aren't your natural state. After we are born, we begin the departure from our spiritual power and descend into more of what this damaged world wants us to be. We become more about acquiring, hoarding and comparing instead of creating, helping and adventuring. Awake human beings work on elevating their Soulset in the serene hours before daybreak, in the sanctuary of solitude, silence and stillness. Through hope-filled contemplation of the finest version of yourself, without errors in your character. By marvelous meditation on how you wish to show up during the day ahead. By thoughtful consideration of the quickness of life and the suddenness of the exit. And by rich reflections on what gifts you aim to materialize so you leave the world in better shape than you encountered it, on your birth. These are some of the ways you can raise your Soulset game.

"Yes," continued the billionaire, the vulnerability of his open-hearted delivery displaying itself even more potently in his now soft voice. "You two have a brave, loving and wildly powerful hero at your foundation. I know to most people this idea sounds crazy. But it is truth that I speak. And by spending some time on your Soulset during your Victory Hour, you'll improve your awareness of—and relationship with—this most magnificent part of you. So you are consistently serving society instead of gratifying the ego hungers of your smaller self."

"And with better daily awareness of our Mindset, Heartset, Healthset and Soulset, we'll make the better daily choices that will guarantee better daily results, right?" pronounced the entrepreneur, reciting *The 3 Step Success Formula* she'd discovered in an earlier mentoring session.

"Precisely," applauded the billionaire. "Exactly," he added, nodding his head.

"And please, always stay sincere to what's most important in a life greatly lived," pleaded the billionaire. "Be not seduced by the super-ficialities that suffocate the human spirit and divorce us from the best within us."

He pulled a thin wallet out of a front pocket and read the words of Tolstoy from a tattered piece of paper that had been folded in a sleeve. Here's what you would have heard him say in his raspy yet dignified voice, if you were in that SUV with them:

"A quiet secluded life in the country with the possibility of being useful to people to whom it is easy to do good, and who are not accustomed to have it done to them; then work which one hopes may be of some use; then rest, nature, books, music, love for one's neighbor—such is my idea of happiness."

The three companions were now standing outside the magnate's house. An owl was perched on a lemon tree. It hooted terrifically as it saw the billionaire. He replied with a simple wave.

"Nice to see you, buddy," the billionaire said. "What took you so long to come home?"

History-Maker Focus #4: Day Stacking

"Remember that each of your prized days represents your precious life in miniature," the billionaire observed. "As you live each day, so you craft your life. We all are so focused on pursuing our futures that we gener-ally ignore the exceedingly important value of a single day. *And yet what we are doing today is creating our future.* It's like that sailboat over there," expounded Mr. Riley, pointing to a water craft off in the distance.

"A few navigational shifts, seemingly irrelevant and infinitesimal, when done consistently over a long voyage, make the difference between ending up in breathtaking Brazil or fantastic Japan. All you need to do to pretty much guarantee a hugely successful and a splendidly meaningful life is Own the Day. Make those 1% course corrections and improvements over each twenty-four-hour allotment you receive, and these days will slip into weeks and your weeks into months and your months will slip into your years. The Spellbinder called such daily personal and professional optimizations 'micro-wins.' Enhancing anything in your day, ranging from your morning routine to a thought pattern to a business skill to a personal relationship, by only 1% delivers at least a 30%—*yes, 30%*—elevation only a month from starting. Stay with the program and, in just one year, the pursuit you've been focusing on has elevated 365%, at least. The main point I'm making here is concentrate monomaniacally on creating great days—and they'll stack into a gorgeous life."

"Small daily, seemingly insignificant improvements, when done consistently over time, yield staggering results," reinforced the entrepreneur, recalling one of the brain tattoos she'd been schooled in during this magical adventure.

"Yes," declared the billionaire cheerfully, as he stretched and then touched his toes while whispering to himself, "Life is good, and I must help these two kind souls become great—before it's too late."

"Here's the real takeaway," the billionaire carried on. "Elite producers and everyday heroes understand that what you do each day matters far more than what you do once in a while. Consistency really is a key ingredient of mastery. *And regularity is a necessity if you're amped to make history.*"

In that moment, the entrepreneur's attention was stolen by her phone as the screen lit up. Stunningly, the following words showed up in lettering that resembled blood dripping, leaving her trembling and shaken:

A killer IS coming

"Baby—what's up?" asked the artist, revealing more of the growing intimacy of their relationship.

"Yes—what happened?" wondered the billionaire on seeing the ghost-white face of the entrepreneur.

"It's . . . um. . . It's . . . well . . . it's . . ." she sputtered.

She fell to her knees, in a flower bed close to where the chauffeur had parked the SUV. Almost as quickly, she stood up again.

"It's another death threat. They're telling me someone is on the way to kill me. The investors again. Pushing me to leave the firm. Guess what, guys?" the entrepreneur said, pivoting into a posture of high confidence and mighty defiance. "*I'm not leaving*. I built this company. I love what I do. I would do anything for my team. Our products are incredible. And growing the enterprise has given me great fulfillment. I'm ready to fight them. Let's go! Bring it on, I say!"

"It's being handled," murmured the billionaire, echoing what he'd said at his beach, on first learning about the situation. "Just stay fully present to the teaching you're learning and this special opportunity of being a new member of The 5 AM Club. Keep having a blast here with me in Mauritius. Continue this little love story unfolding between you and my tattooed friend over here," smiled the billionaire. "And keep strengthening the awareness of your natural power, as a leader, performer and human being. I'm really happy to see your progress. You already seem braver, lighter and much more peaceful. Good on you."

"Getting up at 5 AM is getting easier as each day passes," the entrepreneur said, feeling comforted and sounding composed. "The insights you're sharing are valuable. I'm growing a lot. I can't wait to go granular on how to make the habit stick and learn *The 20/20/20 Formula* so I know exactly what to do during my Victory Hour. I've been practicing some yoga and walking along the sea in the darkness before the sun comes up, yet I'd love some help on a more specific ritual. I know you have one. But the philosophy, so far, has been remarkably helpful."

"The precise methodology is coming soon. At this point I simply want you to know that the concept I've just shared with you both is called *The Day Stacking Foundation*. Winning definitely does start at

147

your beginning. Own your morning and the quality of your day rises exponentially which, in turn, upgrades the calibre of your life exceptionally. You'll be so much more energetic, productive, confident, excellent, happy and serene—even on the most difficult of days, when you calibrate the front end of it. Okay, now you two go and have an amazing day together. I love the words of the poet John Keats, who wrote: 'I almost wish we were butterflies and lived but three summer days—three such days with you I could fill with more delight than fifty common years could ever contain.' Pretty great, right?"

"Totally," voiced the artist as he tugged on three dreadlocks, patted his stomach and then laced up a black combat boot. "Totally agree."

"And what time should we meet tomorrow, cool cats?" inquired the billionaire, with a look that confirmed he was quite sure of the answer.

"5 AM," the entrepreneur and the artist replied enthusiastically, in unison.

CHAPTER 11

Navigating the Tides of Life

"The best and most beautiful things in this world cannot be seen or even heard, but must be felt with the heart." —Helen Keller

The entrepreneur had learned to sail as a child. She'd loved the sensation of salt water on her young face and the feelings of freedom that being out on the vast sea brought her spirit. She wondered why she had stopped sailing. In that instant, she also considered why she'd given up so many of the pursuits that had brought her such harmony. And she cherished the fact that in this basic moment, in a small boat gliding through the endless Indian Ocean, she was truly open. And wildly alive.

"Our culture measures success by how much money we have, the amount of achievement we complete, and how much influence we reach. Yet," thought the entrepreneur, "while both The Spellbinder and Mr. Riley agree that those victories are important, they've encouraged me to consider how well I'm running my life by another series of metrics as well. By my connection with my natural power and by my intimacy with my authenticity and by the vitality around my physicality and by the size of my joy. This seems like a much better way to look at success. Being both accomplished in the world yet peaceful within myself."

Her time at The Spellbinder's conference and her wonderful days here on this pristine island with people who still took the time to say "good morning," smile at strangers and show genuine warmth continued to inspire and provoke both tiny and large shifts in her understanding of the true nature of a productive, prosperous and fulfilling life.

The entrepreneur was noticing she was becoming less machine-like and more human. She no longer checked her technology compulsively. She couldn't remember feeling so creative, so available to the miraculous wonders of life. She'd never been so awake to the blessings every day on Earth brings. And she'd never, or at least she couldn't recall a time when she had, felt so thankful. Yes, utterly appreciative—for *everything* she'd experienced. She realized the hard points of her life had strengthened her and made her more insightful, interesting and wise. A fascinating and richly colorful life is stamped with many scars, she began to understand.

She promised herself that she'd exploit the challenge she was facing with her investors to raise her grade of courage. The partners' takeover attempt would simply escalate her commitment to defending the natural heroism she'd learned we all have within us, at our center beneath the layers of fear, insecurity and limitation that we all collect as we advance through life. The behaviors of her untrustworthy partners would only serve to make her a braver, better and more decent person. Often, a bad example teaches us more about who we wish to become than a good one could ever provide. And, in this world of so many hardened human beings who have lost access to who they truly are, she vowed to conduct the remainder of her days modeling excellence, resilience and the utmost of kindness.

As the entrepreneur and the artist navigated their little wooden vessel through the waters that were as clear as crystal, around coral that could be brutal if struck and farther away from the beach where the billionaire had delivered his morning instruction, the entrepreneur spotted the distant land mass where Mr. Riley suggested she and her new love have a picnic.

She also detected an ever-growing affection for the large man who sat next to her. Though they came from entirely different universes, their chemistry was undeniable. It was as if galaxies had collided. And though they had different ways of operating, their compatibility was as nothing she'd experienced before. Her mother had once told her that if you are fortunate enough to fall in love even two or three times within a lifetime, make each of these stories count fully.

Her companion's artistic powers intrigued her. His desire to be great on his own terms attracted her. His occasional hard edges challenged her. His sense of humor amused her. His palpable compassion moved her. And his dark eyes melted her.

"This was a good idea," the artist said as the entrepreneur adjusted the set of the sail and skillfully directed the boat around some buoys placed there by early morning fishermen. "To come out here—away from everything. I needed a break from the learning. I'm loving all the information. I'm getting so much from Mr. Riley. Man, he's a treasure. But my head is full. I don't want to think for a while. I just want to have some fun and enjoy life. Being out here, with you, is special."

"Thanks," replied the entrepreneur simply as her hair waved playfully in the wind and her sparkling eyes stayed fixed on the water in front of her.

"This is the happiest I've seen her look since I met her at the conference," thought the artist. He put an arm around the entrepreneur. She didn't retreat in any way, remaining relaxed as their brightly painted vessel ventured deeper into the ocean.

After a while, the small island they had been heading toward came into clearer focus.

"The billionaire's team stocked us up for a pretty good picnic," noted the entrepreneur. "How about we drop anchor in the shallow area over there and have lunch on the white sand part of the beach?"

The island looked deserted aside from the well-fed seagulls, some with live fish dangling from their skinny yellow beaks, that soared overhead. And the gigantic turtle ambling along the damp shoreline as though he ruled it.

"Cool," the artist replied. "I'm good with that," he added as he took off his shirt unselfconsciously and dove into the water with a wide splash.

The delightful meal the two enjoyed consisted of grilled spicy prawn and a fresh mango salad, along with a humongous chunk of pecorino cheese flown in that morning from Italy. Watermelon mixed with pineapple and kiwi had been provided for dessert.

The entrepreneur shared her longing to build one of the world's greatest companies as they savored the food and relaxed in that sanctuary of peaceful isolation. She spoke of her desire to build a genuine empire and then, perhaps, to retire in style to the rustic side of Ibiza. She also confided even more of her pained childhood, from the terrible divorce of her parents to the depth of her trauma around the violent passage of her beloved father. She spoke in further detail of the series of failed relationships that had caused her to concentrate most of her time on her work and the loneliness she felt when she wasn't in the process of advancing her business.

"Those weren't 'failed relationships,'" mused the artist as he munched joyfully on a chunk of watermelon. "They made you who you are, right? And I really like who you are. Actually," said the artist candidly, "I *love* who you are."

He leaned over and kissed the entrepreneur.

"What took you so long to say that?" she asked.

"I don't know. My confidence has been low for a long time," confessed the artist. "But hearing The Spellbinder at the seminar and meeting you and feeling our amazing vibe and then being on this totally insane yet incredible adventure . . . I don't know. It's making me believe more in myself again. This is all helping me to trust life again, I guess. To open up to someone again is great. I should paint later today. Something special is going to show up. I just know it."

"Yes, you should," encouraged the entrepreneur. "I sense it, too. You're going to be a hugely successful and truly legendary painter."

And then, after a lengthy pause, she added, "I love you, too, by the way."

The romance of that moment being shared by the two new members of The 5 AM Club was suddenly broken by the sound of loud hip-hop music. A figure could be seen in the water moving dazzlingly fast—zigzagging and then racing along straightaways. It soon became evident who this noisy and uninvited intruder was: Stone Riley, riding on a souped-up Jet Ski and wearing a top hat that had been strapped to his chin. Yes, a top hat. And if you looked closely, you would see a skull-and-crossbones symbol on it—the sort that sits on pirate flags.

Soon he, too, was up on the unspoiled beach with the two lovers. Soon he, too, was eating the prawns and mango salad and wolfing down large pieces of the fresh fruit dessert. And soon he was holding hands with the entrepreneur and the artist.

This man was a pure oddball. And a most human hero. The entrepreneur and the artist looked at each other as the billionaire did his thing. They shook their heads, clapped their hands and laughed easy laughs.

"Dudes," shouted the billionaire above the volume of the thumping music as his Jet Ski bobbed in the shallow water. "Missed you two. Hope you don't mind me crashing your picnic," he communicated with food in his mouth. Without waiting for an answer, he turned up the decibel level of the song and sang along to the words.

"Gnarly tune, right?" he asked with all the energy of a power plant.

"Def," replied the artist instinctively. "I mean definitely," he corrected.

The three companions spent the rest of that unforgettable afternoon swimming, singing, dancing and talking. That evening the billionaire hosted a magnificent dinner out on his beach, which was lit with tiki torches, cream-colored lanterns and what you would have guessed were thousands of candles.

A long wooden table, draped with the finest of linens, supported platters of exquisitely prepared food. The Spellbinder also appeared at the banquet, swapping stories with the billionaire while a few of Mr. Riley's other friends showed up later to play the bongos, share in the fabulous meal and sip some fine wine. Even the ultra-professional and exceptionally hospitable attendants were encouraged to join the festivities. It was all surreal. And special.

For an instant, the entrepreneur reflected on the preciousness of the evening and recalled a quote her father had placed on the door of the family fridge. It was from Dale Carnegie, the self-help author, and it read: "One of the most tragic things I know about human nature is that all of us tend to put off living. We are all dreaming of some magical rose garden over the horizon instead of enjoying the roses that are blooming outside our windows today."

The entrepreneur smiled to herself. She realized she would postpone living fully no more. She'd not only fallen in love with a good man. She was beginning to experience a lavish lust for life itself.

———

At 5 AM the next morning, the sound of a helicopter pierced the sereneness that only presents itself at that hour of the day. The entrepreneur and the artist waited on the beach as they'd promised the billionaire they would. They held hands, tightly, and awaited the next lesson he told them he'd share. But the billionaire was nowhere to be found.

An assistant wearing a crisp shirt the color of the sky and pressed Bermuda shorts the hue of a tomato, with red leather sandals, ran down from the home of the titan of industry.

"Bonjour," she said in a highly polished way. "Mr. Riley has requested that I escort you to his helipad. He has a huge gift for you both. But you'll need to hurry. Please. We're on a strict timeline."

The three of them scampered along the beach, up a groomed trail through lush trees, past an herb garden with wooden signs containing quotes from famous leaders as well as one that said "Trespassers Will Be Composted" and, finally, to an expansive manicured meadow. At the center of it sat a gleaming helicopter with its rotors whirring against the radiance of the early morning lightfall.

Inside the aircraft a single pilot could be seen. He wore aviator glasses, a black flat-brimmed baseball cap and an all-black uniform. As his passengers were led inside, the pilot remained silent, manipulating the controls and writing on what appeared to be a detailed checklist attached to a scuffed-up clipboard with the phrase "Rise and shine so you'll escape the misery of mediocrity" written at the top in red. A smiley face emoji was evident below this line.

"Good morning," said the entrepreneur enthusiastically to the pilot. "Where's Mr. Riley?"

The pilot didn't answer. He tuned a dial. Tweaked a knob. And made another tick mark on the white page.

"Good luck, and have a safe flight, you two," announced the assistant as she adjusted the seat belts and placed headphones with a microphone snuggly onto the heads of her VIP guests.

"Where the heck are we going?" demanded the artist, reverting to angry-man status.

No reply. The door shut with a thud. Then locked, with a click.

The engine noise grew louder, and the propeller accelerated its rotations. *Whoosh, whoosh whoosh,* went the sound. The pilot, seemingly in some sort of imperturbable trance and certainly not at all friendly, pushed the control stick. The helicopter began to rise above the grassy field. Unexpectedly, the aircraft tilted to the left dramatically. Then it descended aggressively toward the Earth in a freefall before jerking upward again.

"Total disaster," shouted the artist. "This pilot is incompetent. I hate him."

"Just breathe. All will be well," reasoned the entrepreneur. She looked relaxed, secure and in complete control. Her morning training was working. She pulled the artist closer to her. "I'm here. We'll be safe. This will end well."

Soon, the helicopter was high in the sky and moving steadily, efficiently and gracefully. The quiet pilot fiddled with the dials and tinkered with the controls, seemingly oblivious to the fact he carried two passengers.

"I've seen that watch before," observed the artist as he spied the big timepiece on the pilot's lean wrist.

"Same one Stone had on at The Spellbinder's presentation. This is nuts," he stated in a quivering voice. The painter was sweating like a polar bear in a heatwave.

"Own your morning. Elevate your life," came the singing voice from the front of the helicopter.

"Hi, cats. Bonzour. Enjoying being members of The 5 AM Club this morning?" he questioned in a raspy tone. "Boy, oh boy, you're gonna love the surprise that's coming. Another country for another lesson on the morning routine of legendary leaders, creative geniuses and the great women and men of the world."

The pilot turned his head around radically and whipped off his sunglasses intensely. Then he let out a monumental burp.

It was the billionaire.

"Hey, people. I didn't mean to scare you two glorious human beings. I do have my helicopter pilot's license, you know," said Mr. Riley sincerely, almost apologetically.

"Sure," remarked the artist, still clinging to the entrepreneur like a gambler holding his last chip.

"Got it years ago," the billionaire continued. "Helicopters are ubercool. But with all my business ventures these days, I don't get in the airtime I used to. Sorry for the rough liftoff. I guess I need more practice."

"So where are we going?" the entrepreneur asked as she eased into her supple leather seat.

"Agra" was the billionaire's one-word answer.

"What does that mean?" asked the artist. "What's an Agra?"

"I'm taking you guys back to the airport," said the billionaire. "Gotta keep us moving on this once-in-a-lifetime adventure we're on."

"We're leaving Mauritius?" wondered the entrepreneur with disappointment. Her bracelets dangled and knocked against each other as she said this.

"What about everything you still have to share with us?" the artist asked. "We still haven't learned *The 20/20/20 Formula* you say will revolutionize our lives. You told us that it's pretty much the foundation of The 5 AM Method. I've been waiting to learn it," argued the artist, punching a fist into a hand again. "And I really, really love Mauritius. I wasn't ready to leave."

"So do I," agreed the entrepreneur. "I thought you promised us you'd get into the detailed tactics around what to do after we get up at 5 AM. And at The Spellbinder's conference you promised that you'd share practical productivity hacks so I could scale up my business and some key techniques to build my own fortune. And me and my man only had one picnic together. And you crashed it with your loud music and your pimped-up Jet Ski!"

No one spoke for a moment. Then, slowly, everyone in the helicopter began to giggle.

"Relax, guys!" hollered the billionaire. "My home is your home. You can come back to Mauritius any time you want. I'll send the same drivers and the same jet, and I'll make sure you feel the same love from me and my awesome team. No sweat. Happy to be helpful. Always."

He adjusted another dial before adding, "I've got a plane waiting for us on the runway right now. You lovebirds have been *tremendous* students. Absolutely first-rate. You've passionately embraced The Spellbinder's teachings. You've been up with the sun and on time every morning. I've seen all your progress. So I wanted to give you a great present today."

"A present?" the artist queried. "I'll need to get back to my studio at home pretty soon. I've got some serious restructuring of my craft and fixing of my life to do after all this."

"And I'll need to be at my company soon, too," the entrepreneur said. Some of the worry lines returned to her forehead as she pronounced these words, though there were many fewer than before she had joined The 5 AM Club.

"Well not yet, guys. Not yet—please," pleaded the billionaire. "We're going to Agra."

"I have no idea where that is," admitted the entrepreneur.

"Agra is in India," the billionaire explained. "I'm taking you two to see one of The Seven Wonders of the World. And get set to learn the next part of The 5 AM Method. Everything you've learned so far has been preparation for all that's coming. Lock and load, dudes. We're now ready to get into the *advanced* information to help you drive exponential productivity, maximum performance, legendary leadership and a towering life that upgrades the world. Get set to receive the most practical information you could ever learn on the morning routine of world-builders and history-makers. The best is about to come."

The billionaire expertly landed the helicopter next to a pristine private jet that had its turbines running. Unlike the first one, this aircraft was all black. But like the one that brought the two students to Mauritius, it had 5AC emblazoned on the tail, also in a hue of orange similar to a mandarin.

"Let's go to incredible India!" exclaimed the billionaire energetically.

"Let's go, then!" replied the entrepreneur and the artist.

One of the most valuable experiences of their extraordinary escapade with Stone Riley, the eccentric magnate, was about to begin.

Chapter 12

The 5 AM Club Discovers
The Habit Installation Protocol

"I hated every minute of training. But I said, 'Don't quit. Suffer now and live the rest of your life as a champion.'" —**Muhammad Ali**

The next morning's lesson was scheduled to be on how the most productive leaders and performers on the planet install the habits that make them superstars. And live fascinating, adventurous and purposeful lives. In reply to Mr. Riley's request, both the entrepreneur and the artist had arranged to extend their time away. They understood the profound value of the training they were being exposed to. And they knew their smartest move was to embrace it fully.

"Hi, cats," shouted the billionaire, running up to his companions as the Indian sun rose timidly against a horizon that was at once barren and electrifying.

It was precisely 5 AM.

The tycoon wore a black Nehru-collared shirt, cargo shorts and black sandals. He was smiling broadly. He still glowed from the sunshine of Mauritius. And, today, he wore a turban.

"This morning, I'll be walking you through The Spellbinder's insights on installing the peak performance regimes that will help you activate your greatness in business and in life. As I shared with you in

159

an earlier lesson, what makes the best the best is not their genetics but their habits. And not the extent of their gifts, but the strength of their grit. Today's lesson will walk you through what the science and research tell us we must do to let go of the behaviors that weaken us and to code in the ones that will serve us."

"What's grit?" asked the entrepreneur, paying attention to every word the billionaire spoke. Today, she had her hair in a ponytail and simple shoes on her feet.

"It's a term popularized by social psychologist Angela Duckworth, who studied elite performers in the fields of business, education, the military and sports. She found that what makes the most successful achievers so great isn't their inherent talent but their levels of commitment, discipline, resilience and perseverance. 'Grit' is her word to describe these traits."

"Cool, brother," said the artist. "That inspires me not to give up on a painting when I hit a wall of self-doubt. Or when I get frustrated by my lack of progress. Or when I get scared others in my field will laugh because I'm producing art that is fresh and original instead of copied and derivative."

"Good," responded the billionaire as he rubbed his muscular abs. "Albert Einstein wrote 'Great spirits have always encountered violent opposition from mediocre minds. The mediocre mind is incapable of understanding the man who refuses to bow blindly to conventional prejudices and chooses instead to express his opinions courageously and honestly.'"

"Love that," spoke the artist exuberantly, displaying an expression that showed his growing pride in trusting his personal vision when it came to his craft.

"Anyhoo, let's get back on track and keep jamming on the most potent ways to install world-class habits that last versus ones that dissolve after a few weeks of trying to make them stick. Of course, this morning's mentoring class is absolutely essential for you two because, even though you guys are up at 5 AM daily now, we want the discipline to become a lifetime routine. Oh, and an essential part of world-class habit installation involves learning how the pros build remarkable self-control and unleash rare-air amounts of willpower. So, we should start there."

The three companions were standing in front of the Taj Mahal. They were alone. The structure was unspeakably sublime as they stared at it, a genuine testimony to the rewards of architectural and engineering mastery.

"I love India so much," declared the billionaire. "One of the greatest nations on Earth. And this place, well, it's one of The Seven Wonders of the World for a reason. Breathtakingly beautiful, right?"

"True," admitted the entrepreneur as she sipped some very hot coffee.

The billionaire held a large water bottle in his left hand. It had a statement printed on it, as his water bottles often did, which he read to his two students with gusto:

The hero does not become great during periods of comfort. The illustrious and noble souls of our world became strong, brave and moral whilst standing resolutely in the storms of adversity, difficulty and doubt. It is in the moment that you face your deepest weakness that you receive the chance to forge your greatest strengths. Real power, then, comes not from a life of ease but one of intense effort, devoted discipline and demanding action in the direction of what your supreme self knows to be right. To continue at a time when you ache to stop. To advance when you long to quit. To persist in the instant when you feel like giving up is to claim your membership among the great warriors and honorable characters who led humanity to a better place through their earned invincibility.

"Wow," uttered the artist. "Some great poet wrote that?"

"Nope," mentioned the billionaire. "Those words are all mine."

Mr. Riley then raised a hand into the air—and you know what happened.

Out of the early morning mist appeared an impeccably dressed and very attractive aide. "We're all so happy you're back in India, Sir. We have missed you," she uttered. "Here's what you asked for."

The billionaire bowed slightly and gave his assistant a friendly smile.

A spectacularly ornate pashmina shawl was handed to the titan, who stretched it out in the light. As you know, pashmina is a fine type of wool from Kashmir. The term itself translates into "soft gold" in the Kashmiri language. And if you saw it, you'd agree it looked so.

Detailed stitching had gone into the fabric and, as the two students focused more closely on it, they could see *The 5-3-1 Creed of The Willpower Warrior* sewn into the shawl. Below this title was a series of statements that explained what the "5-3-1" meant. It was all quite unique.

Here's what the handcrafted stitching said:

The 5 Scientific Truths Behind Excellent Habits

Truth #1: World-class willpower isn't an inborn strength, but a skill developed through relentless practice. Getting up at dawn is perfect self-control training.

Truth #2: Personal discipline is a muscle. The more you stretch it, the stronger it grows. Therefore, the samurais of self-regulation actively create conditions of hardship to build their natural power.

Truth #3: Like other muscles, willpower weakens when tired. Recovery is, therefore, absolutely necessary for the expression of mastery. And to manage decision fatigue.

Truth #4: Installing any great habit successfully follows a distinct four-part pattern for automation of the routine. Follow it explicitly for lasting results.

Truth #5: Increasing self-control in one area of your life elevates self-control in all areas of your life. This is why joining The 5 AM Club is the game-changing habit that will lift everything else that you do.

The 3 Values of Heroic Habit-Makers

Value #1: *Victory demands consistency and persistency.*
Value #2: *Following through on what is started determines the size of the personal respect that will be generated.*
Value #3: *The way you practice in private is precisely the way you'll perform once you're in public.*

The 1 General Theory of Self-Discipline Spartans

To regularly do that which is hard but important when it feels most uncomfortable is how warriors are born.

The billionaire closed his eyes and repeated this phrase: "I don't wish for an easy life because there is no growth of my powers there. Give me a challenging life—one that brings out the finest in me. For this makes an iron will. And an unconquerable character."

"This shawl is my gift to you two," the industrialist went on. "Please do study the five scientific truths and the three values along with the one general theory that make up *The 5-3-1 Creed of The Willpower Warrior*. It will serve you brilliantly as you encode habits that endure."

Within a few moments, an auto rickshaw sped up from an empty parking area off in the distance. Out came a smiling young man dressed smartly in a dark gray jacket, perfectly pressed trousers and polished brown shoes.

"Namaste, Arjun," said the billionaire as he clasped his hands together.

"Hey, Boss," was the warm reply of this assistant. Though his words were casual, the way he articulated them demonstrated immense respect for his employer.

"You two know the story behind the Taj Mahal?" the billionaire asked as the aide stood off to the side, looking ready to offer any help Mr. Riley required.

"Please tell us," the entrepreneur requested. She carried a single legal notepad with a simple black rollerball pen. All the billionaire's early talk

163

of how the misuse of technology leads to the destruction of creativity and an extreme reduction in productivity was having a major impact on her. Today, she wore a bangle engraved with the words "Dreams don't come true while you're sleeping."

"Sure—it's a rad story," gushed the billionaire, retreating to more of his California surfer slang.

"Like you two sweethearts, the Mughal emperor Shah Jahan who masterminded this marvel was very much in love. As a symbol of his devotion to and adoration of his wife, Mumtaz, after her death in 1631, he committed himself to the construction of a monument the likes of which the world had never seen. One so extravagantly sensational, staggeringly inspirational and structurally exceptional that all onlookers would understand the depth of this man's affection as they experienced all its splendor."

"It does something to my heart when I look at it," murmured the artist, staring at the marble facade that glimmered in front of him. He squinted as the early morning rays struck his eyes. He was looking more fit, calm, confident and poised than the entrepreneur had ever observed.

"Me too," agreed the billionaire with a note of melancholy in his voice. "Seeing the Taj Mahal isn't just an excursion of the intellect. It's also a resurrection of the spirit. It wakes even the numbest person up to what we, as human creatures, are capable of producing. But to continue, once the maharaja set his bold intention, his workers started the process of translating that lofty vision into a definite reality. Because, as you both now know, *ambition without implementation is a ridiculous delusion.* You two are now much more fluent in the insight that anything legendary requires generous amounts of industry, artistry and persistency. Mastery isn't a sudden event. It really is a ceaseless *process* that may take years of painstaking craftsmanship, practice, sacrifice and suffering before the finished project intensifies to a level that moves the world.

"This is yet another GCA—a Gargantuan Competitive Advantage," continued Mr. Riley. "To remain loyal to your noble ideal not only during the weeks after you thought up the dream but over the long months and perhaps extended years in the parched desert of creative implementation while you endure rejection, exhaustion, the stones of jealous peers, the skepticism of your loved ones, being diverted by other attractive opportunities and finding your way through the isolated winters of self-doubt. This is what separates the also-rans from the icons. Anyone can be great for a minute. The sport of icons is sustaining genius-grade performance over a lifetime. And that takes unusual grit and patience uncommon in these superficial times. The kind that the majority of society today has sadly failed to develop. Know what I mean?"

The billionaire was animated, energetic and completely jacked up. He threw an arm into the air and flashed the universal victory sign with two fingers. It seemed he did so just to protect his inspiration. And to insulate the fire that had been activated within his heart.

"Many decades ago, Albert E.N. Gray delivered an address for salespeople in the insurance industry. He called it *The Common Denominator of Success,* and it distilled what the author had identified over thirty years of study as the greatest key to fortune in one's business, family, health, financial and spiritual lives."

"What was it?" inquired the entrepreneur with acute interest as she sipped her now tepid coffee.

"Well," offered the billionaire, "from my recollection of the pamphlet that was made from the talk and then widely circulated to top sales professionals, he said, 'I had been brought up on the popular belief that the secret of success is hard work but I had seen so many people work hard without succeeding that I became convinced hard work was not the real secret.'"

"So, what was it?" implored the artist impatiently.

"Dude, I'm getting to it," the magnate replied playfully. "So, Albert Gray said, 'This common denominator of success is so big, so powerful...'"

"And it is?" interjected the entrepreneur, equally unable to wait for the answer.

"Gray explained that 'the common denominator of success—the secret of success of every man and woman who has ever been successful—lies in the fact that *they formed the habit of doing things that failures don't like to do.'*"

"Simple. And profound," observed the artist as he ran one hand down one dreadlock. He, too, sipped some now cold coffee.

"Top producers make it a habit to do the high-value activities that average ones don't feel like doing—even when they, too, don't feel like doing them," the billionaire continued. "And by practicing the desired behavior over and over, their self-mastery and personal discipline grows. And the new routine becomes automated."

The artist nodded, then stroked his goatee. He was thinking about his art.

"I truly have been limiting myself because of my insecurities," he thought, once again. "I'm so worried about what others will say about my work that I'm not creating enough. And Mr. Riley's right. I'm not being patient and building the self-control that doing difficult but valuable things brings. I sort of just do what I want, anytime I want. Some days I have some drive, and other times I sleep all day. Sometimes I'm lazy. Some days I work hard. I'm like a cork bobbing in the water, with no steady direction. No real structure. No real discipline. I play video games a lot, sometimes for many hours. And I have this habit of rushing to create paintings that sell fast when I need some money instead of slowing down and concentrating all my skill on the one opus that will define the extent of my expertise. And turn my whole field on its head by its genius."

"So," the billionaire expounded, returning to his story about the making of the Taj Mahal. "For twenty-two years—not twenty-two days and not twenty-two months—twenty-two *years*, over twenty thousand workers toiled in the scorching Indian sun. Block of marble by block of marble carried from immense distances by over one thousand elephants, the army of craftsmen steadily erected the structure you're seeing. They faced architectural roadblocks, environmental extremes and unexpected tragedies along the journey. Yet, they were focused, fearless and relentless, dazzlingly committed to doing whatever it took to get the emperor's gorgeous dream done."

"Really incredible, you know," said the artist, as he surveyed the landmark. A butterfly sailed by. A few raindrops sprinkled on his face. And, believe it or not, more doves soared high above the billionaire's head.

"What's with all the doves, rainbows and butterflies that seem to surround you a lot of the time?" pressed the entrepreneur as she adjusted the t-shirt she was wearing. It had a quote from Oscar Wilde on it that seemed to fit the newfound awareness of the businesswoman. It read, "Be yourself. Everyone else is already taken."

"We all have the magic. Most of us don't know how to use it," was the baron's brief and mysterious reply.

"So, getting back to the Taj Mahal, after two decades, this mausoleum was complete," he remarked in a hushed tone. "And humankind was given one of the greatest products of poetic audacity it has ever received."

"I'm beyond inspired," confided the entrepreneur. "Thank you so much for bringing us here to Agra. I'm ever so grateful."

"The emperor must have really cared for his wife," mused the artist, delivering a penetrating reveal of the wonderfully obvious. He then looked intently at the entrepreneur. Her radiance went far beyond the basic beauty of starlets, models and women of high glamour. Hers was a quieter, more profound loveliness, the kind that makes sunrises special and moonbeams enchanting. He thought to himself that this woman's magnetism comes from a place deeper than merely an attractive face. It was a charm born of struggle, an electricity emanating from hurt, an energy emitting through a formidable intellect and a prettiness formed by her robust resolve to step into a person of true power, wisdom and love.

"The Taj Mahal is such a direct metaphor for you cats to consider on the subject of staying with the commitment to a new habit through whatever hardships show up. And remaining sincere to your ideals

not only in the seasons of comfort but especially when it all gets terrifically difficult. And that's why this morning's coaching is so exceedingly important. What you're about to learn will help you *implement*
so much of the philosophies I've shared with you up until now. The
Spellbinder has carefully developed the model I'm about to reveal, over
many, many years working with business-builders, masterful achievers
and change-makers like myself. Today's session isn't so much about
why you should embrace the morning ritual of rising before the sun.
It's much more about how you can get this routine done. As a *lifetime*
regime," explained the industrialist as he rubbed an earlobe like an
imaginative child rubbing a magic lamp.

"Awesome," said the artist. "I need this. The practical ways to make
sure I don't stop getting up at 5 AM after this adventure ends."

"Cool," indicated the billionaire. "Then let's go!"

Two burly security guards then led the billionaire, the entrepreneur and the artist through a private entrance into the complex, usually
reserved for heads of state, members of royalty and other global leaders. Once inside the monument, which was dark and still, the billionaire
began his discourse.

"This is a fascinating, riveting, confusing and exciting period in
the lifeline of the world. For those showing up as victims each morning, and every day, the future will be very hard, dangerous and
frightening because they won't know what hit them. And they'll be
absolutely unprotected to deal with the environmental, economic and
societal upheaval that is coming. Yet for the dedicated minority who
have habituated a battleproofed morning routine to defend their gifts,
cultivated heroic personal restraint and developed a bulletproofed character through the rigorous training of their muscles of self-discipline,
the times ahead will be phenomenally rich, harmonious and ultra-
productive. Those who have armored themselves against the turbulence
on its way by installing a world-class and carefully granulated morning ritual will actually be in a position to leverage all the messiness

into humongous opportunity. And transform all the confusion into a supreme sense of clarity, genius and calmness that allows them to win."

The billionaire rubbed his turban and then, for some reason unknown to his two students, began to whisper.

"The first insight I'll offer you here is that your brain is constructed for expansion. Yes, I'll agree those who are stuck in their pro and personal lives and those who are working under a mentality of can't versus running a psychology of possibility will argue that there's no way they can make the improvements they need to make by wiring in great habits like being members of The 5 AM Club. They'll fight to the death on the 'reality' of why it's impossible for them to accelerate their creativity, productivity, prosperity, performance and impact. They'll totally try to get you to believe their rationalizations for being unable to materialize an amazing career and manifest an exquisite private life. They have given away their power to make change for so long, they've come to believe their powerlessness represents the truth. Neglect your power long enough and you'll eventually believe you don't have any. But, the reality of their conditions is a very different story. The fact is that such people— good, well-intentioned, talent-filled people—have allowed the forces of their sovereign selves to become corrupted so often they've succumbed to a state of acute passivity. Yes, most people are passive instead of active builders of the ambitions within them. And then unconsciously they've manufactured a series of excuses about why they can't show up as leaders in their work and capable creators of their lives because they're so scared to leave the safety of their stuckedness and make the very improvements that would bring them to glory."

The billionaire stopped to draw in a giant gulp of air. A ray of golden sunlight peeked into the Taj Mahal. Then he carried on.

"Science now confirms that our brains can continue to grow throughout our lives. This beautiful phenomenon is called neuroplasticity. And it speaks to the fact that the human brain, like personal willpower, is a lot more like a muscle than previously understood. It's plastic in a way. Push it and it'll expand. Flex it and it'll extend—and become more potent for your use in the tallest expression of your most radiant gifts. So, you want to make sure you exercise your brain aggressively to make new habits like getting up early your new normal. *Neurons that fire together, wire together*, you know? As you repeat the routine you wish to add to your lifestyle, it becomes easier—and more familiar. That's a really important point to contemplate. And then act on."

"I've never been aware that we actually have the ability to grow our brains," noted the entrepreneur excitedly. "And I guess what you're saying is the more we practice a fresh habit, the more our brains will work with us and evolve to make it part of who we are. Right?"

"Yup," responded the billionaire. He loved seeing how the two human beings he was mentoring were improving through his sharing. Real leaders always feel great joy when they shine a light on the talents of others.

"Powerful idea," he went on with his finger now on the wall of the wonder of the world. "You don't have the brain you want, you have the brain you've earned. Or to put it another way, you don't have the brain you desire, you have the brain you deserve—based on how you've been operating it. Spend your days diverted by your devices, tethered to television and majoring in mindless pursuits and your brain will be weak and flabby through your mistreatment of it. Just like other muscles, it will atrophy. And this will result in weaker cognition, slower learning and lower processing power. Your competition will destroy you and your targets will elude you. On the other hand, when you use your brain intelligently by expanding its limits and running it like a titan, it will expand and increase its connectivity causing important gains in your productivity, performance and influence. The brains of London taxi drivers were studied and the area responsible for spatial reasoning, the hippocampus, was found to be significantly larger in them compared to the brains of ordinary people. Guess why?"

"Because of the complexity of the street system in London," the artist responded confidently.

"You got it," applauded the billionaire. "So, just as you develop your biceps in the gym by lifting dumbbells or doing push-ups, the cabbies in London flexed their hippocampi as they drove each day. And, like I said, given that the brain is a lot more like a muscle than neuroanatomists previously understood, that part of it grew stronger. See how powerful we human beings are? This is a superb example of the neuroplasticity we all have at our disposal. The brain can be strengthened, sculpted and optimized—if we choose to make it so. When you guys get home, study this phenomenon as well as the awesome process of neurogenesis, which describes the brain's natural ability to actually breed new neurons. The emerging neuroscience explaining the availability of mastery to every single person alive today, no matter where they live or how old they are or what they do or how hard their pasts have been, is so incredibly exciting," the tycoon gushed.

"Anyhoo," he added, "for now, please just know that the brain has a malleability and a muscularity to it. And what makes the great ones the great ones is they truly understand that daily discomfort is the price of enduring success. And that pushing ourselves hard builds the kind of brain that generates military-grade discipline. It's such a myth that the superproducers had easy lives!"

The billionaire reached into a pocket, pulled out a sealed envelope and handed it to the entrepreneur.

"Please open this. And read it for us—with as much conviction and passion as you have," the baron instructed politely.

Inside, on a neatly folded piece of fine stationery, the businesswoman found the following words of the illustrious philosopher Friedrich Nietzsche:

Do not talk about giftedness, inborn talents! One can name great men of all kinds who were very little gifted. They acquired greatness, became "geniuses" (as we put it), through qualities the lack of which no one who knew what they were would boast of: they all possessed

that seriousness of the efficient workman which first learns to con-
struct the parts properly before it ventures to fashion a great whole;
they allowed themselves time for it, because they took more pleasure
in making the little, secondary things well than in the effect of a daz-
zling whole.

"Flip the page over. Please," requested the billionaire as his eyes twin-
kled in the light entering the Taj Mahal.

The entrepreneur read a second quote that had been carefully written with what she guessed was an indigo-inked fountain pen. The phrase
was from the English poet William Ernest Henley. Imagine these words
infusing the deepest and most unstained part of your soul:

It matters not how strait the gate,
How charged with punishments the scroll,
I am the master of my fate,
I am the captain of my soul.

"The masters and the geniuses and the heroes of civilization all lived
hard lives," expanded the billionaire. "They trained tough. They 'played
through pain,' to borrow a term a lot of superstar athletes use these days.
They pushed their potential fiercely. They were ambitious, ceaseless and
ferocious when it came to the complete capitalization of their grandest
potential. The Latin root of the word 'passion' means to 'suffer.' These
women and men suffered for their visions, ideals and aspirations. They
suffered for the increase of their skill and sacrificed for the realization of
their prowess. They endured enormous anguish as they advanced their
crafts and abandoned their temptations. And I must tell you, these illustrious performers also suffered for the state of the world. Playing small
with your promise demotes our world, you know. Because the planet
becomes a poorer place without your greatness in it."

Suddenly, the billionaire fell to his knees. He lay flat on the floor and closed his eyes, folding his arms over his heart. The tycoon then began to snore. Loudly.

"What the heck are you doing now, brother?" asked the artist, appearing both confused and amused.

"Voluntary discomfort," was the speedy reply.

More snoring.

"I want my teddy bear!" he cried. "And my jammies."

Stone Riley then began to suck his thumb.

"He's unreal," laughed the entrepreneur, clearly entertained by yet another stunt of this maverick industrialist.

One could see the billionaire was now smiling, apparently impressed with his comedic skills as well as his unusual ability to make a teaching point.

Remaining on the ground, he said: "The single best way to build your willpower is to voluntarily put yourself into conditions of discomfort. The Spellbinder calls these 'Strengthening Scenarios.' When I was much younger and my ability to command myself to do what I needed to do when I didn't feel like doing it was much weaker, I'd give in to my lesser urges so easily. My self-discipline muscles were very flabby because I wasn't exercising them. The Spellbinder knew I needed to become a lot stronger so I could install the 5 AM routine—in a way that stayed with me my whole career. So, he had me actively put myself into situations of hardship. And it worked like magic."

"What kind of situations?" asked the artist.

"Once a week, I slept on the floor."

"You're serious?" quizzed the entrepreneur. "Really?"

"Absolutely," the billionaire confirmed. "And I began taking cold showers every morning. Twice a week I'd fast, like so many of the most accomplished women and men of the world have done to capitalize on and manifest their primal power. It's remarkable how much time I'd save during the fasting windows when I wouldn't eat. And striking how clear my thinking would be and how much energy I'd have. Oh, and when I'd be at my loft in Zurich, to promote my toughness and grit, I'd do some hard winter training by running in the snow with only a t-shirt and a pair of shorts on."

The billionaire stood up.

"It's exactly what I've been suggesting since we got to the Taj Mahal: you have the capacity for world-class self-control. Science confirms it. The real key is to push your brain to develop new neural pathways and to force your willpower muscles to flex and stretch, intentionally working these natural resources up to their highest level. This is how anyone can become so strong, courageous and undefeatable that, no matter what obstacles they face and difficulties they experience, they continue on their quest to meet their glorious goals. Why do you think Navy Seals and members of the SAS—true willpower warriors—actively expose themselves to such potentially spirit-crushing scenarios? All those long runs in the rain, with heavy backpacks on. Crawling through thick mud in the middle of the night. Eating brutal food and living in a spartan setting. Confronting their fears by performing tests like jumping into the ocean from cliffs, backwards, with blindfolds on, or enduring exercises involving psychological degradation so they train themselves to transcend what most limits them. Look, cats, bravery—and the capacity to do the difficult things that are necessary for the fullest expression of your greatness—isn't a divine blessing. Nope. Not at all. It's a voluntary practice. Toughness—and a will of iron—takes devotion. So, I very much suggest you begin to suffocate your demons, slay your dragons and hug your monsters by doing more demanding things. This is one of the surest routes to masterful achievement and a private life you'll be ever so proud of at the end. You know, this makes me think of the Irish playwright George Bernard Shaw. Boy did that dude have a cool beard," the billionaire said awkwardly.

"Ever seen it?" he kept on.

"I have not," the artist responded.

"You should, it's gnarly," the mogul noted.

He then snapped his fingers eight times. After this, an unknown

174

voice bellowed from somewhere within the mausoleum, "The reasonable man adapts himself to the world: the unreasonable one persists in trying to adapt the world to himself. Therefore, all progress depends on the unreasonable man."

The voice grew silent.

"George Bernard Shaw wrote that in his play *Man and Superman*, a four-act drama that he produced in 1903. All I'm trying to say is this: when it comes to fulfilling your gifts, talents, admirable ambitions and instinct to change the world in whatever way most resonates with you, never, ever be reasonable with yourself."

The billionaire paused. And then did something his two students had not seen anyone do before. He kissed the area of flesh between the index finger and thumb of his left hand. "You gotta love yourself before you can lift the world, by the way," he muttered with a grin before proceeding with his mentoring.

"Inspiring," the artist admitted. "What George Bernard Shaw said."

"Research proves that training yourself so your willpower becomes maximized is one of the crowning achievements of an epic life," the billionaire continued. "The Welsh explorer Henry Morton Stanley observed that self-control is more indispensable than gunpowder."

"Definitely inspiring," the entrepreneur echoed.

"Look," said the billionaire. "It's such a myth that celebrated athletes and legendary artists and revered statesmen and stateswomen had more natural willpower than the rest of us. That's just a big lie. What's real," he declared, "is that these exceptionalists began as ordinary people. And through relentless practice and constant drilling to wire in excellent daily habits, their power to manage themselves against their cravings and temptations grew stronger until the culture perceived them as superhumans."

"Small, daily, seemingly insignificant improvements, when done consistently over time, yield staggering results," commented the artist, happily reciting the valuable brain tattoo that he'd embraced on this wondrous journey.

He reached over and grasped the hand of the entrepreneur.

"That's right," acknowledged the billionaire. "What looks to the human eye like invisible and infinitesimal optimizations around your willpower—when performed daily—are what make you into a Michelangelo or a da Vinci or a Disney or a Chopin or a Coco Chanel or a Roger Bannister or a Pelé or a Marcus Aurelius or a Copernicus over extended periods of training. The true geniuses all started out as ordinary people. But they practiced building up their strength so much and so often that showing up at world-class became automated. Here's another brain tattoo The Spellbinder taught me: *Legendary performers practice being spectacular for so long that they no longer remember how to behave in non-spectacular ways.*"

"So, practically speaking, where do we start?" the entrepreneur asked. "Because I know both of us want a lot more self-discipline, and to have excellent habits that last a lifetime. Especially getting up at 5 AM."

"Follow me," instructed the industrialist.

Mr. Riley led them down a corridor of the monument, past a series of dim rooms and into a small chamber. In one corner sat a blackboard. The billionaire picked up a piece of chalk and proceeded to draw this diagram:

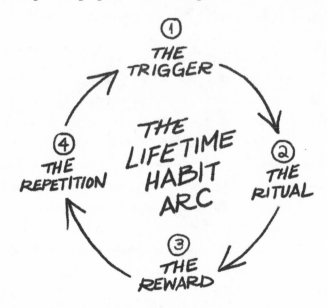

"This simple model is based on the latest studies on how habits are formed," he began. "Your starting point is to create some kind of a trigger. To embed the early-rising ritual into your mornings, this could be as simple as having an old-school alarm clock next to your bed that goes off at 5 AM. When we get to Rome, I'll explain why you shouldn't have any technology in your bedroom."

"Rome?" the entrepreneur and the artist exclaimed at the same time.

The billionaire ignored them.

"Once you've got the trigger of your alarm clock in place, the next step—as you can see from my diagram—is to run the routine you want to encode."

"So, we just get out of bed, right?" queried the entrepreneur.

"Yup," said the billionaire. "It sounds obvious, but jump straight out of bed before your reasoning mind—the prefrontal cortex—can give you a bunch of excuses about why you should go back to sleep. It's in this very moment that, by getting out of bed, you build the early-rising neural circuit in your brain through the power of neuroplasticity. And remember: brain pathways that fire together wire together into a potent neural highway, over time. It's in the very instant when you're faced with staying on the mattress or standing up and starting your morning in a great way that you have the chance to make your willpower stronger. It's uncomfortable at the start, I know."

"All change is hard at first, messy in the middle and gorgeous at the end," interrupted the artist, reinforcing another of The Spellbinder's brain tattoos.

"Yes," agreed the billionaire. "The next step of the four-part pattern to program in a new ritual is to make sure you have a preset reward in place. The reward is what kickstarts and then grows your drive to get the new habit done. Always use the power of rewards for the advancement of your triumphs. So, let's assume you do what you know to be right instead of following what's easy and sprint out of bed fast—as soon as the alarm goes off. I'll explain exactly what to do during your Victory

Hour from 5 to 6 AM when I walk you through *The 20/20/20 Formula.*"

"Man—are you ever going to teach it to us?" the artist interrupted again. He wasn't being rude. If you were in that chamber with those three, you'd sense that he only spoke that way because he was so interested in The 5 AM Method. That's all.

"*The 20/20/20 Formula* is the subject of tomorrow morning's coaching session," the billionaire offered with the utmost grace. "For now, let's stay centered on the third step. You need to set up a reward. That's what the eminent researchers on willpower tell us is essential to create behaviors that stick. Your reward for rising with the sun could be a nice piece of dark chocolate for dessert at lunch. It could be taking a nap later in the day, another favored rite of the planet's greatest creatives. It could be treating yourself to the book you've been wanting to buy for your library. You can figure out what feels right for you."

"Got it," said the entrepreneur. She was now sure that all this information would significantly elevate her business game and dramatically uplift her Mindset, Heartset, Healthset and Soulset—leading her into a truly excellent life.

"Good. That brings us to the final point in the pattern," said the billionaire as he touched the piece of chalk to the word "repetition" on the blackboard, in that room of the Taj Mahal.

"The way to annihilate the weakest impulses of your lower self and to free yourself of the cravings and temptations that are blocking your best is through ceaseless repetition of the new behavior you're working hard to install. The word that comes to mind here is *steadfast.* Be steadfast in your commitment to remaining a lifelong member of The 5 AM Club. Be absolutely dedicated and excuseless in following through on this life-altering self-promise. Each time you follow through, you'll deepen the relationship with your sovereign self. Each time you rise at dawn, you'll purify your character, fortify your willpower and magnify the fires of your soul. I guess what I'm trying to help you two wonderful people appreciate is that the real measure of your majesty is shown not in your outer moments before an audience, but in the soft and early light of lonely practice. You become undefeatable in the world by what you do when no one's watching."

"I've read a fair amount about championship sports teams," said the entrepreneur. "Really helped me build superb squads at my company. And if there's one thing I've learned, it's that what took the winning team to victory was less how they played in the last seconds of a close final game and more how disciplined they were at practice."

"Exactly," agreed the billionaire. "The brilliant moves in the last seconds of the championship match were *automatic*—the result of tireless hours of repetition of those splendid moves during training."

"Cool point," the artist thought to himself.

"I want to get to one remaining learning model this morning before I let you cats go, one that will make it incredibly clear how installing a habit follows a sixty-six-day process. Yet, before I do, I did want to share a few more fast practical points on self-discipline."

"Great," the artist replied. "Today's lesson has been big for me. I know it'll help me beat procrastination, and I'm sure it'll improve the quality of my art. And I've already been making progress on calibrating my physical fitness."

"He has," agreed the entrepreneur with a wink.

"Well, just remember that willpower weakens once it gets tired. Scientists call the condition 'ego depletion.' See, you wake up each morning with a full battery of self-control. That's why I want you to do the activities that are most important to the rise of your inner empires at the time when your capacity is strongest—at 5 AM. Here's the thing: as you go through your day, going to meetings, checking messages and performing tasks, your ability to self-regulate decreases—and so does your capability to handle temptations and manage weak impulses. The fact that human discipline muscles get tired from all the decision fatigue explains why so many massively successful people end up doing something foolish that destroys their careers. They gave in to the urge that causes their downfall because all day long they were making important decisions. By the time it was evening, they had no willpower left in their battery to manage the craving."

"Super-fascinating," remarked the entrepreneur. "This explains a lot."

"So, the key is rest and recovery of the self-control muscle," explained the billionaire. "Never allow it to get too tired. Your willpower really is weakest when you are most tired. Key awareness to build on here. We make our worst decisions and our lowest choices when we're exhausted. So, don't allow yourself to get exhausted. Period. I have a powerful mentoring session on how the best in the world protect priceless assets like their willpower through the lost art of personal regeneration planned for you later."

Mr. Riley began to cough. A concerning, throaty cough. Not an insignificant one.

"Oh," he added, regaining his composure. "Please also know the research also supports the idea that external order increases your discipline. That's why Steve Jobs made sure the workplace at NeXT was minimalist and painted all-white when he was there. Mess lowers your self-control as well as steals your cognitive bandwidth."

"Maybe that's why so many so-called geniuses wear the same uniform every day," the artist commented. "They want to keep order and structure in their lives. And they understand that each morning we wake up with a limited amount of willpower as well as mental focus. So, rather than wasting these valuable gifts by spreading them over many trivial choices like what to wear and what to eat, they automate as many basic things as possible, so they can concentrate their highest powers on just a few important activities. Now I'm getting how geniuses become geniuses even more. If all I did every day was my art and only a handful of other things, I wouldn't suffer from 'decision fatigue,' as you call it. And that would mean I wouldn't waste so much time in the evening—and make so many bad choices as the day ends, like watching stupid TV shows, eating so much junk food and sipping too much tequila."

"Okay," declared the billionaire. "You folks clearly now know 'all change is hard at first, messy in the middle and gorgeous at the end.' That insight should be well on its way to settling in as a default belief of your Mindset. Now, let's deconstruct that powerful brain tattoo of The Spellbinder into a potent model which explains the three phases every habit installation goes through so you have even more firepower to lock in the regime of rising at dawn. You'll absolutely love what you're about to learn. Promise me you'll turn up the volume of your listening as we go through this? Then we'll call it a morning."

"We promise," the entrepreneur and the artist expressed together.

"Pinky promise?" asked the billionaire, putting out a little finger.

"Yes," responded the entrepreneur as she locked pinkies with her mentor.

"Yes," agreed the artist, as he did the same.

"Terrific," enthused the magnate.

One of the security guards who had led the three companions into the structure walked in and pulled a chart out of a backpack. He shone his flashlight onto it so all could see what had been printed on it. The teaching framework that came into view looked like this:

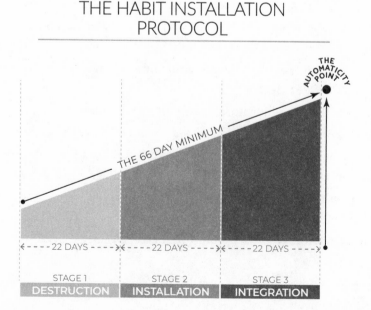

THE HABIT INSTALLATION
PROTOCOL

THE
AUTOMATICITY
POINT

THE 66 DAY MINIMUM

22 DAYS — 22 DAYS — 22 DAYS

STAGE 1 — STAGE 2 — STAGE 3
DESTRUCTION | INSTALLATION | INTEGRATION

"On the coding of any new habit, you'll move through an initial period of destruction," said Mr. Riley as he pointed to the first phase on the diagram. "Keep at it and you'll definitely move ahead into the second stage of the process, where new neural pathways are formed and the real installation begins. This is the messy middle. Finally, as you stick with your practice of making any fresh routine your normal way of being, you'll arrive at the final—and wonderful—stage: integration. The whole exercise takes approximately sixty-six days, according to the research data of University College London. The Spellbinder, in his teachings, calls this powerful fact *The 66 Day Minimum.* Sixty-six days of training to make a new habit yours. So, don't quit after a few days, or a few weeks, or even after two months. *As it relates to becoming a member of The 5 AM Club, stick with your self-promise for at least sixty-six days. No matter what.* Do this one thing and the remainder of your life will be exponentially better. This I promise you from my heart," said the billionaire.

"See, all change is hard at first. That's why The Spellbinder named stage one 'Destruction.' If it wasn't difficult at the start, it wouldn't be real change. It's supposed to be hard because you're rewriting the past patterns of your mind and destroying old ways of operating. And rewiring past programs of your heart and emotions. Do you know why the Space Shuttle uses more fuel in the sixty seconds after liftoff than it uses over the entire orbit around the Earth?"

"It needs to overcome the powerful forces of gravity after it takes off," the artist answered confidently.

"Exactly," the billionaire affirmed. "It requires a large amount of fuel to overcome those initial forces and reach escape velocity. But once it does, momentum kicks in and the craft just goes. The first phase of creating any new habit—The Destruction Stage—is precisely like this. You need to overcome your deeply ingrained habits, dominant rituals and traditional states of performance. You need to rise above your own forces of gravity—until your escape velocity kicks in. It's so challenging at the beginning. I'm not going to lie to you—you both have done very well getting up at 5 AM over the mornings you've been with me. But you will hit a wall over these first twenty-two days while you're in phase one. Nothing wrong—just part of the habit installation process anyone seeking peak productivity and a richer life must go through. For most people ready to get up before daybreak, each day of this first phase is a hardship. They feel like giving up. They complain that rising early just isn't for them. That they're not built for this routine and that it's just not worth the pain. My advice is simple: *Continue at all costs. Persistency sits at the threshold of mastery.* The things that feel hardest are also the ones that are most valuable. Keep remembering that doing difficult things that are very important was how the highest achievers and greatest heroes of our civilization embraced their power. Please also remember this rule: *when faced with a choice, always choose the one that pushes you the most, increases your growth and promotes the unfoldment of your gifts, talents and personal prowess.* So, when you feel like quitting, persevere. You'll get to the next stage soon. And understand the negative thoughts, cranky emotions and strong desires to surrender are a normal part of the process of hardwiring any new regime. The first twenty-two days are supposed to feel like a mild form of torture."

"Because stage one is all about the destruction of old ways of being so that new ones can be set up, right?" the entrepreneur asked.

"Precisely," the billionaire confirmed. "And just because you couldn't do something before doesn't mean you can't do it now," he added while nodding in an encouraging way. "I need to repeat what I said so you absolutely lock it in: if it wasn't hard initially, it wouldn't be real—and valuable—change. Society has programmed us to think that because it's difficult at first, something bad is happening. That we should stop what we're doing. And return to the safe house of our former normal. Zero growth and evolution toward legendary in that mode of operating. Zero."

"So true," agreed the entrepreneur. "Everyone I know repeats the familiar every day. Okay. Maybe not everyone, but definitely most people. Same thoughts, same behaviors and the same moves."

"The truth is not that they can't change," said Mr. Riley. "It's just that they didn't make the commitment to improve and then stay with the process long enough for their neurobiology as well as their psychology, physiology, emotionality and spirituality to work its natural wonders. *Everything* you now find easy you once found hard, you know."

The billionaire then asked for the security guard's flashlight and focused it onto the part of the learning model related to the second stage of routinization. "Thanks, Krishna," he added.

"See here—all change is messy in the middle. Stage two is called 'Installation' because it's like you're going through an interior renovation, of sorts. Former foundations need to be torn down so that much better ones can be put up. This stage will make you feel confused, stressed out and frustrated. You'll feel like quitting even more—and dismissing your decision to join The 5 AM Club as a terrible one. You'll long to go back to staying in your warm bed and counting more sheep. Just know and trust that all is good. *Very* good, actually. And though you can't see it, you're advancing even further in the habituation of making the early-rising routine yours for the rest of your life. Things are about to get easier. They really are. You're just going through the second stage of the procedure. And it only *feels* messy. And, it only looks chaotic. The reality is you're growing beautifully. And closing in on a whole new grade of performing. 'In all disorder there is a secret order,' said famed psychologist Carl Jung.

"So, when you're wiring in this priceless new morning routine, the entire structure of your brain really is in upheaval as you manufacture new neural pathways. Your whole system really is being restructured. You're honestly in seriously unfamiliar territory. Sprouting green shoots. Going blue ocean. Conquering new territories of self-potential and accessing higher universes of human optimization. Cortisol, the fear hormone, is elevated at this time so you'll feel scared a lot of the time. All that's happening within your brain is consuming huge reserves of energy. So, you'll be exhausted often at stage two of habit installation. The ancient sages, seers and philosophers called such a profound personal transformation 'The Dark Night of the Soul.' What was once a caterpillar is messily—yet almost magically—becoming a butterfly. The mystics wrote of deep and real change as a journey involving a series of little deaths. *The old you must die so a better you can be reborn.* The Spellbinder says that 'for you to upgrade to greatness you must undergo an annihilation of your weakness.' Dramatic words, I'll admit. But the guru speaks truthfully. In stage two, sometimes you might even feel like everything's falling apart. But actually, all is coming together—even better. Your human perception is often not reality, as you've learned. It's just you seeing the world through a lens. The fact is that the illusion of safety is always so much more deadly than your rise toward personal mastery. Stay in stage two of the process for around twenty-two days. And just know that *unfathomable* rewards are coming."

"I love all that you just said," interjected the artist. "I'll install the early-rising ritual for the rest of my life—even if it kills me trying," he promised to himself.

The billionaire grew quiet.

"I've been through this shedding and transforming process many, many times. Each time I go for a new habit, or greater skill, or even a more evolved core belief, I go into this death-and-rebirth cycle. And I need to tell you that it does feel like the end. You'll be so scared at times, tired a lot for a while and confused by what the dark voice of your ego will say. You'll even feel like you're going crazy sometimes. That's why so few people do this work. And why so few reach the rare-air of epic performance and make a worldwide impact on the culture. It's a sport only for outright warriors. It requires enormous courage, immense conviction and uncommon strength of character. You have all this in you. Just resolve to apply it. As I said, with practice and patience, it'll all get easier. And eventually automatic.

"Okay, cats," spoke the billionaire as he clapped his hands together like an encouraging football coach. "I know you're getting this beautifully. So, let's keep jamming. Stick with the process of new habit installation through the breakdown of old patterns, which happens in stage one. Then continue through the formation of new circuitry in your brain, which happens through neuroplasticity and the manufacturing of better pathways in your emotional core in stage two. Do that, and you'll most certainly reach stage three, the final part of your ascension: 'Integration.' Remember: all change is hard at first, messy in the middle and *gorgeous* at the end."

The billionaire paused, smiled gently and then touched his toes. He kissed the flesh between his fingers again. Then he went on.

"This final stage is when it all comes together," he explained, "and you get to experience the benefits of your fantastic commitment to being a lifetime member of The 5 AM Club. You're nearing the end of the roughly sixty-six-day period required for a human brain—and being—to encode a routine. So now it's success time. You've advanced through the initial disruption, you've made it through the dangerousness and chaos of the middle phase and you've come out the other side stronger, more skilled and with greater intimacy of your most supreme—and invincible—nature. You're now the next version of your greatest self, able to bring on a bigger game, influence more people by the glorious power of your example and be more useful to the world because you've owned more of your primal heroism. All your hard work, sacrifice and suffering, careful consistency and brilliant bravery come together in this stage as the new habit you've been working on integrates at a psychological, emotional, physical and spiritual level. And becomes your new normal."

"Normal?" wondered the artist. "Life gets easy?"

The billionaire suddenly fell to the marble floor of the Taj Mahal and started doing more push-ups. He looked sort of like a boxer training for the main event.

"What the heck are you doing now?" questioned the entrepreneur, amused. "He's crazier than I ever imagined," she thought. "I do love him."

"The primary purpose of life is growth: to be continuously pushing yourself to materialize more of your potential. My daily push-ups not only keep me in a state of continual optimization toward world-class. It's also a tremendous way to keep myself feeling young, happy and alive. Boredom kills the human spirit."

The industrialist stood up.

"For the A-Player, the top of one mountain is the bottom of the next. The installation of one great new habit brings on the outstanding opportunity to begin the next. I do one thousand push-ups a day, you know. Superb exercise. One of the best. So simple. Keeps me lean and chiseled. Good for my core. And the exercise also recruits my glutes," the billionaire said with an awkward expression.

"But doing a thousand push-ups a day is also a ritual to remind me to keep going. Keep expanding. Keep elevating my Mindset, Heartset, Healthset and Soulset and escalating my rise to my best. Honestly, I'm not afraid of failing. That's just part of learning to fly. I'm just horrified of not growing."

"Got you," the entrepreneur said, scribbling frantically on her notepad.

The billionaire then moved an index finger across the teaching model and rested it at the area that said, "The Automaticity Point."

"The exciting fact is that once you arrive at the automaticity point, you no longer need any willpower to get up at 5 AM. The new regime's implementation into your human operating system is complete. Awakening before dawn becomes second nature. And easy. Here's the real gift from your excellence and devotion over the sixty-six or so days: *the willpower you were using to lay down the early-rising habit is now freed up for another world-class behavior,* so you have the chance to grow even more productive, prosperous, joyful and successful. This is the hidden secret of all pro athletes, for example. It's not that they have more self-discipline than the average person. It's just that they capitalized on whatever impulse-control they had for sixty-six days until the game-winning routines got installed. After that, they redirected their willpower to something else that would improve their expertise. Another practice that would help them lead their field and achieve victory. One habit installation after another habit installation is how the pros play. Over time, their winning behaviors became automated. Systematized. Institutionalized. Absolutely no effort was required to run them once they got hard-wired. And these superstars practiced their habits of victory so often, they've arrived at a place where they forgot how to *not* do them."

"They got to a point where it was easier to run them than not to run them, right?" commented the entrepreneur.

"Absolutely correct," responded the billionaire.

The artist was excited. "So valuable to me personally and to my work as a painter. And, so I completely understand this process fully, each of the three stages—Destruction, Installation and Integration—takes about twenty-two days, right?"

"Right. And at around the sixty-six-day mark it locks in as an automatic routine. That's The Automaticity Point, because habits take around nine weeks to implement. Don't stop getting up at 5 AM after a week. Don't give up when it gets messy in the middle of the process. Stay relentless through the entire exercise through all its trials and challenges just like Shah Jahan did as he and his workers constructed the Taj Mahal, building it into one of the wonders of the world. Awesome takes patience. And genius takes time. Stay true in your dedication to carving out an hour for yourself as the sun rises and while the majority sleeps to develop your Four Interior Empires that will set you up to realize all the outer ones that your big hearts long to actualize. Do not neglect the call on you to deploy your fullest talents, magnify your spectacular strengths, multiply your happiness and discover a paradise of peace within you that no outer event can ever reduce. This, my friends, is how you become undefeatable, unbreakable and a true master of your domain. As well as a wonder of the world, in your own unique way."

"Love it," beamed the entrepreneur. "Bravo. Totally helpful. Explains why so few people have the habits necessary to achieve mastery. They just don't stay with their initial commitment long enough for it to work. They could. But they don't."

"Yup," agreed the billionaire. "That's why information and education, learning and growing are so vitally important. The majority just don't know this life-changing model and the practical insights that I've revealed to you around it. And because they don't know, they can't apply. And knowledge unimplemented leaves potential undercapitalized. We're all built for triumph, in whatever way we choose to define it. Sadly, most of us have never been schooled in the philosophy and methodology that The Spellbinder taught to me. The same teaching I'm now paying forward to you. You just need to make sure you tell as many people as possible about The Spellbinder's work. Please. This way, we can help people leave the darkness of apathy, mediocrity and scarcity and find their inherent power to do astonishing things with the rest of their lives. God, we need to make this world a better, healthier, safer and more loving place."

"For sure," the entrepreneur and the artist promised, together.

The entrepreneur then stopped to take in the unforgettable nature of the scene that enveloped her. She was standing next to a man she'd unexpectedly fallen in love with over a bizarre, beautiful and marvelous adventure. She was standing inside one of The Seven Wonders of the World, located in India, a nation she'd always longed to visit for the breathtaking sights, exotic delights and the country's extraordinarily special citizens.

She paused to consider what had unfolded back in her usual world. The manipulations, the thievery, the disloyalties and the treachery. In that moment, she laughed. Not some forced laugh that so many of us hear at business meetings where good people in quiet fear wear social masks in an effort to fit in, appear powerful and look cool. No, this was the palpable joy of a person who'd just discovered some of the true treasures of a life wisely lived.

The entrepreneur, in that instant, realized how blessed she was.

The takeover attempt would resolve itself since life always has a way of working things out for the best. Sure, she'd learned not to repress the natural feelings of anger, disappointment and sometimes sadness that were arising within her from time to time when she'd think about the situation. That was just her being human and real and even brave, not weak. Yet, she also now understood there were things more important than wealth, acclaim and fame. And that many financially rich people are actually desperately poor.

"Nothing's as valuable as my happiness. Nothing's as priceless as my peace of mind," the businesswoman thought.

She'd found love. She was still in excellent health. She had so many things to be grateful for: two eyes to see the splendors of this wonderful world, two legs to explore it all, food on her table each night at a time when billions have empty bellies. And a roof over her head for ample shelter. She had wise books to read in her library, work that fed her creativity and, as the billionaire said so often, an opportunity to achieve outright mastery not only to benefit herself but also in service of society.

And so, inside that majestic mausoleum that has electrified the inspiration of so many visitors from across the Earth, and as the sun rose into the abundant Indian sky, the entrepreneur found it in her heart to do something we all need to do more of.

She forgave.

She let go of her hostility toward her investors. She released her resentments for her detractors. And she let go of every single one of her weighty disappointments. Life is too short to take things too seriously. And at the end of her life, what would matter most would not be whether those venture capitalists had ownership of her enterprise, but who she became as a human being. And the quality of the craft she produced. And how many people she helped. And how much she laughed. And how well she lived.

The billionaire was right: every human being does the best they can do based on the level of consciousness they are currently at and on the grade of true power they can command. And if her investors had known better, they would have done better. These people generated pain and suffering for her because, at a deep and subconscious level, they are in pain. And because they are suffering. Those who hurt others silently loathe themselves. Yes, this sort of higher way of seeing things is not so common in our civilization. But maybe that's why our world is filled with so many wars, so much danger and so much hatred. Just maybe, she considered, these corporate bandits were her teachers. Sent by life's better nature to push her to the edge so she would reach such a place of disheartenment and despair that she'd have to change. And learn to soar. Just maybe all she'd experienced was, as the billionaire taught, precious preparation for who she needed to become to fulfill the potential of her most luminous gifts and realize the promise of her most high destiny, in a way that benefited humanity. And, perhaps, it's when we face losing everything that we come to know our grandest selves.

This strange, quirky and most genuine mentor in front of her, Mr. Stone Riley, was pouring his heart out, explaining how the simple yet not initially easy daily discipline of joining The 5 AM Club could, and indeed would, transform the productivity, prosperity and well-being of any person who applied the method. He'd kept each of the lofty vows he had made at their bizarre first encounter, at The Spellbinder's mesmerizing conference. He'd shown himself to be a titan, not only of industry but also of integrity. And decency.

"We need more of his kind," she thought. "Women and men who are pure leaders. People who influence not through the strength of a large title and by the threat of a big position but via the power of their characters, the nobility of their expertise, the compassion in their hearts and by their unusual dedication to leaving everyone they meet better than they found them. Leaders run less by the selfish addictions of the ego and more by the selfless dictates of our greater wisdom."

The entrepreneur remembered the words of the poet Maya Angelou: "My wish for you is that you continue. Continue to be who you are, to astonish a mean world with your acts of kindness."

The instructions of Mother Teresa also entered the mind of the entrepreneur in that instant: "If everyone would only clean their own doorstep, the whole world would be clean."

And so, on that very special early morning, inside one of the splendid monuments of the world, she not only forgave—she made a pact with herself. Understanding, as never before, that optimizing one's self is the best way to improve the state of the world, and that developing the genius within was the fastest way to uplift her relationship with everything externally, the entrepreneur forged an agreement. She made herself a promise not only to never again consider taking her own life. She also pledged that every day, for the remainder of her days, she'd rise at 5 AM and give herself the gift of that Victory Hour free from all trivial diversions, unimportant stimulations and unnecessary complications. So that she could continue. Continue calibrating her Mindset, purifying her Heartset, fortifying her Healthset and escalating her Soulset.

She would demand this of herself no matter what excuses and rationalizations the weaker and scared part of her personality would argue for. Because she deserved to experience her greatness. And because she hoped to be one of the heroes that we all are waiting for.

"Anyhoo," the billionaire shouted, inappropriately loudly. "Three final and ultra-practical tactics to help you lock in new habits. I've spent a lot of time on this subject because it's so absolutely essential to your success. I'll quickly walk you through three techniques that research confirms will help The 5 AM Club morning routine stick. Then we're out of here."

He pulled out the flashlight and focused its rays on the ceiling of the chamber. The following brain tattoos slowly appeared:

#1. To make a habit last, never install it alone.

#2. The teacher learns the most.

#3. When you most feel like quitting is the time you must continue advancing.

The billionaire smiled again. "Pretty simple instructions, right? Profoundly simple because they're simply profound. The first point will remind you that rituals run deepest when performed in a group. That's why being a member of The 5 AM Club is so potent. You're not installing this morning routine alone. We're all in this together. And my sincere wish is that, when you cats get home, you bring as many people as you can—people who are ready to rise early so they can do world-class work and craft phenomenal lives—into the club. Support groups have long been a proven way to make improvements that last. So, leverage this concept brilliantly, please."

The billionaire coughed. Then he rubbed his chest, as if he were in pain. He pretended no one noticed. And advanced the dialogue.

"The second point will remind you to actually teach the philosophy and methodology you've been learning from me. As you do so, your own understanding of the material will deepen even more superbly. In many ways, educating others on all I've shared will be a gift you provide to yourself."

"I've never looked at it that way," observed the entrepreneur.

"It's truth," informed the billionaire. "And the final line you see on this ceiling is the most important. Remember that persistency is necessary for all forms of mastery. In that moment you feel you can't go further lies an enormous opportunity to forge an entirely new level of willpower. When you feel you can't continue, progress a little longer. Your self-discipline muscle will be amplified considerably. And the degree of your self-respect will increase vastly. And few things are as essential to exponential productivity, leading your field and the creation of a life you adore as raising the appreciation you have for yourself."

Stunningly and without any clue about what was coming, the billionaire flipped over and held a headstand. With eyes closed, he recited a phrase from Gerald Sykes, the writer and philosopher, that went like this: "Any solid achievement must, of necessity, take years of humble apprenticeship and estrangement from most of society."

"You two amazing humans deserve to materialize your best selves and realize epic achievements," the billionaire said as he returned to earth. "Do not betray the powers that sleep within you by staying too late in a soft bed that keeps you sedated. The great men and women of the world became so not because they lounged glamorously under the covers, but because they set sublime ambitions that they then proceeded to *do*—even as the majority called them crazy. World-class takes time and commitment and sacrifice and patience—like the Taj Mahal shows us. And heroism never occurs in a single season. Encode the 5 AM habit. Stay with the process indefinitely and move ahead when you most feel like stopping. Doing so will make you a legend. And seal your fate as someone who is worthy of worldwide influence."

Stone Riley then stood up. Hugged his two students. And disappeared down a marble passageway.

CHAPTER 13

The 5 AM Club Learns
The 20/20/20 Formula

"Early in the morning, when you are reluctant in your laziness to get up,
let this thought be at hand: 'I am rising to do the work of a human being.'"
—Marcus Aurelius, Roman emperor

"Rome is in my veins. Its energy courses through my blood. And its unique type of magic resets my spirit," thought the billionaire as his jet taxied along the tarmac of that city's private airport. The song "Magnolia" by Italian music group Negrita pulsed through the speakers of the aircraft as the tycoon swayed his taut shoulders to the beat.

"The fierce pride, fantastic passions and glorious hearts of the Romans inspire me so much," he affirmed to himself. "The way the light falls on Trinità dei Monti, the church that crowns the Spanish Steps, never fails to lift my soul—and often brings tears into my eyes. The exquisite food, including the mozzarella di bufala, cacio e pepe, amatriciana and carbonara along with the fire-cooked abbacchio, feeds my desire to maximize the enjoyment of my life. And the painstakingly handcrafted architecture in this open-air museum of a city, where I love to walk in the rain, speaks to both the warrior as well as the poet within me," the magnate reflected as his jet neared the gate.

The billionaire had spent many of the finest years of his fantastic though far from perfect life in Rome, staying at an apartment in the historical center on Via Vittoria. Zurich and his other homes were the places he'd go mostly to work on projects and manage his global commercial pursuits. But Rome, well, Rome was to fuel his sense of awe. And to nourish his appetite for joy.

Inhaling the fragrance of gardenias at springtime and taking long treks past the temple that sits at the lake in the park called Villa Borghese were two of his favorite things in life. Rising at 5 AM, before Rome's dense traffic could stifle some of its magnificence, and riding his mountain bike past the Trevi Fountain, up to Monti and by the Colosseum, and finally over to Piazza Navona to just sit and embrace the marvelousness of the church in that exalted square, reminded him of the brilliance that only early morning brings. Much more than his wealth, such experiences made him feel prosperous. And alive.

You should know that the greatest love of his life hailed from Rome. The billionaire met her in an English bookstore just off Via dei Condotti, the fabulous street where Italy's iconic fashion houses have their flagship stores. Though he was in his late thirties, the titan was still a bachelor at that first encounter, something of a playboy and a man known for his taste in the finer pleasures of the world. He still remembered the book he sought her help to find: *Jonathan Livingston Seagull* by Richard Bach, that wonderfully transformational novel about a seagull who knew he was made to fly higher than the flock and embarked on an unforgettable journey to make that inner knowing real.

Vanessa put her hands on a copy quickly, was exceedingly polite yet frustratingly aloof and then moved on to help another customer.

It took the billionaire over a year of visiting that cramped bookshop with books arranged on old wooden shelves that lined the timeworn walls for this young woman to agree to have dinner with him. The billionaire's quest was driven by her under-the-radar kind of beauty, her ardent intelligence, her bohemian personal style and her awkward laugh that made him feel as happy as a family of bees in a huge honey pot.

They were married in the enchanting seaside town of Monopoli, in the southern Italian region of Puglia.

"What a special day that was," the baron mused wistfully. "The music that rang through the main square as we all danced with wild abandon under the melting glow of a full moon. The farm-fresh burrata cheese, the orecchiette pasta made by the chef's grandmother. The townspeople joining the lively party, displaying their boundless Italian hospitality by bringing bottles of homemade Negroamaro and Primitivo wine as wedding gifts. The whole experience still touched him considerably.

The billionaire's relationship with Vanessa had been both sensational and volatile, as in many epic love stories. Sometimes—often, actually—intense romantic connection raises deep-rooted pain. With that special person, we finally feel safe to take off our social armor and show our truest selves. And so, they get to see us in the fullness of our wonder, passion and light. Yet, that also brings intense glimpses of the shadow side we all have, the side that develops from the hurts we've had, as we've lived.

In *The Prophet*, Kahlil Gibran wrote, "When love beckons to you, follow him, though his ways are hard and steep. Though the sword hidden among his pinions may wound you. Though his voice may shatter your dreams as the north wind lays waste the garden. All these things shall love do unto you so that you may know the secrets of your heart." Yet, despite the turbulent nature of their marriage, the billionaire and his statuesque wife made it work, for decades.

Though she had passed away suddenly many years earlier, he never remarried. He wouldn't allow himself to fall in love again, preferring to concentrate on growing his business empire, expanding his philanthropic pursuits and enjoying the genuinely lovely life he'd earned, alone.

The mogul took out his wallet and slowly removed a creased photograph of Vanessa. He stared at it, transfixed by the image. Then he started coughing again. Vigorously.

"You okay, Boss?" inquired one of the pilots from the cockpit.

The billionaire remained silent, looking at the photo.

The entrepreneur and the artist had flown to Rome a few days earlier and had been mesmerized by the sights, splendor and rarities of The Eternal City. With hands locked together, taking in the energy and beauty of Rome, they traversed the cobblestone streets previously walked by great builders and noble emperors.

Today was the day they had waited a long time for. This morning they'd learn *The 20/20/20 Formula* that rested at the core of The 5 AM Method. The two students would be taught, with granularity, precisely what to do within The Victory Hour, that window of opportunity that runs between 5 and 6 AM, so they'd consistently enjoy amazing days.

Today they would discover, in intimate detail, how to use their mornings well, to create a world-class existence.

As requested by the billionaire, the two stood at the very top of the Spanish Steps. It was precisely 5 AM. If you stood on the platform under the obelisk that's there and looked down to the steps beneath it, you'd see the exact spot where the mentor and his two students met on this morning.

The first rays of the Roman sun kissed Trinità dei Monti as the lovers looked out over this city of such culture. The early Romans were remarkable for the grandeur of their visions, for the scale of their buildings and for their otherworldly ability to construct monuments that betrayed engineering reality. The two of them could see St. Peter's Basilica and the tomb of Emperor Augustus, as well as the Seven Hills that were so central to the protection of the empire that began as a tiny village on the banks of the Tiber River—and grew to what now included forty different countries spanning Europe, Asia and Africa. The air was fragrant with a blend of floral notes and smokiness, as if a fire were burning in the far distance.

"Buongiorno!" cried a voice amid the tranquility. "Own your morning. Elevate your life," the billionaire shouted with the kind of enthusiasm you'd hear from Roman soldiers on achieving a crucial victory.

Mr. Riley walked into the first embers of the lightfall, smiling a man in the magic of life type of smile. He had chosen to wear a pair of chic Italian sunglasses for this all-important coaching session. He also wore an Italian windbreaker over a black t-shirt with the initials SPQR emblazoned on it, black sweatpants and orange running shoes.

"Tutto bene?" he asked cheerfully.

"We're good," said the entrepreneur, happily, understanding a few words of Italian.

"Really good," offered the artist.

"Big day, cats. Today's lesson, to be taught to you by me—your cheese-gulping tonnarelli pasta–gobbling mentor—is all about *The 20/20/20 Formula*. We're finally here. We're finally ready to calibrate your morning routine so you both materialize your promise for genius and lead a life of limitless joyfulness. You'll so love what you're about to hear. The rest of your life will never be the same," the illustrious industrialist declared.

As the sun slowly ascended, for the first time a tattoo could be seen on the back of the billionaire's left hand. It had numbers on it. They simply read "20/20/20."

The rays of light congregated over his head to give the appearance of a halo. The entire scene was ethereal. You would have been impressed.

"Is that new?" wondered the artist, showing a clear curiosity. "Didn't notice it before."

"Yep," responded the tycoon. "I had someone in Trastevere do it for me last night. Cool, right?" spoke the billionaire, appearing as innocent as a newborn.

"Sort of," pronounced the artist as he let out a monstrous yawn, then sipped from a takeaway cup of coffee. "Great coffee here in Italy," he added.

"Well, the tattoo is temporary," admitted the billionaire. "I got it because today's *The 20/20/20 Formula* day. It really is one of the most important of all our training days together. I feel blessed to be here with you two. I'm starting to feel we're family now. And to be back in Rome is so incredibly special. I stopped coming here after my wife, Vanessa, passed away. Just hurt too much to be here without her," he confessed, before looking away.

Stone Riley then dug into a pocket of his sweatpants and pulled out a wishbone. He carefully placed the object on one of the steps that had a series of mysterious drawings on it. Just so you know what it looked like, it looked like this:

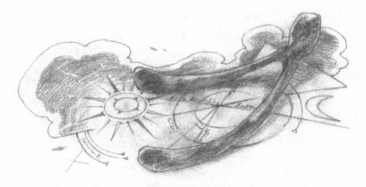

The billionaire asked his two guests to make a wish, before instructing them to pull it apart as a sign of good luck.

"I brought this to our session this morning not only to create even more great vibes for you cats," continued the billionaire. "I also want you both to remember that a wishbone without a backbone doesn't really get you very far," he explained.

"Sort of the 'part-time commitment delivers part-time results' insight we learned earlier?" queried the artist.

"And the 'no idea works without doing the work' insight," reinforced the entrepreneur as she did a yoga stretch into the increasing sun.

"Sort of," replied the billionaire. "I know you both long to lead productive, excellent, happy and meaningful lives. Being a member of The 5 AM Club truly is the one habit—of all possible habits—that will guarantee this mighty ambition comes true. It's the single-finest practice I've ever encountered to translate the intentions of living gloriously into an everyday reality. Yes, dreams and desires are just wishbones. Rising before daybreak is your backbone to get them done.

"The power of getting up early really comes from the daily application of *The 20/20/20 Formula*," the magnate continued. "And you're now just a few seconds away from being exposed to this astonishingly potent morning routine."

"It really is about time!" said the artist as he put on his own green-lensed sunglasses to shield his eyes from the light which was now beginning to wash into the empty spaces around the Spanish Steps and down onto the cobblestoned square that features a famous fountain built around Bernini's sculpture of an old boat.

"Give me a hug before we get going, people!" bellowed the billionaire affectionately as he embraced the artist and entrepreneur. "Welcome to my beloved Roma!" he added as the song "Come un Pittore" by the group Modà began to play from an open window of a nearby apartment. A curtain hung out of it, flirting with the soft breeze.

"Okay. Let's rock this piece. Please know that your creativity, productivity, prosperity, performance and usefulness to the world as well as the quality of your private life won't transform by simply rising at 5 AM alone. It's not just rising early that makes this regime so powerful. It's what you do over the sixty minutes after you wake up that makes The 5 AM Club so game-changing. Remember this: your Victory Hour gives you one of life's greatest windows of opportunity. As you now know, the way you start your day dramatically influences how it unfolds. Some people get up early but destroy the value of their morning routine by watching the news, surfing online, scanning social feeds and checking messages. I'm sure you both understand that such behavior comes from the need for a quick pleasure rush of dopamine—an escape from what is truly important. This way of acting causes members of the majority to miss out on doing the things that would allow them to leverage the quietude of this special time to help them maximize greatness so awesome days show up consistently."

"And as we create each day, so we craft our life, right?" asserted the artist, confirming a key piece of information he'd learned on the beach of the billionaire's oceanfront compound. "That's *The Day Stacking Foundation.* And it's one of *The 4 Focuses of History-Makers* that you explained to us. I still remember that model."

"Absolutely correct," applauded the billionaire. "And I need to say that beginning your day intelligently, healthily and peacefully isn't only about optimizing your public and private success. It's also about protecting it."

Suddenly, a man driving a horse carriage and dressed as a gladiator rolled through the square known as Piazza di Spagna and shouted, "Buongiorno Mr. Riley," and then continued on his way.

"A dopo," replied the billionaire loud enough for the man to hear. "Gnarly costume, right?" he said to his students.

The billionaire rubbed his fake tattoo and looked toward the Colosseum.

"That man we just saw makes me think of the Auriga, a type of slave in ancient Rome, who would transport important Roman leaders and was chosen for his trustworthiness. Here's the neat thing: another key job of the Auriga was to stand behind the military general known as the 'Dux' and whisper the words 'Memento, homo' carefully into his ear as he placed the laurel crown on his head."

"What does that mean?" asked the entrepreneur. Today she'd dressed in faded jeans, a bright red t-shirt with a V-neck and white running shoes. Her hair was styled in the ponytail that she liked. She had her bracelets on. And she absolutely radiated optimism.

"'Memento homo' is Latin for 'remember you are only a man,'" the billionaire answered. "The Auriga did this to keep the leader's arrogance in check and to help the leader manage the inevitable invitation to egotism that all great success inescapably brings. The ritual was a profound discipline to ensure the Dux remained monomaniacally focused on his true mission of making himself, and the empire he ruled, even better—and not diluting all his energies on the amusements and excess that cause dynasties to fall."

"You know what?" indicated the artist. "I've seen some artistic geniuses blow up their creative empires and destroy their good reputations because they didn't manage their success properly. So, I hear you."

"Def," said the entrepreneur. "I mean, definitely," she quickly corrected as she clasped the hand of her new boyfriend. "I've seen so many rocketship companies lose their market share because they fell in love with their winning formula. They lost their fire. They got bloated and cocky. They bought into the faulty belief that because there were long lineups for their excellent products, there would always be long lineups—even without iterating their goods, improving customer service and ensuring that every single employee continued to raise their leadership performance. So, I hear you, too, Mr. Riley."

"Awesome," was his one-word reply.

"As you apply *The 20/20/20 Formula*, always remember to keep improving the way you run it each morning. Stay hungry. Keep a whitebelt mentality around it. Because *nothing fails like success*. Once you experience how transformational the practice is, it'll be easy to start coasting—and maybe even neglecting—a few steps of the process."

The billionaire touched an index finger down to one of the steps. He closed his eyes and quietly recited these words: "It's time to stop being a fugitive from your highest self and accept membership into a new order of ability, bravery and understanding of the call on your lives to inspire humanity."

He then walked across the stone platform atop the Spanish Steps and raised two fingers of his right hand to show the universal sign for peace. Next, he waved an arm in the direction of a man on a seat heating up chestnuts in Piazza di Spagna, near the foot of Via dei Condotti. The man wore a gray shirt that had wrinkles over the chest area, navy blue trousers and yellow running shoes.

On seeing the sign, the man immediately stood up and darted through the square, up the steps—three at a time—all the way to the peak, where the billionaire was stationed. He lifted his rumpled shirt, revealing a bulletproof vest—and pulled out a laminated sheet of paper from beneath it.

"Here you go, Grande. Good to see you back in Roma, Boss." The man spoke with a rich Italian accent and a voice as gritty as sandpaper.

"Grazie mille! Molto gentile, Adriano," the billionaire said as he kissed the palm of a hand before extending it for a handshake.

"Adriano's on my security team," noted Mr. Riley while studying the page that had been presented to him. "He's one of my best. He grew up in the town of Alba in the Piemonte region of this exceptional nation. You cats like tartufo?"

"What's that?" queried the artist, looking a little confused by the scenario that had just played out.

"Truffles, baby!" enthused the billionaire. "My goodness, they taste incredible. On tagliolini pasta with melted butter drizzled over it. Or when grated over jiggly fried eggs. My, oh my, food of the emperors it is!" The billionaire's eyes were as wide as a prairie while he imagined the meal he was describing. A razor thin line of drool meandered out of the right corner of his mouth. Yes, a line of drool. Beyond weird, right?

Adriano, who had remained in position, discreetly handed his employer a handkerchief. He looked at the entrepreneur and the artist with a glance that seemed to say, "I know he's strange, but we love him, too."

And then all four people perched upon that overwhelmingly alluring site started to laugh. Together.

"Have a great morning, Boss," Adriano said as he prepared to leave. "I'll meet you in Testaccio this evening. Thank you so much for inviting me to eat with you tonight. Are we eating cacio e pepe, as usual?"

"Si," confirmed the billionaire. "A presto."

"Alba is where white truffles come from," explained the billionaire. "Specially trained dogs sniff them out. Or pigs. Maybe in the future, I'll take you guys on a truffle hunt with me. I promise you it'll be unforgettable. Anyhoo, have a look at this fantastic learning model. The Spellbinder actually deconstructed The Victory Hour and *The 20/20/20 Formula* for us. Zero questions about how to run your morning routine now. No room for excuses. It's all laid out for you. Just run the play and you'll own your day. Procrastination is an act of self-hatred, you know?"

"Really?" asked the artist.

"Absolutely. If you really loved yourself, you'd relinquish all your feelings of not being good enough to be great and renounce all slavery to your weakness. You'd stop focusing on your deficiencies and celebrate your amazing qualities. Just think about it: there's no person on the planet today who has the unique stack of gifts that you have. Actually, in all of history, there's never been even one person exactly like you. And there never will be. Yes, you're that special. That's an indisputable fact. So, embrace the full force of your lavish talent, luminous strengths and breathtaking powers. Let go of the destructive habit of breaking the commitments you make to yourself. Failing to keep self-promises is one of the reasons so many of us don't love ourselves. Not following through on what we tell ourselves we'll do so destroys our sense of personal worth and dissolves our self-esteem. Keep behaving like that and the unconscious part of you will begin to believe you're not worth anything. And remember the psychological phenomenon known as The Self-Fulfilling Prophecy I walked you through earlier. We always perform in a way that is aligned with the way we see ourselves. And so, our thinking creates our results. And the less we value ourselves and our powers," he went on, "the less power we have access to."

The billionaire watched a group of butterflies fly by before continuing.

"That's just the way it all works. So, my suggestion is that you stop putting things off, flex those willpower muscles we talked about inside the Taj Mahal, and make the remainder of your life an exercise in audacity, a testimony to exceptional productivity and a rare expression of unstained beauty. Honor all you truly are by living your genius instead of loathing yourself, by denying your specialness. Procrastination is an act of self-hatred," the billionaire repeated. "So really go all in on installing *The 20/20/20 Formula* as the core way of managing your morning."

The billionaire showed the framework to the entrepreneur and the artist. It looked like this:

THE 20/20/20 FORMULA
DECONSTRUCTION

POCKET #1

	WHAT	WHY	BENEFITS
05:00 AM — 05:20 AM **M O V E**	• INTENSE EXERCISE • SWEAT HARD • LEARN • HYDRATE • BREATHE DEEPLY	• CLEANSES CORTISOL • BDNF FLOWS • DOPAMINE RISES • SEROTONIN INCREASES • METABOLISM ELEVATES	• MORE FOCUS + PRODUCTIVITY • FOCUS + BRAIN OPTIMIZED • ENERGY GROWS • LESS STRESS • LIVE LONGER

POCKET #2

	WHAT	WHY	BENEFITS
05:20 AM — 05:40 AM **REFLECT**	• JOURNAL • MEDITATE • PLAN • PRAY • CONTEMPLATE	• GRATITUDE BOOSTED • AWARENESS SOARS • HAPPINESS LIFTS • WISDOM DEVELOPS • SERENITY EXPANDS	• GREATER POSITIVITY • DECREASED REACTIVITY • HIGHER CREATIVITY • STRONGER PERFORMANCE • RICHER LIFE

POCKET #3

	WHAT	WHY	BENEFITS
05:40 AM — 06:00 AM **G R O W**	• REVIEW GOALS • READ BOOKS • CONSUME AUDIOBOOKS • LISTEN TO PODCASTS • STUDY ONLINE	• THE 2x3x MINDSET • KNOWLEDGE DEEPENS • ACUMEN ESCALATES • CONFIDENCE ACCELERATES • MASTER CHANGE	• BETTER INCOME + IMPACT • CRAFT CALIBRATES • DOMAIN DOMINANCE • PERSONAL GROWTH • INSPIRATION RISES

"As you can see from this learning model, there are three twenty-minute pockets to install and then practice to mastery-level. The first twenty-minute pocket of *The 20/20/20 Formula* requires that you *Move*. Simply put, doing some sweaty exercise first thing every morning will revolutionize the quality of your days. The second pocket encourages you to *Reflect* for twenty minutes. This segment is designed to help you reaccess your natural power, boost self-awareness, dissolve your stress, fuel your happiness and restore your inner peace in an era of acute over-stimulation and excessive activity. And you'll round out this sixty-minute Victory Hour of personal fortification with twenty minutes centered around ensuring that you *Grow*, whether that means investing some time reading a book that will improve your understanding of how the best lives were made or an article that will refine your professional prowess or listening to an audio session on how the virtuosos accomplish their unusual results or watching an educational video that will show you how to lift your relationships or increase your finances or deepen your spirituality. As you cats now know, the leader who learns the most wins.

"One of the most helpful things I've ever learned from The Spellbinder was that starting my mornings with a strong workout—pretty much right after I jumped out of bed—was of the *utmost* importance. I still remember his actual words—and they were firm: 'You must begin your day with intense exercise. This is a non-negotiable. Otherwise *The 20/20/20 Formula* won't work. And I'll take back your membership in The 5 AM Club.'"

Three doves flew over the billionaire. He eyed them with a giant grin, blew a kiss to one and then advanced his discourse on the morning routine of history-makers.

"Training rigorously first thing in the morning is a total game-changer. Moving vigorously shortly after you get up will generate an alchemy in your brain—based on its neurobiology—which will not only wake you up fully but electrify your focus and energy, amplify your self-discipline and launch your day in a way that makes you feel on fire. Now, to be ultra-practical for you two, I'll say that your workout could mean taking a spinning class or performing a bunch of jumping jacks and burpees or skipping like the pro boxers love to do or doing wind sprints. Not sure what will work best for you. The real key here, though, is to make sure you sweat."

"Why?" asked the artist, now taking copious notes.

"For the reason you'll see on the diagram. As you know now, cortisol is the hormone of fear. It's made in the cortex of the adrenal glands and is then released into the blood. Cortisol is one of the main materials that stunts your genius and devastates your implicit opportunity to make history. Very good scientific data confirms that your cortisol levels are highest in the morning."

"Fascinating information," observed the entrepreneur, as she performed another stretch in the Roman sunshine.

"Yes, it is. So, exercising from 5 to 5:20 AM—for just twenty minutes—will significantly lower your cortisol and, therefore, dial you into your top performance. Fantastic way to start a morning, right? Science has also shown there's a vital link between physical fitness and cognitive ability. The sweating from a powerful workout releases BDNF—brain-derived neurotrophic factor—which supercharges that organ for a winning day."

"Wow," said the entrepreneur, also taking notes at a furious pace.

"BDNF has been shown to repair brain cells damaged by stress and accelerate the formation of neural connections, so you think better, and process faster," expounded the billionaire. "Another Gargantuan Competitive Advantage, for sure. Oh, and it also promotes neurogenesis, so you'll actually grow new brain cells. What's that alone worth to you?"

"Wow times two!" shouted the artist, sounding very corny versus displaying any hint of cool.

"My business will be untouchable and I, personally, will become unbeatable as I execute on all these ideas you're so generously sharing with us," offered the entrepreneur. Modeling what she'd seen Mr. Riley do when others had been kind to him, she performed a slight bow to show her appreciation.

"Absolutely," agreed the billionaire. "And by exercising intensely during the first twenty-minute pocket of *The 20/20/20 Formula*, you'll also release dopamine, which you well know is the neurotransmitter of drive, along with elevating your amounts of serotonin, the wonderful chemical that regulates happiness. This means that by 5:20 AM, while your competitors are counting sheep, you're already amped to lead your field, achieve excellent results and make the day ahead epic."

"Would it be possible for you to be specific about what we need to do in order to make sure we're up with the sun?" requested the entrepreneur. "I mean, can you get into a little bit of detail about what behaviors we must perform so we actually get out of bed when that alarm clock goes off? I hope that's not a dumb question. Is that too basic?"

"It's a great question," said the artist as he stroked his girlfriend's back.

"It's a fabulous question!" exclaimed the tycoon. "And sure. Like I've suggested, buy an old-school alarm clock—that's what I use. As I said in Agra, you never want to sleep with any technology in your bedroom. I'll explain why soon. Once you have your alarm clock, advance the time on it from the actual time to thirty minutes ahead. Then set the alarm for 5:30 AM."

"Really?" indicated the artist. "That seems odd."

"I know," admitted the billionaire. "But it works *like magic*. You trick yourself into thinking you're getting up later, but you're actually rising at 5 AM. This tactic just works. So, do it. Next, and this sounds obvious but it's another key hack, as soon as the alarm goes off bolt out of bed before your weaker self sucks you into all the reasons to stay in bed. Before your rational mind can come up with reasons to remain under the covers. You just need to make it through that sixty-six-day habit installation process so that waking up at 5 AM reaches The Automaticity Point. And it becomes easier to get up early than sleep later. When I first joined The 5 AM Club, I slept in my workout clothes."

Mr. Riley looked slightly embarrassed. Then more doves and butter-flies passed by. And a wisp of a rainbow could be seen spreading across the Spanish Steps.

"You're kidding me brother, right?" laughed the artist as he twirled a dreadlock. "You really slept in your exercise gear?"

"I did," admitted the billionaire. "And my running shoes were laid out right next to my bed. I did whatever it took to eliminate the death grip that common excuses could have over me."

The entrepreneur was nodding. She appeared stronger and happier as each day passed.

"Anyway, let me keep jamming on the point about exercising first thing in your morning. By working out intensely, you'll stimulate that natural pharmacy of mastery which will make you feel fundamentally different than when you first woke up. The way you feel when you first wake up really isn't the way you'll feel only twenty minutes later at 5:20 AM, when you run this strategy to bulletproof your neurobiology and battleproof your physiology. Please remember that! Obviously, the sweaty movement also transforms your psychology over time. Even if you're usually a 'non-morning person' and grumpy at the beginning of your day, you'll change—the whole 'neurons that fire together, wire together' thing. You'll feel the confidence every leader without a title needs. You'll have the focus to stay on task for hours and hours, so you get your most brilliant work done. And you'll feel much calmer. See, the boost in norepinephrine that fierce morning activity generates not only improves your attention, it leaves you feeling significantly more serene. And more good research proves that exercise regulates the amygdala in the limbic system, the ancient brain we discussed in an earlier class at my beach in Mauritius, so that your responses to stimuli ranging from a hard project or a difficult client to a rude driver or a screaming baby are much more graceful instead of hysterical."

"Pretty marvelous benefits," remarked the entrepreneur. "You're right, Mr. Riley. I couldn't put a price tag on having all these weapons of mass productivity in my arsenal."

"Precisely," said the billionaire as he hugged the entrepreneur. "I do love you two," he added. "I'll miss you both."

In that moment, the mentor's usual hopefulness shifted into some unknown sadness. "Our time together is coming to an end. Maybe we'll meet again. I really hope so. But I don't know . . ."

His voice trailed off, and he looked away again, up at the white church that stood behind where they had gathered, a glorious tribute to the brightest examples of visionary architecture. The billionaire reached into a pocket of his black sweatpants and pulled out a pill, popping it into his mouth like a child consuming a tiny piece of candy.

"Anyhoo, as you can also see on the deconstruction," he went on, holding up the model, "working out first thing in the morning also elevates your metabolism—and it fuels the fat-burning engine of your body so you burn any excess more efficiently and lean out more quickly. Another valuable triumph, right? Oh, and as you optimize your fitness you'll set yourself up to stay healthy your entire lifetime. 'Train harder. Live longer' is a smart motto I built my empires by. You now know that one of the keys to legendary is longevity. Do not die. You can't own your game and change the world if you're pushing up daisies in a cemetery," the titan of industry articulated energetically.

"The primary point that I'm trying to offer on the first part of this calibrated versus superficial morning protocol is essentially this: your life will feel and work a hundred times better when you're in the finest physical condition you've ever been in. Sweaty exercise as your first move after rising with the sun really is a total life-changer. Period. So, do whatever it takes to code in this habit. Whatever it takes, cats."

"Can I ask you another question, Mr. Riley?" the entrepreneur asked politely.

"Go for it," said the billionaire.

"What if I want to exercise for longer than twenty minutes?"

"Totally cool," noted the billionaire. "This morning routine isn't written in stone like those words carved into that obelisk up there," he added as he pointed up to the monument sitting on a small platform just above the Spanish Steps. "Take all I'm sharing and then make it yours. Customize it to fit your preferences and make it bespoke, to suit your lifestyle."

The billionaire inhaled a fresh breath of Roman air—the same air the emperors, gladiators, statesmen and craftspeople breathed a thousand years ago. Just imagine breathing that air. And standing there with these three fascinating members of The 5 AM Club.

"This brings me to the second twenty-minute pocket of *The 20/20/20 Formula* that you need to run over your Victory Hour. The time between 5:20 and 5:40 AM is when you 'Reflect.'"

"What exactly do you mean by 'Reflect'?" asked the artist, exemplifying his newfound confidence in being a great student. He rubbed his goatee as he voiced the question. His arm rested around the entrepreneur's shoulder.

"As I've been suggesting during our time together, managing your morning well is a main skill of exceptionalists. Using the front end of your day expertly is such a key determinant of business eminence and personal magnificence. And one element of a cleverly granulated morning routine is a period of deep peace. Some quietude and solitude for yourself before the complexity starts arriving, and your family needs your energy, and all your other responsibilities take over. *Tranquility is the new luxury of our society.* So, during this segment of your Victory Hour, savor some stillness. Contemplate how you're living and on who you hope to become. Be thoughtful and intentional on the values you want to be loyal to over the hours ahead of you. And how you wish to behave. Consider what needs to happen for this to be a great day amid the construction of a legendary life."

"This pocket will be super-important to me," remarked the entrepreneur as her bracelets clinked together. One of them was shiny and new. It bore the phrase "All these early mornings will make me an icon someday."

"I agree with you," expressed the billionaire. "Reflecting on what's most important to a life beautifully lived will leave you with what The Spellbinder calls 'residual wisdom' throughout the rest of the day. For example, thinking quietly about the weighty value of purely producing work that represents mastery or remembering your commitment to treating people kindly and respectfully during the second pocket re-anchors those virtues within your awareness. And so, as you experience the remainder of your day, the residue of your reconnection with this wisdom stays in focus, infusing every single moment and guiding each one of your choices."

Another butterfly flitted by. Three more soon followed the first, almost poetically. The billionaire decided to deepen his explanation on reflection, but first popped another pill. He put a hand on his heart and looked at the sensational view of Rome. "The way the light falls here really is like nowhere else," he thought. "I'll miss my Roma."

The billionaire stared down the steps at the white boat sculpted by Pietro Bernini and then glanced at the flower shop, also in the square below.

"In so many ways, reflection is a main source of transformation because once you know better, you definitely can do better. During this twenty-minute segment of The Victory Hour, all you need to do is get serene, stay silent and enter the stillness. What a gift you'll give yourself in this era of such scattered attention, worry and noisiness."

"That would be a giant gift to give to myself—and to my business," acknowledged the entrepreneur. "I'm realizing I spend so much of my time doing and reacting, and so little of my time deliberating and planning. You've talked about how the great ones leverage periods of isolation. I've read that many famous geniuses had a habit of sitting in solitude for hours with nothing more than a pad of paper and a pen for capturing the insights that would start flashing across the screen of their imaginations."

"Yes," commented the billionaire. "Developing a tremendous imagination is a highly important portal into a celebrated fortune. One of the things that makes the historic sites here in Rome so special is the sheer size of the structures. What vision and confidence the Romans who created them must have had! And what skill to have turned the ideas into something real. My point is that every single one of the sensational edifices in The Eternal City is the product of the imagination of a human being, properly used. So, yes, you should also use the reflection pocket to invent, visualize and dream. 'Twenty years from now,' a quote I think comes from Mark Twain says, 'you will be more disappointed by the things you didn't do than by the ones you did do. So, throw off the bowlines. Sail away from the safe harbor. Catch the trade winds in your sails. Explore. Dream. Discover.'"

"All great artists dream about a future few believe is possible," stated the artist sagely.

"Yup," nodded the billionaire. "Another tactic you can practice at this time is to write out what The Spellbinder calls a *Pre-Performance Blueprint*. This is simply a written statement of your ideal day ahead. Researchers confirm that pre-commitment strategies work beautifully to increase your focus and discipline to get things done. You'll have a clear and calibrated script for your day ahead, so it unfolds the way you want it to. Of course, nothing in business and life is perfect. Still, that doesn't mean we shouldn't do our best to pursue it. The heroic women and men of the world were all perfectionists. They were *maximizers*, immensely obsessed with being remarkable at all they did. So, take at least ten minutes to write out your perfect day."

The mogul peered over at the flower shop again. He raised his left index finger up to the Roman sky. A volcanically attractive young woman, with high cheekbones, tortoiseshell glasses, a gray linen blouse and fashionable trousers, stood up, holding a metal attaché case. She then sprinted up the steps like a cheetah chasing its dinner.

"Hi, Vienna," said the billionaire as she arrived.

"Salve, Mr. Riley," replied the young woman respectfully. "We are delighted to see you back in Rome. Sir, I have your items."

The aide entered a code into the lock and the case sprung open. Inside were three luxuriously crafted journals, bound by the most supple Italian leather. The billionaire handed one to the entrepreneur and one to the artist. He lifted the last one, clutched it close to his heart and licked it. Yes, he actually licked his journal.

"When we're at the magical vineyards of South Africa, I'll explain why I just ran my tongue over my diary," the billionaire enthused with ever-increasing mystery.

"South Africa?" quizzed the artist loudly. "When are we going?"

"Magical vineyards?" queried the entrepreneur.

The billionaire ignored them both.

"You're good, Vienna," spoke the billionaire to his assistant. "Really good. Ci vediamo dopo," he added, as she walked down the ancient steps and hopped onto the back of a black scooter that had been waiting for her, before it raced away.

As the entrepreneur and the artist opened their journals, they saw a carefully detailed framework on the first page.

"Another learning diagram for us?" asked the artist in a grateful tone.

"Si," noted the billionaire.

"Brother, I love these models," the artist said. "Priceless teaching tools to make confusing concepts incredibly clear."

"And super-relevant," added the entrepreneur. "Clarity breeds mastery. Right?"

"Truth," affirmed the industrialist. "And you're welcome, cats. But it's been The Spellbinder who has invested decades of his rich life creating these frameworks to explain the philosophy and methodology of The 5 AM Club. They look simple because it's taken him his entire professional lifetime to handcraft them. It takes long years of extreme attention and ardent isolation to strip away the complexities of any work to reach the simplicity that sits at the touchstone of genuine genius. It's like when an amateur looks at a masterpiece. It looks simple because he doesn't comprehend the expertise of the master in taking away all that was unnecessary. Removing the non-essentials to produce the gem takes years of dedication. And decades of devotion. Making things look simple to the untrained eye is the mark of a maestro."

The learning model in the lavish leather journals looked like this, just so you have a clear sense of what the three companions saw on that sunny morning in Rome:

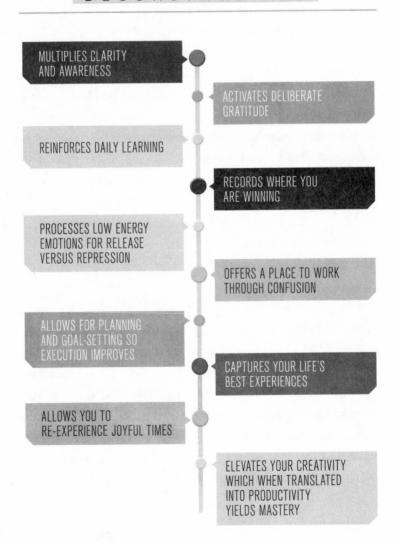

THE JOURNALING HABIT
DECONSTRUCTION

MULTIPLIES CLARITY AND AWARENESS

ACTIVATES DELIBERATE GRATITUDE

REINFORCES DAILY LEARNING

RECORDS WHERE YOU ARE WINNING

PROCESSES LOW ENERGY EMOTIONS FOR RELEASE VERSUS REPRESSION

OFFERS A PLACE TO WORK THROUGH CONFUSION

ALLOWS FOR PLANNING AND GOAL-SETTING SO EXECUTION IMPROVES

CAPTURES YOUR LIFE'S BEST EXPERIENCES

ALLOWS YOU TO RE-EXPERIENCE JOYFUL TIMES

ELEVATES YOUR CREATIVITY WHICH WHEN TRANSLATED INTO PRODUCTIVITY YIELDS MASTERY

"Let me get to the point of these gifts my assistant brought us," the billionaire continued. "During the 'reflection' pocket of *The 20/20/20 Formula*, another absolutely winning move is to write in a journal. And so I had these made for you by an Italian craftsperson. Hope they work wonders for you."

The magnate looked down Via dei Condotti. Street cleaners were hard at work. Tourists were strolling along the avenue, taking selfies and buying trinkets from street vendors.

"The Spellbinder loves hanging with me here in Roma. If we're lucky, we'll see him later this morning. I know he went running at daybreak along the river to Prati before heading off to a fishing excursion at a place a few hours from here. Oh, by the way, he formalized writing in a journal for at least a few of the minutes between 5:20 and 5:40 AM with the term 'Daily Diaries.' The key when you do this is just to write. Don't think too much. Simply download your commitments for the hours ahead, record your precious ambitions and activate your gratitude by listing what's good in your life right now. Please also use your journal as a place to process through any frustrations, disappointments and resentments in your heart so you let them go. It's miraculous how you'll release toxic emotions and low energy from your system when you write down your suppressed hurts, freeing up maximum creativity, premium vitality and unmatchable performance."

"A super way to fireproof and fortify my Heartset, right?" said the entrepreneur.

"Yahoo!" applauded the billionaire, who then placed a finger upon the learning model on the first page of his journal.

"Here are some of the rewards you'll receive when you invest ten or perhaps the entire twenty minutes of pocket number two of your Victory Hour in writing your Daily Diaries. And to repeat so I reinforce, I suggest you don't write only the positive elements of your current life but also those aspects of your experience that are causing discomfort and pain. Because the quickest way out of hard emotions is to have the wisdom and courage to go straight into them. Feel them to heal them. Name them to let go of them. Put a written voice to the dark energy of life's burdens to dissolve them. These are breakthrough insights I'm revealing to you two here. Because once you reclaim the power blocked by layers of toxic emotions and the wounds of the past, your Mindset, Heartset, Healthset and Soulset will all soar exponentially. And when your four interior empires escalate through your effortful self-purification, your supreme self begins to assume command. This then yields the external empires you both hope to see more of. What I'm trying to explain is this: difficult feelings that you don't find a healthy way to remove become repressed, which creates stress, poor productivity and even disease."

"Cool diagram," acknowledged the artist. "Are you saying that if I don't feel the uncomfortable feelings, they build up and get stuck inside me to the point where I could get sick?"

"Yes, what you just said is pretty much what I'm suggesting," Mr. Riley confirmed. "Those stuck toxic emotions layer over your gifts, talents and higher wisdom. This is one of the primary reasons most people on the planet have forgotten the heroes they are. When we avoid feeling, we lose access to our most powerful selves and forget the truths of life: that each of us can accomplish astounding things, and produce astonishing works, and realize radiant health, and know true love, and live a magical life, and be helpful to many. I speak fact here. But most of us have so much fear, pain, anger and sorrow built up over our real selves, we have no sense of the opportunities that sit right in front of us. All that dark energy blinds us from seeing them. And blocks our access to our primal genius. The great people of history had this access. Today, the majority have lost it."

"A magical life?" stated the entrepreneur. "You keep speaking of magic. Sounds a little far out. A little granola."

"Yes, a magical life," responded the billionaire firmly, but politely. "I'll explain how you enter the magic available to all of us when we get to South Africa. Once you learn what I'll teach you in the vineyard there, your ability to manifest more money, better health, greater joyfulness and deeper inner peace will grow dramatically. But I can't share anything about how to live in the magic yet. I'm not allowed to," commented the billionaire mysteriously.

"You need to feel a wound to heal a hurt," the billionaire continued with precision. "I've endured a lot of suffering in my life. Business defeats, personal losses, physical failures. I'm actually going through something right now that's creating sorrow in my heart." The billionaire's high-spirited demeanor suddenly began to fade. For an instant, he looked older. He hunched over. And his breathing grew labored. But then he recovered.

"Anyhoo, the good news," he said energetically as he raised both arms high into the Roman air, "is that I'm not carrying much past pain in my wonderful present and into my fantastic future. I used the Daily Diary practice during the 'Reflect' pocket of *The 20/20/20 Formula* to move through and release it all. This skill alone is one of the reasons I'm so full of wonder, gratefulness and peacefulness, most of the time. And how I've been able to achieve so much. Living in the past steals so much energy from most people, you know? This is a massive explanation for why most people are so unproductive. The Spellbinder's the only person I've ever met who made the link between poor performance and emotional turbulence. But think about it. It's totally true. So imagine what doing your Daily Diaries each morning will do for your accomplishment and the success of your business, especially as you navigate what you're going through." The billionaire spoke with palpable empathy as he placed one lean arm around the entrepreneur and the other over the shoulder of her new boyfriend. "And for your art," he added, turning to the artist.

"And carrying past pain is so exhausting," the artist agreed. "We all get defeated—and sometimes nearly devastated by life."

The billionaire kept on with his discourse. "I also encourage you to find at least a few moments during the second pocket, between 5:20 and

5:40 AM, to meditate. The Spellbinder taught me how to do so, and it has profoundly helped my concentration, my confidence, my performance and the calm that I feel, while running a sophisticated business portfolio. *And calm performers are the highest achievers.* There's nothing crackerjack about meditation, so get over any biases you might have around the skill and go ahead and lock it in. It's simply one of the world's best ways to strengthen your focus, preserve your natural power and insulate your inner peace. There's a lot of wonderful science confirming the value of a regular meditation ritual, so, even if you want to dismiss the method, the data says it works—phenomenally—as a human optimization habit. Current research proves that regular meditation helps lower levels of cortisol, thus lowering your stress. It's also a strong way to grow the relationship you have with yourself. You need to make more time for *you*. To scale your fluency and intimacy with your higher nature. To reconnect with your best part, that side of you that understands the impossible is mostly the untried and that knows of your hidden reservoirs of luminosity, audacity and love. That portion of you that still can see the greatness in others, even when they behave badly, and that models positivity in the world—even when such virtues are not replied to you. Yes, go into this twenty-moment sanctuary of silence and stillness each morning and *remember all you truly are.* Truth speaks in the solitude of the day's earliest light. And then carry this breathtaking knowledge with you, through the remaining hours of the gift we call a day."

The billionaire fell to the ground. And did a series of rapid push-ups. Then, a plank pose followed. You're now very familiar with this quirky tycoon's bizarre maneuvers.

"I need to get on to the third pocket of *The 20/20/20 Formula* so we can wrap up today's mentoring session. I've got a series of meetings set up for later, and then I'm off to a splendid dinner with Adriano, The Spellbinder and a few other old friends," the billionaire said cheerfully.

"Sure," said the artist. "No sweat."

"Of course," said the entrepreneur. "We heard about a restaurant close to Campo di Fiori that makes great carbonara. We're trying it tonight."

"Yummy," acknowledged the billionaire, sounding more like a five-year-old than a captain of commerce. He then continued his discussion on the morning routine of empire-builders, superachievers and the saviors of our civilization.

Suddenly, the billionaire clutched his stomach, wincing in pain.

"You okay, Mr. Riley?" the entrepreneur asked as she rushed toward her mentor.

"Absolutely," he replied, pretending everything was fine. "Let's keep moving. I'm totally committed to making sure you learn everything that was taught to me about The 5 AM Club before I leave you. Please, just make sure you share The Spellbinder's teachings with as many people as you can. You'll be improving the world as you do. I might not be able to," he said as his voice trailed off.

"Okay," the industrialist carried on. "Let's keep going. Pocket three of *The 20/20/20 Formula* is designed to help you 'Grow' daily. Remember *The 2x3x Mindset*: to double your income and impact, triple your investment in two primary areas, your personal mastery and your professional capability. So, 5:40 to 6:00 AM, the final segment of The Victory Hour, is when you deepen your base of knowledge, increase your acumen, improve your expertise and outlearn your competition."

"Leonardo da Vinci said, 'One can have no smaller or greater mastery than mastery of oneself,'" said the artist.

"I love you even more today," the entrepreneur said.

"Well, I adore you more every day," he replied with a grin.

"Oh, brother," laughed the billionaire. "I'm caught in a love fest. Right here on the Spanish Steps."

He closed his eyes and recited these words of stoic philosophy by Seneca, the Roman statesmen: "'Each day acquire something that will fortify you against poverty, against death, indeed against other misfortunes as well; and after you have run over many thoughts select one to be thoroughly digested that day.'"

The billionaire opened his eyes and stated simply, "Leadership on the outside begins within." He added, "During the final pocket, from 5:40 to 6 AM, of *The 20/20/20 Formula,* work on becoming more valuable, to your industry as well as to society. See, you don't receive success and influence only because of what you want. You attract it into your life *based on who you are*—as a person and as a producer. Private desire without personal development is like dreaming of having a gorgeous garden but not planting any seeds. *We magnetize ourselves to excellent rewards by raising the value of our selves.* I made my fortune from this idea. As I improved, my capacity to improve the lives of more people improved through the elevated quality of my service. As I made myself more knowledgeable, I became more valuable to the fields in which I conducted my businesses, which lifted my income and my impact. Here's a concept fairly foreign in today's age: read a book. Study the lives of the greatest men and women of the past by consuming their autobiographies during the 'Grow' pocket. Learn about the latest advancements in psychology. Devour works on innovation and communication, productivity and leadership, prosperity and history. And watch documentaries on how the best do what they do—and grew into who they are. Listen to audiobooks on personal mastery, creativity and business-building. One of the traits all my billionaire friends and I have in common is we absolutely love to learn. We grow—and capitalize on—our gifts and talents relentlessly. We invest in expanding ourselves—and our pro games—constantly. We are all totally into reading, improving and feeding our limitless curiosity. Fun for us is going to a conference together. We go to one, at least one, every three months so we stay inspired, excellent and absolutely switched on. We don't spend much time on meaningless entertainment because we're just too invested in endless education.

"Life is very equitable, you know," said the mogul, sounding quite philosophical and now looking much stronger. "You'll receive from it what you give to it. Key natural law there. So, give a lot more by becoming a lot better."

"Okay. So now you have it," Mr. Riley summed up exuberantly. "A beautifully engineered, flawlessly calibrated morning routine for a world-class business and personal life. Embrace it fully, run it daily, or at least five days a week, and your productivity, prosperity, sense of joy and serenity will accelerate potently along with the value you are able to deliver to our world."

"What's next?" inquired the artist.

"We'll now go visit the dead," was the billionaire's only reply.

CHAPTER 14

The 5 AM Club Grasps the Essentialness of Sleep

The Roman sun rose even higher as the three companions gazed over the rooftops and at the Vatican. The streets were now noisy. The Eternal City had come to life.

Again, the titan's hand went up into the air. Again, one could see another assistant appearing out of nowhere. This time a man who appeared to be in his early forties ran across the square, stood in its center and pulled out a device that he spoke into, quickly and loudly. Within a minute, three women with scarves over their hair—like you would see in those wonderful Italian films of the fifties—appeared on three sparkling red Vespas. They parked them at the foot of the Spanish Steps, right by the sculpture of the boat, before disappearing down Via delle Carrozze.

"Let's go, people!" exclaimed the billionaire. "It's time to ride."

"But what's this about visiting the dead?" asked the entrepreneur, the creases on her forehead reawakened and her arms now crossed.

"Trust me. Hop on your scooter. And follow me," the billionaire instructed.

The three companions wound their way through the ancient streets of Rome. Even the most unknown church or innocuous obelisk left them in a dreamy state of awe. The sunshine was dazzling now as both the Romans and the tourists filled the boulevards. The city felt so alive. In one square they passed, a remarkably talented opera singer with a man standing next to her to collect money touched the hearts of bystanders by singing like she had no tomorrow. As the billionaire, the entrepreneur and the artist continued their trek along the roads of Rome, they saw yet another surreal sight: The Pyramid of Cestius, built between 18 and 12 BC as a tomb.

"An Egyptian-style pyramid in the heart of The Eternal City. Unbelievable," thought the artist as he tried to keep his eyes on the avenues.

Soon they were out of the city walls. The billionaire was still leading. The entrepreneur noticed, for the first time all morning, that the back of his t-shirt carried the wise words of Benjamin Franklin, one of the founding fathers of the United States, who said, "The early morning has gold in its mouth." And, on the back of his helmet was printed lettering that read, "Rise First. Die Last."

"This man is a marvel," she thought. "One of a kind." The entrepreneur knew this sensational adventure would soon be coming to an end. But she hoped Mr. Riley would remain in her life. She not only had grown to admire him. She felt she needed him.

They rode for a while and then the billionaire motioned that they should stop on an eerily desolate side street. After they parked the scooters, without saying a word, he beckoned his students to follow him, past a stone bust of the great Roman military general Julius Caesar, down a series of stairs and into a dark and dusty tunnel.

"Where the heck are we?" asked the artist. Beads of sweat had formed on the delicate skin under his eyes. Imagine you were right there with these three human beings. And just picture how the artist looked at this moment.

"We're in the catacombs," announced the billionaire. "This is where the ancient Romans buried their dead. All these subterranean passageways are burial grounds—cemeteries—that date from the second to the fifth century."

"And why are we here?" questioned the entrepreneur.

"I brought you to this crypt to make a point," stated the billionaire in his usual warm tone.

At that instant, the sound of footsteps could be heard, coming from the end of the tunnel. The artist glanced at the entrepreneur, eyes wide open.

The billionaire didn't say a word. The footsteps could be heard growing closer. And more forceful.

"I don't have a good feeling," commented the entrepreneur.

The footsteps continued as the hazy light of a candle struck a decrepit wall of the catacomb. Then the whole place went quiet.

A lone figure slowly emerged, holding a tall candle and with a hood over his head, the kind monks wear. No words were exchanged. It was all extremely mysterious. The intruder stood before the three friends. The candle was raised higher—and moved in four circular motions. Then the hood came off.

The face that was revealed was a familiar one. A face that had appeared at stadiums across the planet. And one that had inspired many millions to do amazing work, accomplish epic dreams and lead legendary lives.

It was The Spellbinder.

"My God, you scared me," the artist said, still sweating profusely.

"Sorry. Stone told me to come down here. I got a little lost," apologized The Spellbinder. "Extraordinary place, these catacombs. It's a little creepy in here, though," he added, looking healthy, happy and relaxed.

"Hey, buddy," declared the billionaire as he hugged his adviser and best friend. "Thanks for showing up."

"Of course," The Spellbinder replied. "Well, let me get straight to the insights you wanted me to share with these two. You know I always come to play," he added with a low five like you see pro basketball players giving teammates after making a successful free throw.

"Mr. Riley asked me to share my thoughts on the value of deep sleep as an element of sustained elite creativity, peak productivity and rare-air performance with you. And he told me he wanted to do it down here because not only are the inhabitants of this crypt in an endless slumber, but science now confirms that one of the primary ways we bring on an early death is by not sleeping enough."

"Really?" asked the entrepreneur, folding her arms once again. The light from the candle disclosed a simple silver engagement ring on a finger.

"No. You guys didn't," gushed the billionaire, glee emanating from his raspy voice. He did a quick, quirky dance move he hadn't done before.

"We did," the entrepreneur and the artist responded, together.

"And you're both invited to our wedding. It'll be small, but special," the artist added.

"You're welcome to have the ceremony on my beach in Mauritius," offered the billionaire. "Heck, I'll treat you two cats by handling all costs. For you both and for your families and for all of your friends. The whole thing's all on me. It's the least I can do for you two new members of The 5 AM Club. You trusted a crazy-looking old man. You came on this wild odyssey. You've been open to all the teachings. You've been doing the work. You two are my heroes."

The billionaire let out an urgent cough. Perhaps it was from the dust of the passageway. He then placed three fingers against his chest— right where his heart sat. And coughed again.

"You okay?" asked the entrepreneur, unfolding her arms and touching one of his muscular shoulders.

"Yes."

"So," said The Spellbinder, "let me offer some insights on why it's not only the calibration of the first hour of your day that's mission essential for leadership excellence and exponential productivity *but also the management of the last hour of your evening*, if you're truly serious about experiencing premium results."

He held the candle under his face, creating a near-mystical effect.

"What makes genius-level performance is a delicate balance between the mastery of your morning routine and the optimization of your nightly ritual. You won't be able to orchestrate *The 20/20/20 Formula* Stone walked you through this morning if you don't sleep properly."

"I'm almost always sleep-deprived," acknowledged the entrepreneur. "Sometimes I struggle to function. My memory is off. And I feel exhausted."

"Yeah," agreed the artist. "My sleep's a mess. I'm up a bunch of times through the night. But since I've been on this trip, I've slept good each night."

"That's great to hear. Because we're in midst of a ferocious global sleep recession," vocalized The Spellbinder, clearly articulating the dramatic languaging he'd become internationally known for. "The internet and social media and the widespread absorption with our devices are fueling much of it. Research is now confirming that the blue light emitted from our tools of technology reduces the amount of melatonin within us. Melatonin is the chemical that informs your body that it needs to get sleep. There's zero doubt that checking your gadgets all day long impairs cognitive function, as you've learned. And there's no question at all that being in front of your screens before bedtime causes sleep dysfunction. I could go deeper and explain how the light of your devices activates photoreceptors called 'intrinsically photosensitive retinal ganglion cells' that limit melatonin production and negatively affect your circadian rhythm, which hurts your sleep—but you get my point here."

"I do," confirmed the entrepreneur. "I really do. I'll restructure my pre-sleep routine so that I wake up at 5 AM feeling better and full of energy. I promise to do this so I rest well and so I can implement *The 20/20/20 Formula* flawlessly."

"For *The 66 Day Minimum*—until it becomes an automatic habit," interjected the artist. "And then for the rest of my life, so it actually becomes easier to run The 5 AM Method than to stay in bed sleeping."

"When we don't sleep enough," The Spellbinder picked up, "not only is it fiercely difficult to get up early, but a number of other highly damaging things impair your productivity and minimize your performance along with reducing your happiness and eroding your health."

"Tell us," requested the entrepreneur.

"Yes, tell them," encouraged the billionaire, now squatting in the catacomb. "This posture's really good for your lower back as well as for your digestion," he added, oddly.

"Well, when you sleep—and the key here is not only the quantity of sleep but the *quality* of your sleep states—your neurons shrink by 60% as cerebral spinal fluid washes through your brain. It's also been discovered that the lymphatic system, which was previously believed to be only in your body, is in your skull, too. All this means that we, as human beings, have evolutionarily architected a powerful process to essentially wash the brain so it stays in optimum condition. And this cleansing mechanism only happens while we sleep."

"Unbelievably interesting," the entrepreneur noted.

"Tell them about HGH," implored the billionaire.

"Sure," said The Spellbinder. "HGH, human growth hormone, is produced in the pituitary gland of the brain and is important for healthy tissues in your body, a strong functioning metabolism and a long lifespan. Increased levels of HGH raise your moods, cognition, energy levels and lean muscle mass, while reducing your cravings through the regulation of leptin and ghrelin. Here's the main point: while HGH is released through exercise, which is part of the reason pocket number one of *The 20/20/20 Formula* is such a game-changer, 75% of HGH production happens when you sleep! And here's the real key: to maximize the process of the brain being washed properly and HGH being produced excellently so you expand your creativity, productivity, vitality and longevity, you need five complete ninety-minute sleep cycles. That's what the scientific studies are now confirming. That's seven and a half hours of sleep each night. You also should know that research proves that it's not only sleep-deprivation that kills. Over-sleep, nine or more hours, also has been shown to shorten life."

"Do you have a learning model for us that explains all this, so our awareness gets super-clear and calibrated versus vague and lame?" asked the artist.

"Good job, Stone. You taught them *The 3 Step Success Formula*," applauded The Spellbinder.

The billionaire, still near to the dirty floor of the crypt, nodded. Then he burped.

"Yes, I do have a framework for you," confirmed The Spellbinder. "I've deconstructed my own evening routine that has helped me consistently sleep wonderfully over all these years."

The Spellbinder then pulled out a flashlight that had been hidden in his robe. He unscrewed the top portion, revealing a secret compartment in the tube. From it, he extracted two thin scrolls, handing one to the entrepreneur and the other to the artist.

The following diagram appeared on each scroll:

THE PRE-SLEEP RITUAL OF ICONIC PRODUCERS
DECONSTRUCTION

07:00 PM – 08:00 PM	• Last meal of the day • All devices turned off • Isolation from overstimulation
08:00 PM – 09:00 PM	• Time for real conversations with loved ones • Optional second period of meditation • Frequent reading/audiobooks/podcast time • Regular session for re-creational pursuits • Periodic epsom salt bath
09:00 PM – 10:00 PM	• Preparation for sleep in a cool, dark + technology-free bedroom • Organization of exercise gear for Pocket #1 • Evening gratitude practice

"I don't know how to thank you," the entrepreneur said. "Both of you," she indicated, looking over to the billionaire, who was now doing sit-ups in the candlelight while whispering, "Great fortune and weighty wisdom keep coming my way. I'm always a leader, never a victim. A lion, not a sheep. I love my life and am making it even better every day. And the more people I help, the more happy I am."

"I second my beloved's gratitude," commented the artist. He reached over and lovingly stroked the entrepreneur's hair.

"If the world knew and applied the philosophies and methodologies of The 5 AM Club, every human being alive would transform," the entrepreneur reinforced. "And I now get that awakening with the sun isn't at all about getting by on less sleep. It's more the old 'early to bed, early to rise' point."

"And as each of us does our part to make our personal revolutions, every relationship in our life—from the one we have with our craft to the connections we share with each other—improves with us," offered the artist.

"Sort of like Mahatma Gandhi's words 'Be the change you wish to see in the world,'" added the entrepreneur, her face glowing in the soft light of the candle as she rubbed her new ring. "I read a little about his life before I went to sleep last night."

"With all due respect," pronounced The Spellbinder compassionately, "Mahatma Gandhi's actual words have been adjusted over the years, to become a sound bite that suits a culture experiencing a collective deficit of attention."

"What he actually said," interrupted the billionaire, "was, 'If we could change ourselves, the tendencies in the world would also change. As a man changes his own nature, so does the attitude of the world change toward him. We need not wait to see what others do.'"

"Awesome job, Stone," remarked The Spellbinder, smiling. "But I do appreciate your larger point," he said kindly to the entrepreneur. "And, of course, you're right. My personal ask of both of you is that you'll share as many of the principles and mental models as you can with as many people as possible. Because, yes, if every business leader, commercial worker, scientist, artist, architect, political influencer, sports performer, teacher, mother, firefighter, father, taxi driver, daughter and son simply installed the morning routine and nightly ritual we've shared with you, *we'd have a whole new world.* A lot less sadness, rudeness, mediocrity and hate. And so much more creativity, beauty, peacefulness and love.

"And now, I need to leave," announced The Spellbinder. "See you tonight at dinner, Stone. Cacio e pepe's on the menu, right?"

"Of course," replied the billionaire as he stood up. He began to cough again and appeared unsteady for a moment. His left hand trembled. A leg wobbled.

The Spellbinder quickly looked away.

"I need to go," was all he said before dissolving into the darkness of the tomb.

The three who remained made their way out of the crypt, back up the stairs and into the blinding Roman sunlight.

The billionaire started his scooter and waved for his guests to follow. They ventured down a maze of narrow streets, past an antiquated aqueduct and back through city walls. Soon they were navigating the congested streets of the historical center and traveling down Via dei Condotti.

After parking their scooters, the entrepreneur and the artist followed the billionaire up the Spanish Steps.

"Well," he declared. "This brings us full circle to where we began this morning's mentoring session at 5 AM. Before I let you cats go for today, I have one last super-gnarly model for you two. The Spellbinder taught it to me when I was much younger, and it proved itself to be priceless. I know it'll wrap up this morning's teachings with a very neat bow."

The billionaire clapped his hands with a thunderous *whap*. A whirring noise could be heard in the distance, emanating from Villa Borghese. Soon, the sound grew louder. And closer.

An object hovered above the heads of the billionaire, the entrepreneur and the artist. Tourists sitting on the Spanish Steps, sipping espresso and eating gelato, turned their eyes toward the heavens, trying to figure out what was going on. You would have enjoyed being there, at that fabulous moment.

"Mamma mia," cried an elderly woman in a free-flowing flowery dress. She was holding a baby in one arm and a bouquet of glamorously colored tulips in the other. "It's a drone!" yelled a teenage boy sporting a snapback cap, a denim jacket with "Doubt Is Not an Option" stitched into the back of it and ripped jeans with humongous holes at the knees. For some unknown reason, he was barefoot.

The billionaire began to expertly pilot the little aircraft to a precise landing as smooth as the surface of a lake on a sweltering summer afternoon. He winked at his two students. "Still got the gift," he beamed.

The drone carried a wooden box that, when opened, contained a thin sheet of glass with a learning model on it. Here's what the diagram on the glass looked like:

THE AMAZING DAY DECONSTRUCTION

TIMELINE	ACTIVITY	SHOW NOTES
4:45 AM	• Optimal rise time • Personal care	• Pre-flight runway period • Leave your workout gear by your bed the night before • Hydrate as it fuels the mitochondria of your cells to release ATP, which elevates your energy
5:00 AM - 5:20 AM	• Intense Exercise • Must sweat [Releases BDNF] • Hydrate further • Podcasts/Audio/Video/Music	• Pocket #1: Move • Shifts you from tired to on fire by 5:20am • Exercise lengthens telomeres • Activates The Neurobiology of Greatness
5:20 AM - 5:40 AM	• Meditate • Pray • Journal • Gratitude Practice • Script Pre-Performance Blueprint	• Pocket #2: Reflect • Meditation reduces and slows aging • Planning + sequencing increases focus and productivity
5:40 AM - 6:00 AM	• Read • Audiobooks • Podcasts • Learning + Inspirational Videos	• Pocket #3: Grow • The 2x3x Mindset • Fuels your hope + your craft • Breeds Inspiration • Builds UndefeatAbility in your industry
6:00 AM - 8:00 AM	• Family Connection • Personal Pursuits • No social media • No news • No message checking	• Enriches well-being + reduces digital dementia • Elevates the tone of your morning • Promotes joy and calm
8:00 AM - 1:00 PM	• The 90/90/1 Rule • The 60/10 Method • World-class work	• The Twin Cycles of Elite Performance • TBTF Protocol • Your Personal Menlo Park
1:00 PM - 5:00 PM	• Lower value work • Meetings • Organizing • Break-Fast [optional: The 16/8 Dividend]	• Adminstrivia • Less creative work • Planning • More hydration
5:00 PM - 6:00 PM	• Traffic U • 2WW • 2MP • Decompression + Transition Period	• Sustain game via learning • Personal Renewal Time • Sun/fresh air/refueling
6:00 PM - 7:30 PM	• No digital devices • Family mealtime • Portfolio of joyful pursuits • Nature walks with loved ones	• Social connection • Adventure • Community service
7:30 PM - 9:30 PM	• Reading • Nightly debrief in journal • Pre-prep for early rise • No screens/No technology • Optimal second meditation before sleep	• Nightly sleep rituals • Hot bath with epsom salt • Dark room • Cool temperature
9:30 PM	• Sleep deeply	• Production of HGH • Restoration and regeneration of brain, body and spirit

ZERO-TECHNOLOGY ZONE

ZERO-TECHNOLOGY ZONE

"I thought you guys would find this very detailed step-by-step game plan for an amazing day valuable. Of course, this is just one possible way to carve it out. You'll notice the evening regime is a little different from The Spellbinder's. As usual, how you apply all these tactics we've shared is completely up to you. It's your life—live it as you choose. And yet, this particular framework helped me tremendously because it took many of the powerful elements of *The 20/20/20 Formula* I walked you through earlier this morning along with key aspects of a world-class pre-sleep process and built them into an immensely specific daily map that anyone—and I do mean anyone—can run to experience amazing days, consistently. It's like a food recipe: follow the steps, and you'll get the results."

"And amazing days create an upward spiral into amazing weeks and amazing weeks morph into amazing months," stated the artist, closing his journal.

"And amazing months become amazing quarters and amazing quarters yield amazing years and decades and ultimately . . ." added the entrepreneur, closing her journal.

"An amazing lifetime," the three said together.

"Day by day. Step by step, an epic existence gets handcrafted," summed up the billionaire, wearing his fashionable shades, the kind the in-the-know Romans sport in their effortlessly stylish way that displays an "I don't try too hard to look this phenomenally cool" kind of attitude. More seagulls flapped their wings and made those annoying sounds seagulls seem to enjoy making.

The billionaire was clearly an exceedingly loving soul. Not just rich in money, but also wealthy of heart. But he did detest seagulls and the way they had done a takeover of many of the rooftops in the core of Rome, over the past few years.

"Need to do something about those feathered creatures," he ruminated, displaying uncharacteristic irritation. "Anyhoo, now you know why I brought you to the Spanish Steps. Generating explosive productivity, elite health, exceptional prosperity, sustained joy and boundless inner peace really is a *step-by-step* game. Small, daily, seemingly insignificant improvements, when done consistently over time, do yield staggering results. Daily micro-wins and infinitesimal optimizations really are the surest way to a life that you'll be ever so proud of at the end. This truly is one of my favorite places in the world, you know. I wanted you two to be with me to not only teach you the transformational process of *The 20/20/20 Formula*, but also to reinforce the reality that living remarkably is indeed an upward spiral to the top of a staircase of success and significance. And as you take this journey toward the fullest experience of your highest greatness, step by step, a magic and beauty as obvious as you now witness here will infuse your days and only accelerate over your years. Of this you can be sure."

After carefully scanning the learning model on the glass, the entrepreneur wondered aloud, "What's *The 90/90/1 Rule*? And *The 60/10 Method*? And I don't understand some of these other notations."

"And what do '2WW' and '2MP' on the framework stand for?" asked the artist.

"You'll learn soon enough," the billionaire responded, generating suspense. "You both should know I've saved the best—*and most valuable*—teachings for the end of our time together."

The billionaire then hugged the entrepreneur and the artist, tighter than ever before. They could see tears slowly filling his eyes. Big whales of water.

"I love you two," he said. "Ci vediamo."

And then he vanished.

CHAPTER 15

The 5 AM Club Is Mentored on The 10 Tactics of Lifelong Genius

"If you knew how much work went into it, you would not call it genius."
—Michelangelo

"São Paulo is so special, isn't it?" said the billionaire as the unmarked and economy-class car navigated by a driver in short sleeves stopped and started through the thick traffic of this city of many millions. As in Mauritius, he sat in the front passenger seat.

The three companions had just landed at the jetport and were heading to a boutique hotel in the center of this financial capital of Latin America.

"It's a big city," noted the artist, offering another blinding glimpse of the obvious.

"We so appreciate you flying us down here to Brazil for our wedding," the entrepreneur enthused.

"Thanks, brother," the artist added.

"He really wanted the ceremony to take place at your compound by the ocean," said the entrepreneur, pointing to her fiancé with a warm look.

"I did," stated the artist agreeably. "That place was paradise."

"And, to be honest, I did too. But I wanted to honor my father, given that he was Brazilian," the entrepreneur explained.

"And a happy wife means a happy life," confirmed the artist with a grin.

He then quoted the words from A.A. Milne's *Winnie-the-Pooh*: "If you live to be a hundred, I want to live to be a hundred minus one day so I never have to live without you."

The entrepreneur moved closer to the artist in the back of the car as it sailed past magnificent neo-gothic cathedrals, along great avenues with towering high-rises, down a thoroughfare that showcased the impressive Theatro Municipal de São Paulo and across a roadway where the majestic Ibirapuera Park sat.

What the artist shared made the billionaire think of his wife. He still thought of her every day. And it wasn't the luxurious trips to exotic places that he most recalled. Nor the beautiful meals at the world's best restaurants. His mind drifted to the simplest and most apparently ordinary of moments in her company. Sharing a cheap but excellent pizza with olive oil drizzled over it. Reading books in silence in front of a dazzling fire. Nature walks and movie nights and trips to the grocery store. Dancing in their bedroom to music that reminded them of how much they adored each other. And things like how patiently she taught him Italian, the way she'd snort when she'd laugh really hard—and how utterly devoted she was to their only child. *Life's finest treasures live in its simplest moments*, contemplated the billionaire. In those daily occurrences that most of us take for granted. Until we lose them.

Lifting his hand to proudly display his engagement ring, the artist continued to express the depth of his love while the car rolled along.

"I love her hard, man," he spoke to Mr. Riley. "She's my sunrise. My art used to be all that mattered. Didn't have much of a need for anyone around me, you know. Guess I never knew what real love was. Can't imagine living without her now."

The entrepreneur considered how blessed she was. In the period since she attended The Spellbinder's event, her Mindset, Heartset, Healthset and Soulset were being reordered and upgraded. Radically. And irrevocably.

She was releasing the limiting beliefs that had been forged from her tumultuous childhood and letting go of the toxic emotions that grew out of her past traumas, as well as from the current predicament with her investors. The billionaire was quite right, she was realizing to an even deeper degree: we each do the best we can based on the level of awareness, maturity and personal security we are at. People who hurt others really are hurting within themselves. They are behaving in the wisest way they know how to behave. If they were capable of conducting themselves with greater leadership, generosity and humanity, they would have done so. This profound insight had sown even stronger seeds of forgiveness within the entrepreneur. When she first heard The Spellbinder at his seminar, she was cynical and resistant to a lot of his teachings. She'd since pivoted considerably and was now embracing everything she'd been fortunate enough to learn, wholeheartedly. It was an inspirational evolution to see.

It had been three weeks since the visit to Rome. In that time, the entrepreneur had been doing wind sprints for twenty minutes at 5 AM each morning along with some serious weight training. After that at, 5:20 AM, she'd use the tranquility of the second pocket to contemplate quietly, write lists of the things she was grateful for in her new journal and then meditate. Finally, at 5:40 AM, she'd listen to an audiobook about a business maverick or read something on the subjects of productivity, teamwork and leadership. She'd also, and this was a hard one, broken the addiction to technology that had been her lifeline—as well as her escape from producing her greatest work. And her diversion from being fully present to life. During these fantastic days away from her office, she'd been creating the brightest output of her career, leveraging the phenomenon of transient hypofrontality the billionaire had taught her to orchestrate results at a level of genius she'd never experienced before. And reclaiming the sense of inner well-being she'd lost.

Everything she was applying was delivering enormous rewards. Everything in her life seemed to be clicking again. She was fitter than she'd been in years, happier and more serene than she'd ever known, and more productive—during the periods she was away from the artist, conducting business—than she'd imagined she could be.

All thanks to The 5 AM Club, which she understood, more and more, allowed her to protect her natural talents in a commercial world of such noise, stress and invitation to relentless interruption. The Victory Hour was providing her with an insulated period, at the front end of her day, to build her four interior empires. So she could construct outer ones.

With her newfound hopefulness, confidence and forgiveness, she'd even made excellent progress in negotiating a solution with her investors. She was excited that, shortly, the whole horrible ordeal would be behind her.

And soon, she'd be married. She'd always wanted someone special to share in her delights and successes. And she'd always wished to balance her hunger for fortune-making with her dream of having a family. The kind of family she'd missed being part of as a girl.

Just as the entrepreneur was about to respond to the artist's musings on the extent of his love, a gunshot rang out.

The glass of the vehicle's windshield shattered, instantly looking like a spider's web. Two broad-shouldered men in ski masks, with machine guns over their shoulders, violently motioned for the driver to unlock the doors. When he attempted to accelerate out of harm's way, another bullet pierced the glass, grazing the chauffeur's ear and prompting an outburst of blood.

"Open the door," instructed Mr. Riley, stunningly calmly. "I've got this," he said as he secretly pressed a red button strategically located under the glove compartment.

The doors unlocked. You could hear a *click*.

Speaking in staccato bursts, one of the gunmen screamed, "Everyone out of the car. Now! Or you die!"

As the occupants of the car followed the orders, the other gunman grabbed the entrepreneur by the neck. "We told you to leave the firm. We told you we'd kill you. We told you this was gonna happen," he said.

Suddenly, a long SUV, the sort you see combat leaders in war zones traveling in, raced up to the scene.

Four more people, two men and two women, in flak jackets with pistols raced up on sleek motorcycles.

The billionaire's protection team had arrived.

Fighting broke out in the street, knives were pulled and more shots were fired. The billionaire was whisked away with an efficiency that was striking. He still appeared unruffled and, as if he were a general leading a military mission, said simply, "Save my passengers. They are my family members."

A helicopter was now floating overhead. Yes, a helicopter. It had "SAC" in large orange letters on the side of it, over white paint.

The magnate's security squad quickly disarmed the larger of the two gunmen, the one who had threatened the entrepreneur, and removed her to the safety of the waiting SUV. But the artist, well, sadly he was gone.

"I need to find him!" the entrepreneur screamed at the personnel in the armored vehicle. "I need to find my husband," she added, clearly in a state of acute shock over the entire scenario.

"Stay here," ordered one of the security agents, firmly, holding her by the arm.

But the entrepreneur, in her newly created state of mental toughness, physical fitness, emotional resilience and spiritual fearlessness—thanks to her new morning routine—broke free from the burly guard, kicked open the door that had been left slightly ajar and started to run. Like an elite athlete, she sprinted deftly across a highway with traffic speeding down four lanes. Horns blared, and some passionate Brazilians shouted words in Portuguese, concerned for her welfare. But she kept running, as fast as a gazelle.

She ducked into a café. No sign of her man. Then into a restaurant. Next she raced along a street renowned for its steak houses. The artist was nowhere in sight.

Then the entrepreneur spotted his notebook, the one in which he had made all his notes from the lessons of The Spellbinder and the billionaire. The same notebook she saw him clutching tightly when they first met, seemingly randomly, in the conference hall—when she was at the darkest place of her life. And he, as an angel of sorts, made her feel safer, calmer and happier by his loving presence.

What happened next was tragic. As the entrepreneur slowed down to a walk and turned onto a thin slice of an avenue, she saw blood. Not a pool of blood but drops and specks of fresh blood.

"Oh, God. Oh, God. Please, no," she cried out.

Frantically, she continued following the trail, pushing past a series of parked cars, a mother with a baby in a stroller and a line of elegant houses.

"Please don't let him die," the businesswoman prayed. "Please, God."

"I'm here. Over here," a squeaky voice rang out.

The entrepreneur darted in the direction of the artist's calls. Growing closer, she spied the gunman holding a revolver directly to the head of her fiancé. The thug had removed his ski mask. One could see that he was young. And looked extremely scared.

"Look," declared the entrepreneur, behaving courageously and slowly walking over to the two men. "Look," she repeated. "I know you don't want to hurt him. I know you don't want to spend the rest of your life in a prison cell. Just give me the gun and you can go. I won't say a word to anyone about you. Just give me the gun."

The gunman was frozen. Speechless. And shaking. Slowly he turned the gun away from the head of the artist. And aimed it squarely at the chest of the entrepreneur.

"Just relax," she implored in a fierce yet empathetic voice. She continued walking toward her fiancé and the kidnapper.

"I'll kill you," shouted the bandit. "Stay there."

The entrepreneur took step by careful step while staring directly into the eyes of the gunman. She now had a soft smile on her face. Such was the grade of her newly earned bravery. So was the degree of her considerably enhanced confidence.

After a long pause, the criminal stood up. He stared at the entrepreneur with what looked like a combination of mountainous respect and visceral disbelief. Then, he hurried away.

"Baby, are you okay?" The entrepreneur embraced the artist tenderly.

Gathering his composure, though perspiring unstoppably, he replied, "Born okay, baby. Born okay. Um. You just saved my life, you know?"

"I know," she said. "I didn't do it because we're about to be married, you know. I didn't save you because I love you."

"What?" questioned the artist. "Then why did you do what you just did? I mean, that was *incredible* what you just pulled off! Totally gangster."

"I did it because of the club."

"What are you talking about?" asked the artist, bewildered.

"I did what I did because of the powers I've developed as a member of The 5 AM Club. That's how I was able to do what I just did. *It all really works. All of it.* Everything we've been taught in Mauritius. In India. In Rome. And the main reason I saved your life isn't because you'll soon be my husband and we'll have great kids and then grandkids and a bunch of dogs and cats and hopefully even canaries at our home," she gushed. "No. I saved you only because you're also in the club. And Mr. Riley said we have to stick together. And to have each other's backs."

"Are you serious?" asked the artist, loudly. He wasn't pleased with what he'd heard.

"Of course not! I'm just playing, babe," laughed the entrepreneur. "I adore you. I'd give my life for you any day of the week. Now let's go find Mr. Riley. Let's make sure he's okay."

The next day, after they had recovered from their dramatic experience, they met in the billionaire's penthouse at the chic hotel. Mr. Riley looked lean, focused and very happy.

"Quite the spree yesterday, cats," he stated in a way that suggested that what they'd endured was nothing more than a brisk walk through a flower-filled park.

"That was brutal," the artist replied. "You talk about trauma—that was traumatic."

"You, my friend, were quite the hero yesterday," declared the billionaire proudly while focusing on the entrepreneur. "You, young lady, are a miracle on two legs."

"Thanks," she said, shifting her feet a bit and making sure the artist was okay.

"I watched you roll. I saw your cool. I noticed your concentration under extreme pressure. And your superhuman levels of performance."

"This goddess of a woman here saved my life," the artist acknowledged enthusiastically.

"You two love cats are just beginning to get a taste of the benefits of joining The 5 AM Club. Just imagine you two after applying *The 66 Day Minimum*. Then after six months of running the world-class morning routine you've now discovered. Consider the way you'll capitalize on your potential, optimize your performance—and be useful to our world in a year. Always remember that the greatest of leaders were all servant leaders. The less you make it all about you, and the more your obsession focuses on the upliftment of others, the more you'll increase your identity as a *genuine* empire-builder. And grow into a history-maker."

"Got you," confirmed the entrepreneur as she sipped from a water bottle, making sure she was well hydrated to stay at her energetic best.

"I want to reward you for the heroism you showed yesterday," the billionaire offered. "I have some news that I think will make you love your life even more."

"Tell me, please," the entrepreneur said. "Though I really don't need anything, you know. I did what I did out of love. Simple as that."

"Well . . . are you ready?" the tycoon asked.

"Yes. Ready."

"Well, this morning I had my people buy up all of the equity those nasty investors owned. Let's just say I made them an offer they couldn't refuse. And my legal team had them sign an agreement promising they will never go near your company again and are not permitted to come anywhere near you . . . or the man who will be your husband in a few short hours.

"Gnarly, right?" the billionaire spoke as he tap danced his way across the floor of the penthouse. Yes, he actually tap danced across the entire room. Next, he began flailing his arms manically and grooving intensely to his imagined music. Finally—get this—he started twerking. Yes, the illustrious industrialist who was worth over one billion dollars was twerking in that hotel suite.

"He's the weirdest human being I've ever met—by a factor of a million," thought the entrepreneur. "But truly wonderful. And pretty close to magical."

The entrepreneur and the artist looked at each other and began to giggle. They then joined in—as best as they could, because Mr. Riley could sometimes be a bit of a showman, as humble as he was. After the dancing session they hugged this man who had become their magnificent mentor, exuberant encourager and sincere friend.

The entrepreneur thanked the eccentric baron, profusely, for his generosity in making her difficult situation go away. This spectacular escapade was taking on a near-mystical quality. Everything was improving. All was unfolding even better than she could have dreamed. And now she was free of the very trial that had brought her to the sharpest edge of her life.

In that moment, she realized that on the other side of every tragedy lives a triumph. And beyond adversity exists a bridge into enduring victory, if one has the eyes to see it.

"Anyhoo," said the billionaire, "today's session will be a quick one. "My chief of staff is attending to every detail of your wedding as we speak. You'll have the Casablanca lilies you requested, the music you both suggested and every detail will be calibrated to world-class. It's just the way my team and I roll. Oh, all your guests have been flown in on a series of my jets. Everybody's here. And everyone's full of delight. Especially me."

The titan let out another intense cough. And then two more. His arm started to tremble again as he sat on a modern-looking wooden chair covered by a swatch of white leather, the kind furniture craftspeople in Sweden and Denmark make. For the first time, a look in his eyes revealed hues of fear.

"I'll beat this monster," he whispered to himself. "You're messing with the wrong dude."

He pulled out his wallet, extracted the worn picture of his wife, gone so long ago, clasped it to his heart and centered himself on the essential points of the morning's discourse.

"Now that you know most of what you need to know about The 5 AM Method, I want to offer ten tactics that will quicken your momentum in both your professional and your private lives. These are ten gestures for daily heroism. *The 20/20/20 Formula* will help you use your mornings brilliantly. These ten other routines will complement the regime, so the rest of your day unfolds gloriously. Lock these in and you'll become undefeatable. And experience a meaningful upward spiral of success where every important element of your life rises as your hours pass."

As usual, a hand then went up into the air. Out of the library of the penthouse suite sprang an assistant, struggling to carry what appeared to be a large framed art piece. The billionaire jumped up and rushed over to help his aide.

On the front of the white t-shirt the young, fit and unfairly handsome assistant wore were these printed words: "Everyone dreams of being a legend until it comes time to do the work that legends do."

"This is one of my wedding gifts to you two." The billionaire pointed to a breathtaking painting of Thomas Edison, the great inventor. Over Edison's face, in an edgy modern art script, were the inventor's words: "The best thinking has been done in solitude. The worst has been done in turmoil."

"I commissioned one of my favorite artists, who lives in Berlin, to do this for you. He did a lot of the artwork in my Zurich flat. He hardly paints anymore. Did this as a special favor. You cats could retire if you sold it—trust me on that one. Please flip it over," requested the billionaire politely, sitting down on the sleek chair again and surveying the expansive penthouse that overlooked the skyscrapers of São Paulo. Many of the high-rises had helipads on top of them so the icons of industry who operated within them could skirt around without having to waste precious hours of productivity—and life—sitting in São Paulo traffic. Because as you now know, the hours most people waste epic performers exploit.

On the back of the immaculately framed artwork was a chart with this title on it: *The 10 Tactics of Lifelong Genius.*

The billionaire continued talking. "Thomas Edison exemplifies prodigious creative achievement like few others in history, having recorded one thousand and ninety-three patents over his lifetime and giving us everything from the lightbulb to the motion picture camera and, in 1901, a battery that was later used for electric cars. He wasn't only an inventor. He was also a stratospheric company builder.

"Yup," the billionaire continued. "His life is absolutely worth studying and then deconstructing in your journal so your intimacy and fluency with how he did it grows. Edison once said, 'Being busy does not always mean real work. The object of all work is production or accomplishment.'

"And as you granulate the inventor's achievement formula, please go deep on studying his ability to focus. Edison also observed, 'You do something all day long, don't you? Everyone does. If you get up at seven o'clock and go to bed at eleven, you have put in sixteen good hours, and it is certain with most men, that they have been doing something all the time. The only trouble is that they do it about a great many things and I do it about one. If they took the time in question and applied it in one direction, to one object, they would succeed.'"

"That's on point," observed the artist, who was dressed in black gear this morning and wearing his standard issue combat boots. He'd shaved off his trademark goatee. "It goes to the point you made in Mauritius about us waking up with a limited amount of cognitive bandwidth and every distraction that steals our attention lowers our chance to do masterful work. Because we leave attention residue on every diversion that we allow into our workplace—and lifespace. And if we're not really careful, we'll end up with the digital dementia referred to on the last diagram you shared with us in Rome. I'm getting this piece in a pretty big way today. When I get back home to my studio, I'm definitely going to set up my environment up so it's totally quiet. Zero devices. I also plan to do a big-time technology detox. No social media and no cyber surfing for at least a few weeks, so I get my concentration back. What I'm understanding is that once I'm in the clear space of silence, I should focus only on one project at a time, not spread out my creative power and physical energy on many. That's what I take from Edison's words. Don't diffuse my genius on being pretty good at many things when I have it in me to be legendary by working intensely only on one thing."

"And I'm realizing that even one interruption when I'm thinking about a hot new product or my next blue ocean venture could cost me many millions of dollars—or more," said the entrepreneur excitedly.

"What you two just said is massively important if you are serious about leveraging your talents and expressing the fullness of your inherent greatness," the billionaire affirmed as he beamed cheerfully.

"Edison would climb up the hill to his Menlo Park laboratory and work for hours and hours, and sometimes days upon days, with his team on the one invention that was the center of their inspiration. That groovy cat was a pretty gnarly dude."

The billionaire then pointed to the chart on the back of the painting.

"I know you both need to get going, so you can get ready for the ceremony. Kindly take this gift with you. But first, read what it says here on the back, so you start the process of wiring in these ten tactics that will accelerate your progress in The 5 AM Club and set your gifts, talents and powers ablaze. Rising at dawn and running *The 20/20/20 Formula* is your main move to lead your field and upgrade your personal life. These ten calibrated habits are your amplifiers. They'll ensure that you go from seeing results that are linear to rewards that are exponential."

The learning model looked like this:

THE 10 TACTICS OF LIFELONG GENIUS

THE TIGHT BUBBLE OF TOTAL FOCUS

THE 60 MINUTE STUDENT

THE 90/90/1 RULE

THE WEEKLY DESIGN SYSTEM

THE 60/10 METHOD

THE DREAM TEAM TECHNIQUE

THE DAILY 5 CONCEPT

TRAFFIC UNIVERSITY

THE 2 MASSAGE PROTOCOL

THE SECOND WIND WORKOUT

THE 10 TACTICS OF LIFELONG GENIUS

Under *The 10 Tactics of Lifelong Genius* model, the entrepreneur and the artist read the following list of strategies along with precise explanations about what they mean. And how one was to apply them.

Tactic #1: The Tight Bubble of Total Focus (TBTF)

The Insight: An addiction to distraction is the death of your creative production. Your attraction to digital interruption is costing you your fortune—financially, cognitively, energetically, physically and spiritually. To have the income and impact only a few people currently have, you need to run your days like very few performers currently do. The Tight Bubble of Total Focus is a metaphorical moat that you build around your assets of genius, so they not only stay strong—they increase. The five primary assets that all superproducers defend are mental focus, physical energy, personal willpower, original talent and daily time. Your bubble has a porous membrane that encircles it so that you decide what information, which people and the nature of the activities that enter your orbit. Anything negative, toxic and impure gets blocked at the gate. Essentially, this way of being in the world is your bulletproof defense system to reject any stimuli that would decry your greatness.

The Implementation: The Tight Bubble of Total Focus strategy preserves your focus as well as your primal brilliance by giving you long stretches of time free from trivial fascinations and any influences that dissolve your inspiration—and deteriorate your A-game. Each morning, you enter this invisible bubble of your own making that is completely empty of other people's superficial messages, spam, fake news, advertisements, silly videos, irrelevant chatting and other forms of cyber-hooking that will destroy your life of monumental potential. Part of this philosophical construct is your Personal Menlo Park, the place where—like Thomas Edison—you get lost from the world and go to generate the masterworks that will raise you to industry dominance and global eminence. The real key here is solitude for a scheduled period each day, in a positive environment that floods you with creativity, energy, happiness and the feeling the work you're doing is for the upliftment of humanity. The spaces you inhabit shape the output you produce. This concept can—and should—also be applied beyond your professional routine. So your private time is free of negativity, energy vampires and soul-hurting pursuits. Of course, tinker with this metaphorical wall of armor around your five assets of genius so you have a wonderful social life. And so you don't become a hermit. Using the TBTF in your personal life means you live your days in an alternate universe of your own joyous creation. Remember, the bubble has a porous membrane, so you can carefully choose who you allow into your private reality as well as the elements of beauty, wonder and peace. Specific application ideas include selling your television, avoiding the news for the remainder of your days, staying out of noisy shopping malls where you buy things you don't need, unfriending energy-draining people you follow on social platforms, turning off all notifications while you're in the TBTF and deleting apps with constant announcements.

Tactic #2: The 90/90/1 Rule

The Insight: Doing real work versus artificial work, daily and with absolute consistency, will give you a Gargantuan Competitive Advantage born of mastery. Productivity of virtuoso-level quality is rare. And the marketplace pays most for something that is scarce. Legendary achievers concentrate all their attention and effort on one core project at a time so they harness the fullness of their cognitive capacity and their precious energy on releasing glorious products that turn their industry on their head. To work like this, you need to install the daily habit of exploiting your best professional hours to offer your finest productive results. When you show up for work, it's not the time to shop online, to gossip or to check messages. It's showtime. For the superproducer.

The Implementation: For the next ninety days, schedule yourself to invest the first ninety minutes of your workday on the one activity that, when completed at world-class, will cause you to own your field. This ninety-minute period must be completely free of any noise and interruptions. Place your devices in a bag marked, "for my 90/90/1 period." And then leave that bag in another room. Installing clear boundary fences that block access to temptations is a potent tactic to decrease them.

Tactic #3: The 60/10 Method

The Insight: Research supports that the greatest performers don't work in a linear way—working harder and longer with the hope of arriving at stronger and better results. Instead, the way elite creatives do what they do is by understanding the power of oscillation. They structure their work cycles so that they alternate bursts of deep focus and ferocious intensity of performance with periods of real rest and full recovery. In other words, they work in a balance—and cycle awesome output with times to refuel their assets of genius so they don't deplete them. Armed with data concluding that human beings do their most astonishing work when they are fresh and relaxed versus exhausted and stressed, genuine pros dedicated to the glorification of their genius operate in a mode of pulsation, operating more like sprinters than marathoners.

The Implementation: After you've run the 90/90/1 segment of your workday, use a timer and work at your best for sixty minutes straight while sitting or standing quietly, in your Tight Bubble of Total Focus. Train yourself not to move. Just concentrate. And create the highest results you can possibly make. After your sixty-minute productivity sprint is done, refuel for ten minutes. Ideas for this recovery cycle include going for a quick walk in fresh air, reading a book that will advance your leadership or personal mastery, meditating, visualizing or listening to energizing music with headphones on like many championship athletes do before they step onto the court, so that their brain's attention shifts from the ruminating and worrying behaviors of the left hemisphere into the creativity and flow of the right section.

After ten wonderful minutes of regeneration, go back and perform your next sixty-minute work segment, full of inspiration, excellence and ingenuity. And then your next ten-minute cycle of renewal.

Tactic #4: The Daily 5 Concept

The Insight: Studies show that the most effective business leaders are at their productive peak on the days when, even if they've faced some serious setbacks, they've actively engaged their mindset on the progress they've made. In so doing, they've inoculated themselves from the self-sabotaging influence of the brain's negativity bias. One of the great keys to terrific performance, then, is to train your attention on making consistent 1% wins and micro-achievements throughout each hour of your workday. Small daily achievements, when done consistently over time, definitely do lead to stunning results. And by deliberately reflecting on the areas where you are moving ahead, you'll insulate your ambition, guard your confidence and defeat the dangerous trickster of fear, so you get amazing feats done.

The Implementation: During the second pocket of your Victory Hour, list the five tiny targets you wish to accomplish over the day ahead for you to feel it was one well-spent. This, like so much of what you've learned, is also a practice: the more you do it, the easier this habit gets—and the stronger your execution ability around it grows. So, stay with the process. After just thirty days, you'll have accomplished 150 valuable victories. And after a year, this strategy alone will be responsible for you achieving 1,825 high-value targets, guaranteeing that the next twelve months are the single most productive twelve months you've had yet.

Tactic #5: The 2nd Wind Workout (2WW)

The Insight: You've now discovered the beautiful neuroscience behind daily exercise. Moving the body regularly lifts your concentration, speeds up the processing potency of your brain as well as accelerating its learning capacity, raises your energy, elevates your optimism, helps you sleep better via the production of more melatonin and promotes longevity through the release of human growth hormone (HGH), along with the lengthening of your telomeres. Telomeres keep the ends of our chromosomes from fraying—they're like plastic caps at the tips of shoelaces. Aging shortens our telomeres, which is why they are sometimes compared to a bomb fuse. The powerful point here is that it's well-documented that exercise slows this shortening, helping you stay healthy longer. You should also note that meditation, a diet rich in whole foods, proper sleep quality and intermittent fasting (which The Spellbinder calls *The 16/8 Dividend* because you don't eat during a sixteen-hour fasting window and then break the fast over an eight-hour period) have all proven to protect our telomeres from degenerating. Given the empirically based facts substantiating the absolutely transformative power of exercise, why would you do only one workout a day? Why not use this regimen to increase your vitality massively so you not only outlive your industry peers but hack aging as you enjoy an astoundingly happy and productive life?

The Implementation: To execute The 2WW practice, schedule a second workout at the end of your workday to give you a second wind for a great evening. You'll beat the exhaustion most people feel after work, re-energize your willpower batteries so you improve your evening choices and even find your cravings for sugar in the nighttime are significantly lower. One of the finest activities you could possibly do at this time is a one-hour nature walk. You'll gain another block of time free from digital interruption, letting you do more deep thinking and downloading of valuable ideas. You'll also be rewarded with the benefits that walking within natural surroundings with sunlight and fresh air bring to your Mindset, Heartset, Healthset and Soulset. Naturalist John Muir expressed it well when he said: "In every walk with nature one receives far more than he seeks." Other ideas for your 2WW include going for a sixty-minute mountain bike ride, having a long swim or attending a yoga class. In running this routine, you'll also burn even more calories and speed up your metabolic rate, reducing body fat. The 2WW is a game-changer.

Tactic #6: The 2 Massage Protocol (2MP)

The Insight: Studies have demonstrated that massage therapy is a modality that generates significant improvements in brain performance, mood, your ability to fight stress, and in terms of your general wellness. The benefits of a massage include a 31% reduction of cortisol (the fear hormone) levels; a 31% increase in dopamine (the neurotransmitter of motivation); a 28% elevation of serotonin (the neurochemical responsible for regulating anxiety and raising happiness); reduced muscle tension; improved pain relief via the sending of anti-inflammation messaging to muscle cells; and elevations in the signaling of those cells to make more mitochondria. The key here is to have a deep-tissue massage versus simple relaxation bodywork. It needs to hurt a little for it to work well. This awesome practice also reduces the stress that causes telomeres to degrade, optimizing your good health and maximizing your lifespan.

The Implementation: To apply The 2MP, lock two ninety-minute massages onto your weekly schedule. Because the things that get scheduled are the things that get done. And because vague plans yield vague performance. And because the smallest of applications really is better than the grandest of intentions. Virtuosos bring traction to their vision through their dedication to implementation. You might say you're a busy performer and can't afford the time to get two long massages every single week. In fact, given the proven and marvelous benefits of this protocol for your mental state, cognition, joyfulness, health and longevity, the truth is you can't afford *not* to install this habit. Yes, two ninety-minute massages a week will cost a lot of money. Death will cost you more.

Tactic #7: Traffic University

The Insight: People who commute a total of sixty minutes to and from work each day spend approximately twelve hundred days of their lives doing so—if they live an average human lifetime. That's over three years spent in traffic or on a bus or in a train. And with the rise of the mega-commute, that time period is only growing. Most people sitting bumper to bumper are infecting themselves with toxic news, superficial banter on the radio and other negative stimulation that erodes production and dissolves inner peace. People on commuter trains or buses often sleep, daydream or play with their technology, in a chronic state of apathy. Be different.

The Implementation: Participating in Traffic University is all about leveraging your traveling time—whether to and from work or grocery shopping and errand running—to learn, expanding your professional prowess and personal knowledge. Specific ideas to help you do so include listening to audiobooks and consuming valuable podcasts. The fact is, even one new idea you learn in a book or online course could make you millions or even billions of dollars. Or multiply your creativity, productivity, vitality and spirituality exponentially. There is simply no other investment vehicle available today that will yield a higher return than investing in your education and growth.

Tactic #8: The Dream Team Technique

The Insight: Professional athletes structure a full team to support their rise to Best in World (BIW). In this way, they are freed up to marshal their five assets of genius around the development of the expertise and powers that will cause them to become dominant at their sport. Michael Jordan wasn't his own sports doctor and Muhammad Ali wasn't his own boxing trainer. Superproducers outsource and then automate all activities except those within the realm of their mastery, allowing for purity of focus and freeing up huge amounts of time.

The Implementation: Delegate tasks that not only are a poor use of your hours but also diminish your happiness. Ideally, restructure your entire life so you're doing only the things you're great at—and love to do. With such a setup, you'll not only escalate in your performance because you're prioritized around just a few things, but you'll enjoy significantly more personal freedom. And serenity. As well, because you have people on your Dream Team who are leaders at what they do, your rise to legendary will be swifter since you have great people in your corner. Specific members of your Dream Team could include a fitness trainer who you work with regularly, a nutritionist, a massage therapist, a financial coach to fortify your fortune, a relationship adviser to help you maintain rich bonds with the important people in your life and a spiritual counselor to assist you in staying grounded on the eternal laws of a life well-lived.

Tactic #9: The Weekly Design System (WDS)

The Insight: You now know that things that get scheduled are the things that get done. Designing a week without a granulated game plan for the seven days ahead of you is like attempting to summit Mont Blanc without a climb strategy or hiking into the deep woods without a compass. Yes, spontaneity and room for unexpected miracles are exceptionally important. Yet, this doesn't mean you shouldn't show personal responsibility and human maturity by habituating a practice to architect a thoughtful and clear weekly script that amplifies your energy, organizes your choices and ensures balance.

The Implementation: Carve out and then ritualize thirty minutes early each Sunday morning to create your "Blueprint for a Beautiful Week." Start the process by writing a story in your journal about the highlights from the seven days you just lived. Then record your lessons learned and optimizations for making the coming week even better. Next, on a large piece of paper that has each day running from 5 AM to 11 PM on it, note down all your commitments. The key here is to list more than your business meetings and work projects. Set clear periods for your Victory Hour, your 90/90/1 sessions, your 60/10 cycles and your 2nd Wind Workouts, as well as time for your loved ones, blocks for your portfolio of passions and segments for your errands. Doing this weekly will build extraordinary focus into your days, yield marvelous momentum, enhance your productivity significantly and improve your life's balance noticeably.

Tactic #10: The 60 Minute Student

The Insight: The more you know, the better you will do. Legendary leaders all have boundless curiosity and a limitless appetite to grow into their greatest selves. And education truly is inoculation against disruption. Peak producers are lifetime learners. Be one of the formidable few who reclaim their heroism, cultivate their craft and materialize their genius by getting back to being a world-class student.

The Implementation: For at least sixty minutes a day, study. Do whatever it takes to fireproof your commitment to relentless growth. Learning daily will raise your acumen, deepen your wisdom and incite a blazing fire that stokes your grandeur. You'll become a weighty thinker and an outright superstar. Specific tactics for your sixty minutes include reading every good book you can get your hands on, reviewing your journal notes, working through an online program, talking with a mentor and watching skill-building videos. As you capitalize on your brightest gifts and highest powers, you'll become not only a bigger person but an even more indispensable one. You'll be so exquisite at what you do that your organization and marketplace will not be able to operate without you. You'll evolve into an exceptionally valuable leader in your field. And you'll be able to deliver remarkable streams of value to the teammates, customers and communities you are blessed to serve. The results will be generous rewards returned to you in the form of income, eminence and the psychic joy that comes with being a noble person, doing world-class work and fulfilling a mighty purpose.

"I have another present to honor you two as we go off to your wedding!" exclaimed the billionaire. "It's a verse I memorized for my Vanessa." He was clutching her picture as he said this.

"Every Valentine's Day, it was our tradition for me to present her with one hundred and eight red roses, some terrific chocolates and one other thing over dinner at our favorite restaurant. After that, I'd get down on a knee and recite the poem."

"What was 'the other thing'?" asked the artist.

The billionaire looked a little embarrassed. His gaze fell to the floor of the penthouse.

"Lingerie," was his one-word answer, spoken with a wink.

He then stood up on the sprawling oak dining table that sat in one section of the gigantic hotel suite. Like a child playing hide and go seek, he covered each of his eyes with a hand. Next, he recited an old poem by Spencer Michael Free with thunderous passion:

'Tis the human touch in this world that counts,
The touch of your hand and mine,
Which means far more to the fainting heart
Than shelter and bread and wine.
For shelter is gone when the night is o'er,
And bread lasts only a day.
But the touch of the hand and the sound of the voice
Sing on in the soul always.

"That's so beautiful," said the artist, visibly moved.

It was growing clearer to Mr. Riley that though this bohemian painter had rough edges, he had a soft heart. And though it might appear to an uninformed onlooker that the artist was the more passive half of the romantic couple, this was, in fact, untrue. The reality was that the depth of his great love for the entrepreneur overrode the immature needs of his ego. All his kindness wasn't to be confused with weakness. The artist was a powerful man.

"I've written a poem myself," the artist added. "It's for you, my beloved."

"Read it to me. Please," said the entrepreneur gracefully as she fixed his collar.

"Okay," said the artist with a gulp. "It's called 'May We Never Say Goodbye.' And it goes like this:

MAY WE NEVER SAY GOODBYE
A chance encounter and that very first glance,
Your beauty moved me
And your strength calmed me.
Life's unexpected windows of opportunity
Sent by a knowing intelligence
Asking us to do our part. By taking a risk.

Only those who dare will win.
Only those willing to face rejection will find their salvation.
Only those who reclaim their power will experience a resurrection.

I've never known true love.
I've never believed in double rainbows.
Romantic walks and holding hands at sunrise.
I never imagined that first kiss would lead to this.

When you fall, I will support you.
Should you be scared, I will hold you.
When you are in doubt, I will stand by you.
When you enjoy success, I will raise my glass to you.
And when you feel like leaving, I won't let you go.

I think of you constantly.
I feel you deep within me.
I'm not sure what I've done to deserve you.
But my dream now is to grow old with you.
May we never say goodbye.

The artist went down on one knee and kissed a hand of his soon-to-be bride. She blushed vividly and was profoundly touched. One could then hear loud crying.

The two students handed their mentor a tissue, so he could dry his eyes.

CHAPTER 16

The 5 AM Club Embraces
The Twin Cycles of Elite Performance

"With freedom, books, flowers, and the moon,
who could not be happy?"
—Oscar Wilde

The billionaire was seated alone on the spacious terrace of the private cottage he had rented on a wine estate in Franschhoek, South Africa. As he wrote his Daily Diaries, Mr. Riley reflected on the marvelous happiness, uncommon exuberance and striking beauty that was present at the wedding of the entrepreneur and the artist in São Paulo. They were clearly meant for each other.

"The universe works in interesting and absolutely intelligent ways," he thought. "And if there was a union that would go the distance, it would be this one."

As the magnate made notes in his journal, birds sang their carefree songs and gardeners in blue work uniforms dug into the soil of the vineyard with shiny shovels while speaking energetically in thick South African accents. The tangled yet lovingly arranged vines on wooden stakes spoke of an enchantment that nature alone affords while a mystical wisp of fog slowly migrated from Franschhoek Valley up toward the surrounding mountains.

A little earlier, at 5 AM, the billionaire had taken the entrepreneur and the artist on a mountain bike ride that began on the wine farm, then meandered down Daniel Hugo Street and into the village—past well-used horse stables, lazy dogs that moved as slow as snails on Prozac and rose bushes that had twisted along the white picket fences that had been erected along both sides of the rough dirt road. It really was a near-perfect little place the billionaire had selected as the setting for his second-to-last mentoring session.

The lesson that the billionaire had presented as the three of them rode together centered on the vital importance of balancing elite personal performance with deep self-renewal for sustained masterful achievement. The titan explained the value of alternating time in the world pursuing success at the highest level with time in the wilderness recovering—a symmetry needed to ensure a strong harmony between winning at work and richness in life. And to guarantee that his students played the long game around their assets of genius, the billionaire also explained that massive productivity in society without an abundant heart, an authentic sense of joyfulness and enduring inner peace was no different from the game a hamster plays on a running wheel. It thinks it's moving, yet it remains in a cage.

As the early morning rays melted into the lush greenery, the mogul pedaled his shiny red bicycle, talked excitedly and laughed festive, optimistic, truthful laughs. The kind of laughs we all long to experience more of in our lives. He also continued to cough a lot. One time he even spat up some blood. Yet, because the billionaire seemed vibrant and unusually healthy, the entrepreneur and the artist remained only somewhat concerned for their generous mentor's well-being. Perhaps this was their mistake. But the newlyweds were so in the moment that they didn't spend much time trying to figure out what was going on. In retrospect, they would wish they had.

When the three companions took a break from riding, Stone Riley presented the husband and wife with another learning model, which he pulled out of a blue backpack. It looked like this:

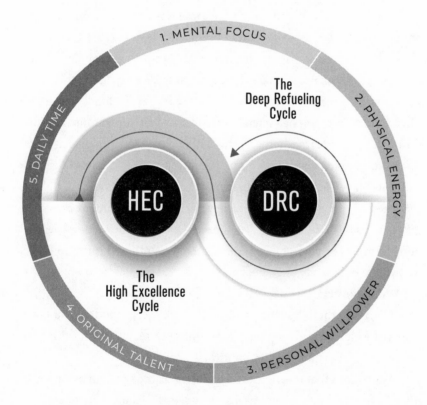

THE TWIN CYCLES OF ELITE PERFORMANCE

PROTECTION OF THE 5 ASSETS OF GENIUS

1. MENTAL FOCUS

2. PHYSICAL ENERGY

3. PERSONAL WILLPOWER

4. ORIGINAL TALENT

5. DAILY TIME

The
Deep Refueling
Cycle

The
High Excellence
Cycle

HEC

DRC

The billionaire taught that "exceedingly excellent creative production without calibrated human asset protection leads to a noticeable performance reduction." What he meant by that was this: *Becoming legendary in your industry is all about sustainability.* And making sure you show up at world-class not just for a month or even for an entire year. The real sport of the captains of commerce, the great masters of the arts, the visionaries of the sciences, the heroes of the humanities and the giants of athletics is preserving your A-game *over a lifetime.*

"Longevity really is a key to legendary," he reinforced. "This," he told his two appreciative students, "is one of the main keys to your rise to iconic. You really must learn how to balance working intensely and brilliantly with deep rest and recovery so you can remain fresh and strong over a long career. As you do this, you won't blow out your gifts by hyperextending them, in the same way that some pro athletes blow out their knees—preventing them from ever playing again. The geniuses all know and apply this remarkably important principle."

As the billionaire sipped sweet, dark coffee, he explained that what makes the great men and women of the world exceptional, in part, is their implementation of a phenomenon known as "supercompensation." Just as a muscle tears when you stress it to the edge of its capacity and then *actually grows during the pause of recovery,* your five assets of genius surge when you actively push them past their usual limits and then allow for a period of regeneration. Mr. Riley pointed to the framework on the paper and said, "See, cats, the little-known key to terrific success over the long term lies in a simple word: *oscillation.* I mentioned it in São Paulo, but you're both ready to go deeper."

"We definitely are," declared the entrepreneur.

"Get this," the billionaire said. "When scientists studied the great Russian weightlifters, they discovered that the secret behind their un-defeatability was their work-rest ratios."

"What does that mean?" asked the artist as the companions walked their mountain bikes along a trail at the edge of a fabulous vineyard.

"Your growth happens when you're resting," replied the billionaire in a straightforward way. "Makes no logical sense, right?" the billionaire went on. "In fact, this productivity rule is one of the most central yet paradoxical truths The Spellbinder revealed to me as I was building my global empires. The mainstream thinking tells us that to get more done, we must put in more hours. To achieve more, we need to do more. But solid research now confirms that that kind of linear approach—'work harder to produce better'—is seriously flawed. It isn't sustainable. It just leads to burnout. Exhaustion. Loss of inspiration and the reduction of your private fire to lead the field—and enhance our world. That old-school way of operating also causes a visceral depletion of the very human resources which, if applied intelligently, will make you the master of your marketplace."

"What you're sharing reminds me of *The 60/10 Method*," remarked the artist happily. He was dressed in the riding gear the billionaire had provided. And, given his now daily practice of *The 20/20/20 Formula* as a member in good standing of The 5 AM Club, he looked significantly fitter, more focused, more energetic and more self-confident than when he showed up at The Spellbinder's conference. His transformation was quite marvelous.

"Superb point," applauded the billionaire. "And you're right. Yet the learning model I'm about to walk you through is so much more than that. Today you'll receive advanced insight on how to alternate work-rest periods to generate exponential productivity. You'll also learn how to have a blast while you're doing it. This morning you'll discover how to work less yet materialize more through what pro athletes call 'periodization.' After we're done, you both will be well beyond any superficial understanding of what it takes to triumph in your sphere while living *beautifully* for the rest of your life."

The billionaire pointed to the part of the learning framework entitled *The 5 Assets of Genius*. "As you've now learned, every morning you wake up with a full battery of creative power. Each dawn you awaken to a full well of five private treasures that, if properly managed, will cause you to overcome the violence of your excuses and avoid the knife blade of your past limits so that the great hero encoded within your soul meets the light of day. And enable you to become all you're meant to be. As a maker of spectacular work, as a leader without a title and as a human being dedicated to living in awe of life's most gorgeous graces."

"I'm all in!" exclaimed the artist.

"And as you now know, *The 5 Assets of Genius*," continued Mr. Riley as he looked at the diagram, "are your mental focus, your physical energy, your personal willpower, your original talent and your daily time. I repeat this so you'll remember this. These primary assets are at their highest early in the morning. That's why you want to start your day well and perform your most important pursuits during your most valuable hours instead of wasting this precious opportunity fooling around with your technology, watching the news or oversleeping."

"Got you," confirmed the entrepreneur, ferociously taking notes in the leather journal she received in Rome. A colorful scarf with elegant patterns on it gave her ponytail a dramatic look this particular morning.

"And the essential point of today's lesson is this," the billionaire spoke as he pointed to the center of the model. "Top performance truly isn't a linear game. Elite accomplishment is much more like a heartbeat, more like a rhythm, more like a pulse. If you want to show up as a great master—over decades so you literally dominate your domain for an entire career and lead a life you love well into old age—you absolutely need to alternate High Excellence Cycles, those periods of intense and fantastic output, with times of meaningful recovery, Deep Refueling Cycles. Please study this," the billionaire requested, tapping an index finger on the printed framework.

"Just so I'm clear," said the artist, as he inhaled the fresh air, "HEC is our High Excellence Cycle and DRC is our Deep Refueling Cycle?"

"Yes," replied the billionaire. Today his black t-shirt had white lettering on it that read, "Yes, I'm in a relationship—with myself." His weirdness was magnificent.

"And so, your main move if you want enduring victory—professionally as well as personally—is to oscillate," the tycoon carried on.

"To cycle periods of passionate, monomaniacally focused and potent work at the highest grade with blocks of time set for refueling, relaxing, recovering and pure fun. It really is like your heartbeat, pulsing."

"I so love this concept you're so kindly teaching us," noted the entrepreneur. "This will be another needle-mover for my business life and for my private world."

"Yes, it will be," agreed the billionaire succinctly. "Growth does happen in the resting phase. That's counterintuitive. Right? We've been programmed to think that if we're not creating and producing, we're wasting our time. We feel guilty if we're not doing. But look at this." The baron unzipped a nylon carrying case that had been fastened around his waist. He pulled out two medals that appeared to be made of gold and placed them around the necks of the entrepreneur and the artist, as one would do in celebration of a champion. On each medal, these words were engraved:

THE LEGENDARY PERFORMANCE EQUATION:
PRESSURE × REFUELING = GROWTH + ENDURANCE

"Tennis great Billie Jean King said that pressure is a privilege," the billionaire reminded his two students. "See, pressure and stress aren't bad."

"They're not?" questioned the entrepreneur.

"Nope. They're actually absolutely *necessary* for the expansion of your capacity," voiced the billionaire.

"You must push your talents hard," the billionaire continued. "Even when you don't want to. Past your comfort zone. Only then will they grow. Always remember this: *The time you least feel like doing something is the best time to do it.* And part of the reason for this, as you also now know, is because when you enlarge your willpower muscle in one important area, your self-discipline in every other area rises with you. The larger point I'm trying to make here is that pressure and stress are wonderful blessings that A-Players exploit. Our gifts don't increase when we stay in our safety circles. Nope. Challenge and stretch your capacities past the normal. Muscles expand only when we take them past our usual limits. And then allow for some time to refuel and recover."

The billionaire surveyed the vineyard. Then he added, "I recall having a fascinating conversation with a pro athlete who showed up at one of my charity dinners. You know what he told me?"

"What?" wondered the artist.

"'I rest to allow all my training to take effect,'" pronounced the billionaire. "Profound way of seeing things. All work and no break depletes your greatness, over time."

"Hmm," murmured the entrepreneur, rolling her mountain bike over to a stake and leaning the seat against it.

"If you want to build stronger abdominal muscles you stress them past their current boundaries," said the billionaire. "If you usually do a hundred sit-ups, you do two hundred. If two hundred is your daily quota, go up to three hundred. This actually causes the muscle to rip apart. The exercise physiologists call the phenomenon 'micro-tearing.' Yet, if you want the muscle to grow, you can't keep exercising it relentlessly or you'll experience injury. You need to rest the muscles for a day or two."

"And it's in that recovery cycle when the actual growth happens," interjected the artist, locking in on the principle he was learning.

"Absolutely correct!" enthused the billionaire. "Growth happens in the resting phase—not in the performing stage. Recall early on in our work together on my beach in Mauritius I told you cats I grew up on a farm, long before I moved to Malibu?"

"Think so," spoke the entrepreneur. "Mauritius feels like another lifetime ago."

"Well, there's a metaphor that I learned at our farm that will help you fully understand *The Twin Cycles of Elite Performance*. Talk to any farmer and she'll tell you about the 'fallow season.' Before it, there's an intense period when the soil gets tilled, crops get planted and serious work gets done. Then there's that season of resting. Seems like nothing's happening. Looks like time is a wasting. Yet here's the neat part: It's in the fallow season that the harvest is really blossoming. All the produce that shows during autumn is just the visible end result."

The billionaire slurped some more coffee. He spilled a little on his t-shirt. The container that held the java had "Dream big. Start small. Begin now" written on it.

A yellow butterfly with tender flapping wings that had blood-red veins along them glided by. Three eagles announced their authority overhead.

"God, I love butterflies," the billionaire said wistfully. "And rainbows, shooting stars, full moons and glorious sunsets. Why be alive if you're not going to be totally *alive*?

"I was like a robot when I was in my twenties," he admitted. "I took myself too seriously. Didn't have a minute to waste. Every hour was scheduled. Every car ride had to have an audiobook running. All flight time was about productivity. Here's the thing . . ." his voice trailed off as his eyes appeared lonely, melancholic and lost.

"I was exhausted a lot of the time. The Spellbinder saved my life. He really did. And the model I'm walking you through this morning helped immensely."

The billionaire took a deep breath, then went on. "My assets of genius became eroded over time. My creativity was floundering—as was my effectiveness. I've since realized that I'm paid by my group of companies to think. To come up with visions and ideas for new products and innovations that will shatter the compass and deliver humongous value to all our clients around the world. But I didn't understand that back then. The Spellbinder assisted me enormously. Taught me *The Twin Cycles of Elite Performance* during our very first coaching session. And insisted relentlessly that I implement them instantly—and consistently. But boy, did I fight him on this one! It was just so against my nature to relax and breathe and to pause. Now I totally get that rest is the very thing that *enables* our primal greatness to unfold."

The entrepreneur nodded her head in understanding. "If I'm not working, I feel super-guilty. Like I'm doing something wrong."

"Self-care is essential to self-love," remarked the billionaire. "All I'm saying is I now understand that balance is vastly important to world-class performance. Working day and night didn't make me more efficient at all. It just made me more tired. And cranky. So, now I make the time to rest, to nourish myself, to mountain bike, to read the books I've always wanted to read, to enjoy a glass of excellent wine like the glass of amazing Pinotage I savored last night in front of the blazing fire in my cottage here in the valley. Ironically, as I've practiced this kind of recovery, my creativity has multiplied, my productivity has soared and my results have skyrocketed. It's just so profound: *I work less, have more fun and yet I get way more done.*"

Mr. Riley then reached into his blue backpack and pulled out a piece of white material, which looked like it came from the sail of a schooner. Remarkably, you could see a drawing of Albert Einstein in a sailboat on it. If you were there, in that precious vineyard with them, you would have seen this:

The industrialist continued his discourse, out in that delightful vineyard. "Oh yes, cool cats, having fun is so very essential to leading your field, upgrading your life and inspiring the world. All of the amazing creatives and productive icons of history had one thing in common, you know?"

"Tell us—please," requested the entrepreneur as her bangles made a "clink-clink" sound. Her new wedding ring shimmered in the morning sunlight.

The billionaire flipped into a quick handstand. He then beat his chest fast with a single fist as he whispered these words to himself:

This day is priceless. All the money in the world will not bring it back again. And so, I seize it and I savor it and I honor it.

This day, I fill my mind with big dreams so there is no space for petty doubts. I replace the psychology of can't with the mentality of can. And I remember that my greatest growth lies at the jagged edges of my highest limits.

This day, I'll recall that until my mission becomes my obsession, my gifts will never become my glory. And until my hunger to serve transcends the insecurities of my self, I'll miss the grand chance of these precious hours to be a vehicle for helpfulness.

This day, I reload my devotion to avoid a counterfeit nobility, staying sincere, humble—with both feet on this sacred ground. Should naysayers and bad actors throw rocks at me, I reply with kindness and love in the face of their bad behavior—even if they don't deserve it. Should critics make fun of me—as they always have since I was a kid—I'll take the rocks they throw at me and make them into monuments of mastery. And should anyone call me strange, as they often do, I'll smile with the blatant wisdom stuck deep in my heart that it's only misfits, oddballs and eccentrics that change our world. Being different is really cool. And eccentricity is very hip.

It was quite a sensational scene. Stone Riley, upside down, beating his chest as if to activate his heart and reciting his poetry.

"Words are creative, you know," he articulated as he stood up and inhaled a big gulp of fresh Franschhoek air. "Speak the words of unchained heroism. Talk the preach of a passionate possibilitarian. Use the languaging of hope, the sentencing of power and the phrasing of leadership—and unbridled love. I manage my words meticulously. Every morning."

The billionaire looked at the vines. "Anyhoo," he added, "all great geniuses really loved to play. They understood that having fun is a potent form of recovery. They all had leisure activities that recharged their empty batteries. Einstein loved to sail. Aristotle and Charles Dickens adored daily walks. Hollywood superstar Meryl Streep used to knit, Steve Wozniak played polo, Bill Gates mastered bridge and Sergey Brin would often be up on a high-flying trapeze. Time away from work isn't a waste," the tycoon reinforced. "It's a must. Offers a space for *incubation* of the very ideas that will make you a fortune. So work less to get more done. That's pretty much what *The Twin Cycles of Elite Performance* model is all about."

"I'm understanding *The 60/10 Method*'s value even more," the artist contributed. "I guess this also means it's okay to have a few days off every week."

"Not only okay but necessary to guard your five assets of genius, the very ones that A-Players leverage to realize industry prominence so their work stands the test of time. To be specific and tactical: *take at least two full days off each week.* No technology. 'Zero Device Days' is what The Spellbinder calls them. Full recovery. And every quarter, take off even more time. For decades I've taken June, July and August to vacation. I sail, bike, sleep, read, swim, chill with my friends, have the happiest times with my daughter and experience life at its best. You cats may not be able to take this much time off. But I need to tell you that during these renewal cycles I do my best thinking and planning and get my best insights. I always return to the office a thousand times more inspired, on fire and alive."

Another butterfly floated by. The vineyard seemed to whisper of wonderful miracles to come. Though the sun now stood in its full radiant glory, a thin slip of a moon competed for attention in the big African Sky. It was breathtaking.

The entrepreneur grasped her husband's hand.

"This is magical," she said.

"You know, guys," Mr. Riley said as he picked up his bike and started walking along the secret back road that he had somehow discovered. "Heaven on Earth isn't some mystical, spiritual place to aspire to. It's not some realm reserved only for saints, seers and sages. Not at all. I've discovered—and boy, have I led a colorful, intense life all these years—that Heaven on Earth is a state, that *anyone* can create."

The billionaire was now deepening the conversation significantly and growing even more philosophical around this particular lesson on work-life boundaries for sustained legendary performance—and a happier existence. Because business victory without a joyful heart misses the opportunity.

"I feel really, really blessed in my life," Stone Riley stated. "I live mostly in the magic."

"The magic?" wondered the artist, now pulling on two dreadlocks and unlacing his biking shoes.

"The magic," confirmed the billionaire, looking serene yet confident, relaxed yet thoughtful, playful yet spiritual. "I've learned that being successful without feeling soulful is the highest of defeats."

The entrepreneur and the artist sat down next to each other on the soil of the vineyard.

The billionaire kept on. "While I've always been passionate about advancing my companies and expanding my commercial interests—

mostly to see how far I can go and to help me fuel my philanthropic work—I am equally dedicated to savoring the magic of a life astoundingly well-lived. Winning without enjoying is nothing."

"Not so sure I get you," admitted the entrepreneur as a truck carrying a gaggle of workers with charismatic smiles sailed by.

"It's a great morning!" one shouted.

"I love my work, so much. And I do get a lot of pleasure from the homes, the goods and the toys I own. But I need none of it. I have my things and my public reputation as a global businessperson. Yet I don't *identify* with it. I'm not attached to any of this. As I grow older, I still love the pleasures of this world very much—but I don't require them for my happiness and peacefulness. I've come to see it all as a big game, a sport of sorts.

"I own my things, but they don't own me," the baron continued. "And though I play in the world I also adore the wilderness, not only meta-phorically but literally—like here experiencing the natural wonders of this ethereal valley in Franschhoek. This, too, is how I live the *Twin Cycles* model. I make time to enjoy life completely."

"The magic," repeated the billionaire as singing birds seemed to croon louder and a flutter of even more butterflies showed up to listen in on the conversation.

"God, life is beautiful. Don't miss out on all of its awesomeness and incredibleness. It's there for you—no matter what you might be going through. See, we all live on borrowed time. And life does whiz by so quickly. You two cats will be old before you know it, probably hanging out with a hundred grandchildren," he said with a chuckle.

"Anyhoo," Mr. Riley spoke in a whisper. "Utopia, Shangri-la, Nirvana and Heaven on Earth are just names for a state of being, not a place of visiting. You enter the magic of life and begin to experience outright bliss daily once you reclaim the inherent power that lurks in your core. And when you don't postpone being grateful for even the tiniest of everyday graces. You'll become a magnet for miracles when you begin being a magician of sorts."

"The billionaire's getting into some pretty mystical and far out territory now," thought the entrepreneur.

"Heaven on Earth," recited the industrialist. "My life is generally a steady stream of beauty, you know? And I've discovered this has little to do with having a lot of money. It has more to do with finding fulfillment, in the smallest of things. The way the fire warmed me and inspired me last evening, for example. It has to do with spending a lot of time in nature, whether that's in vineyards like these," he said, pointing an index finger across the wine farms that filled the valley, "or on walks in a forest, or hiking in the mountains, or being near the sea, or drifting through the sands of a barren desert. It has to do with reconnecting to the awe, wonder and majesty that every human life has available to it by visiting art galleries frequently and letting the energy and genius of the creators infuse your Mindset, Heartset, Healthset and Soulset. It has to do with eating fresh food, simply prepared, with interesting, real, thoughtful, creative and compassionate people who make you feel good. Stepping into the magic also has a lot to do with saying goodbye to your past, embracing the present and making a return to the imaginativeness, innocence, exuberance and lovingness you were intimate with when you were a child. Adults are deteriorated children. Heaven on Earth shows up naturally in your heart when you have the brilliance and bravery to start opening it up again. Like you did when you were little."

"Picasso once said, 'It took me four years to paint like Raphael, but a lifetime to paint like a child,'" contributed the artist energetically. "I'd agree that getting back to being more innocent brings the magic back to our lives."

The billionaire stopped. He rested his bike and waved for his two students to follow him over to an area of the vineyard that had a black metal sign marked "Chenin Blanc" in bright yellow letters. Stone Riley then fell to his knees.

279

The entrepreneur and the artist watched him draw a learning model in the mineral-rich soil of the terroir. It looked exactly like this:

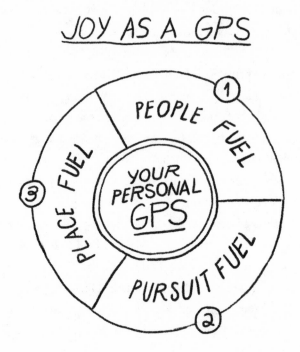

"The magic," the billionaire mused, still whispering, as he stood up straight as a solider. His eyes were closed now. His thick hair fluttered slightly in the mild wind. As he placed one hand to his heart, more doves materialized.

"I'm really into breezes these days. You'd only appreciate them if you didn't have them anymore. Like I'm saying, there's such an enchantment to life. It's right in front of you. Available to anyone. We all can become magicians of sorts. But to experience this higher reality I'm speaking of—to really find it—you'll need to leave the world a lot. Play in common society and succeed in the game it sells you but disconnect from it often, so you're never really owned by it. Because the sport the majority is playing is only an illusion—sort of a waking dream—that too many good people are donating the best mornings of their finest days to as they put money over meaning, profits over people, popularity over integrity, being busy over family and achievement over loving the basic miracles of the now."

The billionaire's eyes remained closed. Next, he lifted both hands toward the heavens, as he liked to do.

"You enter the magic by using your joy as a GPS," disclosed the billionaire, speaking directly to the diagram he'd drawn in the dirt.

"To know ever-increasing amounts of happiness, trust what makes you feel happy. Your heart knows where you need to be. It's so much wiser than your head. Instinct knows so much more than intellect and intuition is smarter than reason, that's for sure. Our intelligence is made up of what those around us have taught us. It's limited. It's confined by logic—and what's been done before. Your sovereign self knows better. It operates in possibility, not practicality. It's visionary. It's *unlimited*."

"Not sure I understand you," said the entrepreneur.

"Follow your joy," instructed Mr. Riley. "Only be around those people who fuel your joy. Only perform those pursuits that feed your bliss. Only be in those places that make you feel most alive. Look, I know it's hard to live this model perfectly. So please see this framework as an ideal to move toward. And like everything else I've taught you, it's a process— not an event. It'll take time. But it begins with being *aware* of this model. And then allowing your joy to be your GPS."

The billionaire started walking with his mountain bike and gently motioned for his two students to follow.

"Ah, the magic that lives at the essence of life. Love it so much. Fills me with more serenity and tranquility than any material object ever has. And this is the importance of balancing being successful with being soulful."

The billionaire clenched his arms tightly and looked as if he was dealing with severe pain, yet again.

"Your heart is always wiser than your head," he repeated softly. "It knows where you must be. Follow it. Trust it. You'll find the magic."

The billionaire gave a signal and instantly, from behind a scarecrow, an assistant dashed across the vineyard to his employer. A silver spade was handed to the billionaire, and a quick hug was exchanged.

The magnate began to dig with gusto. Soon a *clack* could be heard as metal struck metal. Mr. Riley knelt to the ground and began wiping soil from a steel box that had been embedded into the earth. As he did this he started yodeling, much as folk singers in Switzerland and Austria do. It was something else to watch the industrialist as he dug. And to hear him sing.

The entrepreneur and the artist were mesmerized.

The box was then opened, with colossal care. Inside were eleven magic charms, each attached to a letter. In that moment, sunshine radiating over the billionaire created the effect of another shimmering halo.

"I am part of all that is," mumbled the billionaire to himself. "The great power of the universe is within me. All I desire, with active faith, positivity, expectancy and purposeful conviction, is on its way to me. And if that which I wish for does not come, it's simply because something even better is on its way. I know this belief to be true. All wizards know it to be true."

The entrepreneur and the artist stared at each other, eyes wide open.

"What are you doing?" quizzed the artist.

"I'm using one of my incantations," responded the billionaire. He added more yodeling to the end of his sentence, then said, "You can't produce magic in your life until you learn the luminous arts of a real magician."

Abruptly, the box began to rise and hover over the soil for just a moment. The mouths of the entrepreneur and the artist were now as open as a rose in springtime.

The artist was a little unnerved. "Optical illusion someone taught you, right?"

"Maybe yes. Maybe no." Mr. Riley's reply only heightened the mystery.

"Each of these magic charms will help you remember one of the eleven maxims I've been applying over these past decades for increasing my financial fortune and for experiencing an exquisite life. Like I said, my days provide a steady stream of beauty, grand awe and relentless wonder. Heaven on Earth," the billionaire reiterated. "And I want you both to live like this, too. The cool thing is that anyone can create this kind of an existence. But very few people alive today know how to manifest one.

"And each associated letter will bring together some of the key themes I've shared with you on this sensational adventure, sort of to summarize things as we approach the end," the mogul added.

The first charm was a small mirror. Here's what the letter attached to it said:

The Billionaire's Maxim #1

To Create Magic in the World, Own the Magic within Yourself.
Look in the mirror. Your relationship with you predicts your relationship with the world. Remember that you have a primitive longing for silence and solitude—and that it is in quietude that self-awareness rises. French mathematician Blaise Pascal wrote: "All of humanity's problems stem from man's inability to sit quietly in a room alone." Release your need for complexity and immerse yourself in the stillness only the early morning can provide so you get to know yourself again. Because a flight from solitude really is an escape from freedom.

To become an everyday magician, so your life is rich with passion, plenty and peace, grow more comfortable being still. So you start to hear the whispers of the great genius who slumbers within you. In restfulness, you'll remember all you truly are. You'll reaccess that supreme self, abundant with creativity, potency, invincibility and a love that has no conditions. In this sanctuary of silence, you will also be afforded something so rare in this age: time for yourself to *be*. And the more you do so, the more you'll discover how life really works. You'll also begin to differentiate between your beliefs that are merely cultural constraints and those that are actual truths. And between the trustworthy voice of your intuition and the persuasive pronouncements of your fears. In solitude, you'll also receive the disruptive insights that will transform your field. I know it sounds strange but amid serenity, you'll actually visit the alternate reality in which visionaries like Nikola Tesla, Albert Einstein, Grace Hopper, Thomas Edison, John D. Rockefeller, Marie Curie, Andrew Carnegie, Katharine Graham, Sam Walton, Rosalind Franklin and Steve Jobs, among other luminaries, spent much time. Why do you think the legendary scientists, inventors, industrialists and artists all made so much effort to be alone? I've shared with you that long stretches spent in noiseless contemplation is one of the secrets of the advanced mind. Ultimately, you're the only person you'll be with your entire life. Why not strengthen your relationship with your greatest self, fully know your genius and start a lifetime love affair with your most noble nature?

~

The second magic charm was in the form of a flower. The billionaire relished its fragrance. He then smiled and passed the letter associated with it to his students for their review. It read:

The Billionaire's Maxim #2
Collect Miraculous Experiences over Material Things.
The world has burdened and hardened you. As a child, your instinct showed you how to spot the miraculousness of a snowflake, find fortune in a spider's web and adore the splendor of falling leaves on a colorful autumn morning. The pursuit wasn't about acquiring things. It was about exploring life. To switch the lens through which you see life from one that views what's ordinary to one that perceives the extraordinary is to multiply your ability to create miracles. And to re-engage with the lost purity you knew in your youth before a broken society trained

284

you to value objects and cash over joys and delights. Laugh more often, dance more regularly and play more frequently. Please.

"The future holds promises of mysterious good. Anything can happen overnight," said the mystic Florence Scovel Shinn. Be more alive to the wonders that inhabit your days: gentle breezes, squirrels chasing each other in a park and music that is so wonderful it makes you cry. And you will begin to live as royalty along with heightening your primal powers to produce even more magic in your mornings. Never sacrifice your well-being and quality of life for greater annual income or larger net worth. The determinants of a magnificent life have remained the same for centuries: a sense that you're growing and capitalizing on your human potential; effortful work that draws out your finest productivity and is profitable for humanity; weighty connections with positive people who escalate your jubilation; and time doing that which nurtures your spirit as you advance through your days with a grateful heart.

Yes, in Rome I licked my journal. It's one of the rituals I run to actively heighten my aliveness by raising my appreciation of all the good blessings that have been given to me. The more vividly I value everything in my life, the more everything in my life climbs in value.

So, become a collector of awesome experiences instead of a consumer of material things. Simplify your life and make a return to the essential enjoyments that are sitting right under your noses. As you do, you will overcome the forces that have suppressed your fire and tear down the charade of superficiality that so many fine souls among us are stuck in. And as you continue, you will come to know how gorgeous and terrific your life really is.

And please do remember that your past is a servant that has made you all you now are—not a companion to spend much time with in your present or a friend to carry into your spotless future. It's impossible to enter the magic that each fresh morning brings if parts of you are holding on to old disappointments, resentments and hurts. You know that well now.

Lightheartness of being and ancient pain can't stand the sight of each other. So, train yourself through steady and ceaseless practice to immerse yourself fully in this moment. Yes, it takes work and patience. Yet savoring this very instant is an essential move for a dazzling life. This time is all you really have. And it's an empire worth more than any amount of money in the world. One day, you'll see.

~

The third magic charm was a symbol of a door.

"Every ending marks a new beginning. All we experience happens for a helpful reason. And when one door closes, another will always open for you," noted the billionaire. "Trust—always—that life has your back—even if what's unfolding makes no sense."

The attached letter read:

The Billionaire's Maxim #3
Failure Inflates Fearlessness.

"It is impossible to live without failing at something, unless you live so cautiously that you might as well not have lived at all—in which case, you fail by default," said J.K. Rowling.

The mighty goliaths of ambition and the massive behemoth of imagination within you must never be abducted by the tiny cowards of "What would people think?" "What if I get rejected?" and "I'll probably look silly if I try this."

You can allow yourself to become paralyzed by a fear of rejection or you can go out there and astonish the world. But you just don't get to do both.

Life's reality is that you have a transcendent destiny that begs for your attention in this era of crushing complexity. Stop abusing your greatness, deforming your magnificence and denying your radiance by labeling something that didn't turn out as you wanted a failure. We all know that within every seeming setback lies a distinguished opportunity for even greater success.

And start saying yes more often in your life. Courage is an exquisite weapon to defeat the armies of regret that tear away at lives meekly lived.

~

A wooden paintbrush about the size of a finger was the next magic charm that Mr. Riley carefully lifted from the metal box.

"This will reinforce the notion that you are a powerful creator of your life. And a mighty artist around your ambitions. That productive, prosperous, fit and optimistic people got their great fortune by luck is a lie. I've invested a lot of time making sure you understand this point. That such folks made their empires of money, vitality and influence on society because the stars aligned in the right order to breed their success is pure myth. Here, look at this, please," instructed the mentor kindly as he handed over the next letter.

The Billionaire's Maxim #4

Proper Use of Your Primal Power Creates Your Personal Utopia.
Many human beings spend their finest hours in a facade of satisfaction. By this I mean they think and say they are happy, but in reality they are miserable. They rationalize the fact they have betrayed their dreams, neglected their human treasures and minimized the impact they could have on the planet by telling themselves to be satisfied with what they have, instead of evolving into more. Yes, be wildly thankful for all you have. Yet, also consider that such individuals have dead-ended themselves through absolute neglect and outright abandonment of their inherent power. And as a result, all sense of personal freedom and any hope of sovereignty over their lavish talents have been savaged.

To enter the magic of your life, you must become aware of the four creative tools that turn each of your desires into your visible results.

These four resources that will allow you to materialize miracles in the world are your thoughts, your feelings, your words and your deeds. Exercise your mind to think only thoughts that serve your ascent to mastery and happiness. Sit regularly in feelings of gratitude, positive expectancy and love for all that you have in your life. Speak only the words of upliftment, abundance and encouragement as you saw me doing when I was upside down. And do only those acts that are in forceful alignment with the resident hero that sits at your most wise foundation.

Study someone playing small with their potential and you will understand clearly why their conditions are as difficult as they are. They focus their thinking on their lack instead of plenty. They disrespect the potency of the word by speaking continually of "problems"; by labeling their circumstances as "terrible"; and by classifying rewards such as vast success, financial wealth, contentment and energetic service to others as "impossible," failing to understand that it is their own speech that disconnects them from their capacity to craft magic. Words truly are creative multipliers. And in terms of the daily deeds of such stuck performers, they don't work hard at all, doing as little as possible while hoping for a beautiful life, believing no one sees this crime against their humanity. Yet the most-high magician within them—their conscience and their subconscious mind—watches it all. And witnesses this theft from their best.

～

The next object was a *nazar*, an eye-like amulet that some cultures use to ward off evil people. You may have seen one, on one of your travels.

"Look, cats, I don't believe anyone is truly evil," the billionaire said to his students. "Well, maybe a few. But mostly, the more I live, the more I know that every one of us has experienced various degrees of trauma in their lives. And as I shared earlier, only people in pain do painful things to others. Those who are suffering create suffering. And individuals whose behavior is confusing are generally very confused themselves. They're just really hurting. And something has happened to them that has caused them to feel threatened. And so the goodness at their core has contracted and closed. To call them horrible people is a superficial judgement. It's a lot deeper than that quick perception. Anyhoo, having said that, for now, let's just say that for your own maximum productivity, top performance, boundless joyfulness and peace of mind, it's really important to avoid 'bad people,' those who are filled with wounds from the past that they don't have the self-awareness not to project onto you. I was once on a business trip in Barbados, where a taxi driver gave me this piece of wisdom, which has served me very well. 'Avoid bad people.'"

The eye had this letter stuck to it:

The Billionaire's Maxim #5
Avoid Bad People.

Never underestimate the power of your associations. By the phenomenon known as "emotional contagion" as well as through the activation of the mirror neurons in our brains, we model the behavior of the people we spend our days with. Fill your life with exceptionally excellent, enterprising, healthy, positive, ethical and sincerely loving people. And over time, you'll exemplify these lofty traits. Allow dream stealers, energy thieves and enthusiasm bandits into your Tight Bubble of Total Focus and please know you're sure to become like them.

The real key is to avoid trouble creators. People who have grown up in an environment riddled with drama and non-stop problems will consciously and subconsciously re-create drama and nonstop problems because, as amazing as it seems, such conditions feel familiar, safe and like home to them. Stay away from all drama queens and negativity kings. If you don't, sooner or later, they'll dissolve your bigness and destroy your life. It's just what they do.

Relate peacefully, as much as possible, with everyone. Even one enemy is an enemy too many. Pass through life gracefully, taking the high road when conflict shows up. Should someone do you wrong, let karma do the dirty work. And let a world-class life be your revenge.

~

Clipped to the sixth letter in the metal safe box was paper money of a large denomination. It had been folded into a triangle, for some cryptic reason unknown to the entrepreneur and the artist. This letter was longer than the others. It said:

The Billionaire's Maxim #6
Money Is the Fruit of Generosity, Not Scarcity.
Be not misled by the dominant philosophy of the world. Poverty is the consequence of an inner condition, not an outer situation. To believe otherwise is to hand over your capacity to produce the magic of the prosperity that you want to the very things you are complaining of.

Money is a currency that must flow like electricity. Yes, cash is a current. It needs to circulate. Hoarding it stops the flow of it into your business and private life. All genuine magicians know this. So give more to receive more. Leave lavish tips for servers in restaurants, housekeepers in hotels and drivers in taxicabs. Donate to charities. Do wonderful things for your family and friends without a single thought of any return. A tsunami of abundance will be sent to you.

You may wonder why so many of us live in such scarcity. This state of being is due to our money scars. These are the programs hidden deep within our subconscious that were placed there, unknowingly, by the messaging from our parents and the teaching of other powerful childhood influencers. Their common statements, based on the falsehoods that were taught to them, sound like "be happy with what you have" or "rich people are dishonest" or "money doesn't grow on trees." These words planted the dark seeds of lack within us at a tender, impressionable age.

Four practices have helped me make my financial fortune, and so I gift them to you: positive expectancy, active faith, ever-increasing gratitude and extreme value delivery. By positive expectancy I simply mean to tell you that I always maintain a mindset where I expect money will come to me regularly and from highly unexpected sources. Active faith is when you behave in a way that shows life you trust it in its abundance and benevolence. The universe adores gestures of affluence like paying for a dinner you had with your friends at an expensive restaurant when you cannot totally afford to do so. Or buying the tools you need to raise your craft when there's little cash in your wallet. I'm in no way suggesting that you throw yourself into a prison of debt. Not at all. Overleverage is such a destructive force in our civilization today. Just show nature you know prosperity is coming and perform acts that make you feel like you have plenty. Ever-increasing gratitude, well, we've discussed that one a lot over our journey together. Continue opening your heart to everything and everyone in your life. Bless your money when you pay a bill. Bless the cashier at the grocery store and the farmers who harvested your food. Bless the motorist who lets you into a line in traffic and the musicians who write the songs that become the soundtrack of your life. Bless your legs for carrying you all these years, your eyes for allowing you to witness beauty and your heart for allowing you to feel alive. And extreme value delivery just means giving others—teammates, customers, family members and strangers—exponentially more benefit than they ever could expect from you. Because we reap what we sow.

Developing and then armor-plating your prosperity consciousness will realize quantum gains in your income and personal net worth. So, please get this piece right. Much of the sadness in our culture is because too many of us don't have enough money. This need not be so.

～

"What's next?" wondered the artist as he pulled a robust grape off a vine and swallowed it whole.

The billionaire pulled a miniature running shoe from the case saying, "Exercise is definitely a magic charm. Read the letter I wrote for you both that goes with it."

The letter said:

The Billionaire's Maxim #7

Optimal Health Maximizes Your Power to Produce Magic.

Exercising first thing in the morning gets the primary win of taking care of your health out of the way. This all-important activity is now done, leaving your cognition, energy, physiology and spirit primed to create wonders within your day.

When you begin to work out each morning consistently, you'll be surprised by how poorly you feel when you miss a day. You'll realize that this is how you felt most of the time before you embraced this habit. You just weren't aware of it because feeling low was your usual state of being.

Peak health really is true wealth. Those who lose their good health spend the rest of their lives trying to recover it. Uncommon vitality is also a marvelous method to grow your prosperity. When you get into the finest fitness of your life, calibrate your nutrition to mastery-level, dial-in your sleep routine and minimize aging, you'll notice vast increases in your ability to build intimacy with your sovereign self. So, you bring on more of your genius, glory and compassion into our world. This, in turn, will bring you great financial fortune. Much more importantly, you will be placed in a position of being able to make a bigger contribution. And nothing is as glamorous as helpfulness. Every magician knows this truth well.

～

The eighth symbol was of a tiny mountain climber.

"NSI: Never Stop Improving the quality of your mornings along with the excellence of your life," the billionaire explained. He then let out one last loud yodel. The vineyard workers looked over and laughed uproariously. Mr. Riley waved and giggled with them. He then carried on with his discourse.

"The whole game of the A-Player is to always be rising. When you summit a high peak, you'll see the next range of peaks waiting to be scaled. Key metaphor there for you, cats."

He blew some dirt off the letter that corresponded with this magic charm and held it up for his students to see. Here's how it read:

The Billionaire's Maxim #8
Continue Raising Your Life Standards Toward Absolute World-Class.
Hedonic adaptation describes the psychological circumstance where human beings adapt to environmental and life changes. You receive the pay raise you've wanted for years, and you're overjoyed for a day. Then, this new income level becomes your new normal. The joy you felt fades. Or, you move into a noisy apartment close to train tracks, yet over time you stop hearing the trains. Or maybe the dream car you just purchased staggers you with excitement until, after a few weeks, it becomes just another part of the scenery. These are examples of hedonic adaptation in operation. And the phenomenon unfolds for each of us, inside all our lives.

One antidote to this human way of existing is to constantly increase your personal standards and raise the quality of your life. Make each quarter better than the last, and each year better than the previous one. This is how titans and legends roll.

Related to this is a very important philosophy that has served me well: go through life at world-class. Life's just too short not to treat yourself as amazingly as possible. And as you take better care of you, your relationship with others, with your work, with money and with the world will be lifted correspondingly because your relationship with everything outside of yourself cannot help but be a demonstration of your relationship with all that is within you. This is just the way it is.

Invest in the finest books you can buy, and you'll be rewarded in multiples. Eat fantastic food of the highest caliber, even if all you can

293

currently afford is an excellent starter salad at a luxurious local restaurant. Go have a coffee at the greatest hotel in your city. If where you live has a professional sports team that you love, sit courtside for one game rather than hanging out in the cheap seats for a few seasons. Drive the best car you possibly can. Listen to joyful music daily. Visit art galleries, like I have taught you, so the creativity and consciousness of the painters will rub off on your soul. And remember, be around flowers often—they raise your frequency as well as your ability to see the alternate universe all visionaries tap into. Why do you think so many of the great saints, seers, healers and sages kept flowers beside them? You'll be pleasantly stunned at what this does for your powers to generate all that you desire.

~

Magic charm number nine was a heart. And here's what the associated letter said:

The Billionaire's Maxim #9
Deep Love Yields Unconquerable Joy.
Any chance you get, show people love. A quote often attributed to William Penn has guided most of my life and served me wonderfully. It goes, "I expect to pass through life but once. If, therefore, there can be any kindness I can show, or any good thing that I can do to any fellow-being, let me do it now, and not defer or neglect it, as I shall not pass this way again."

Tell people how proud you are of them and how much you love them while you—and they—are still alive. I once met a man who told me he felt abounding happiness at the very sight of a live person. "Why?" I asked him. "Because I've seen so many dead people in my life that meeting someone alive is a special gift," he said.

Not one of us knows when we'll face our end. So, why hold back that which is most valuable: your human capacity to love deeply?

Part of your job as a fully alive human is to make people feel better about themselves. And to make others smile. It may shock you how little it takes to make someone happy. Write old-school love letters to everyone you care about, thank-you notes to those who have helped you and messages of consideration for anyone you think needs some appreciation. Express how you really feel without being limited by the devilish fear of rejection. And always be more interested in other people than being concerned with coming off as an interesting person. Every human being you meet has a lesson to teach, a story to tell and some dream in their heart that longs for your support.

Our best selves will be shackled by the caring words we leave unspoken, the warm feelings we fail to display and the good deeds we leave undone.

~

"Here, take this, please," the tycoon gently requested as he gave his guests a figure of an angel. "What's on this page is especially important. I suggest you read it with a very open spirit."

The letter expressed the following:

The Billionaire's Maxim #10
Heaven on Earth Is a State, Not a Place.
Take daily voyages into awe and regular adventures into wonder. Wonder is such a potent source of happiness and a key skill in the promotion of your ever-increasing genius. All the great women and men of the world learned how to relax into the magic of a day enchantingly spent.

Through my experiments with life, I now understand that what the immortal philosophers, mystics and saviors called "Heaven on Earth" isn't a place to visit but a state you can inhabit. Trust me, as you cultivate your Mindset, purify your Heartset, optimize your Healthset and elevate your Soulset, the way you perceive and experience life will revolutionize your experience. But if you don't do this profoundly important work, you'll never know. And my words will seem like the ramblings of an old eccentric. A sane person in a world gone crazy has always been considered insane, you know?

So, as you dedicate more time to personal mastery, the amount of self-love you feel will expand. And all lavish successes and private joys do depend on loving oneself. What keeps you in bondage to your doubts, insecurities and fears is low inner worth. Because of what people told you about yourself in your early childhood, your subconscious mind discounts your braveness, smothers your highness and chains your greatness.

As you let go of the false beliefs that you were taught are truths, and as you release the emotional wounds that closed you to love—and I'm speaking of something so much more than romance here—you will develop the ability to sense this all-new reality I've been hinting at. It has always been there. But because of the tainted filter through which you were seeing the world, you were blocked from knowing it.

Yet, nothing is wrong. There has been no waste. All is unfolding as it should. At your end, you will realize that very little of what happened to you was an accident. Everything was for your growth. And all was for your good.

~

The entrepreneur and the artist were mildly taken aback when they were shown the eleventh and final magic charm.

"If you really want to play in the magic of life, reflect often on this one," instructed the billionaire as he handed them a miniature coffin.

This letter, unlike the previous ones, was written in red ink. It read:

The Billionaire's Maxim #11
Tomorrow Is a Bonus, Not a Right.
Postpone not your heroism and never delay your peacefulness. Your life can fall apart within an hour. I am an optimist and a genuine merchant of hope. And yet I am also a realist. Accidents, illness, loss and death

happen every day. It's human nature to think these things will never occur. Yet, all wise philosopers teach us of the transience of our existence.

Armed with this insight, connect with your mortality. Understand that your days are numbered. And with the passage of each glorious morning, you grow closer to your end.

Don't put off expressing your gifts and talents. And make certain you enjoy this ride. Have a good time as you rise toward your magnificence. It's so sad how most people postpone having a beautiful, fun and magical life until they are too old to fully savor it.

Life absolutely is a sublime journey. Yes, we all experience trials—and heartbreak. But it's all mostly good. Every hero story needs to have a villain as well as some juicy tragedy along with the triumphs and ultimate victory for it to be a tale worth watching.

And so, keep the shortness of life at the forefront of your focus. Don't put off your happiness until you have more time, or you get the promotion, or you have more money in the bank. These are excuses, born of feelings that you are undeserving. Sense them and then extract them from your orbit so that you can keep ascending into your loftiest realms.

Tomorrow is a promise, not a fact. Enjoy every morning and appreciate each day you have on Earth. Take bold risks yet hedge them with common sense. Balance living like there is no tomorrow with behaving like you'll live forever. So that when the end does come, you'll know you lived your life as a majestic testimony to the capacity for legendary that every human being carries inside of them.

～

The billionaire then proceeded to kiss his students.

"I love you two, you know. I'll really miss you."

Then he disappeared into the vineyard, leaving only his mountain bike.

CHAPTER 17

The 5 AM Club Members
Become Heroes of Their Lives

"Live like a hero. That's what the classics teach us.
Be a main character. Otherwise what is life for?"

—J.M. Coetzee

The helipad in Cape Town, South Africa, is on the V&A waterfront, a place where tourists ride the Cape Wheel, yacht racers replenish their supplies for courage-filled, adrenaline-fueled ocean contests, fishing charters may be booked and strong morning coffee can be found.

The bubbly brunette with librarian glasses made sure the liability waivers were signed by the billionaire, the entrepreneur and the artist. She then stood on a leather sofa, made notes on her checklist and provided her three VIP clients with the safety briefing that was mandatory before their helicopter whisked them to Robben Island.

As you know, Robben Island—a barren, not-so-huge, shark-surrounded, ominous-looking parcel of land sitting not so far from the coast of Cape Town—is where Nelson Mandela was confined to an enormously tiny prison cell for eighteen of the twenty-seven years he was imprisoned. Over time, this great hero of the world was attacked, abused and otherwise mistreated. And yet, he replied to this bad behavior with olive branches, seeing the good in his captors and guarding his hope for a democratic nation where all people would be equals. Speaking about Mahatma Gandhi, Einstein once said, "Generations to come will scarce believe that such a one as this ever in flesh and blood walked upon this Earth." The same could be expressed of Mr. Mandela.

"It's an absolute pleasure to have you here for your short trip over to the island," the woman indicated politely. South Africans are remarkably well-mannered and thoughtful people.

The billionaire wore a black baseball cap with the phrase "To lead is to be of use" stitched on the front of it.

"You'll have to take that off once you step onto the helipad, young man," the woman told him with a golden glimmer in her eye.

The billionaire beamed. "I think she likes me," he whispered to his companions. "Today's our last day together," he added matter-of-factly.

After the safety instruction had been delivered, the billionaire, the entrepreneur and the artist were escorted out of the building and into a paved holding area where two weather-beaten picnic tables sat. Though it was sunny, the winds were gusty. The billionaire removed his hat.

"I feel a little anxious," thought the billionaire. "I've never been to Robben Island. I've read a lot about what went on there under the inhumane and evil system of apartheid, which ranked the treatment of people according to their color of skin with no consideration for the caliber of their character—or the quality of their hearts."

A serious-looking young man wearing a slim raincoat, khaki trousers and boating shoes emerged from one of the empty maintenance bays and requested that the billionaire and his students follow him out to the helipad. An army green helicopter sat at the center of the area with its rotors spinning impressively. The pilot was at the controls, adjusting dials, knobs and the like.

The young man meticulously made sure that all three clients were properly situated in the aircraft for a safe and even weight distribution, then placed a headphone with a microphone onto the billionaire's head.

"Good morning," boomed the billionaire enthusiastically to the helicopter pilot, as the rotors accelerated. The pilot's face could not be seen beneath his helmet, aviator sunglasses and face protector. And he refused to say a word.

"Not so friendly," muttered the billionaire, remaining both somewhat nervous yet positively excited for this once-in-a-lifetime experience that was about to unfold.

The helicopter started rising, slowly initially then ascending quickly.

"The trip will take about five minutes. Winds and sea swells are extra strong today," was all the pilot spoke. And even this he voiced curtly.

The billionaire, the artist and the entrepreneur remained quiet. Each of them simply stared at Robben Island, a land mass that seemed more vast—and even more brutal—as they neared it.

The aircraft landed on a pad surrounded by low trees and, as it did, seven springboks gracefully vaulted by. Yes, seven springboks! At the same time, it began to rain. And another double rainbow, like the one that had appeared at the dolphin swim in Mauritius, extended across the full length of the horizon that intersected with the Atlantic Ocean.

"All very special," observed the artist, arm in arm with his wife.

"We've definitely entered the magic," replied the billionaire in a respectful tone that conveyed an enormous appreciation for the opportunity to experience Robben Island and at the same delivered a sense of sadness for the valuable lives that had been ruined there.

The pilot lingered in the cockpit, pressing buttons and turning off the helicopter while his three passengers exited onto the asphalt landing space and silently took in the scene. From out of nowhere, an old pickup truck with "KSA" marked on the side raced toward them, leaving voluminous clouds of dust in its wake.

"You're not supposed to be here," shouted the driver, clearly a security guard, in a thick South African accent once he had reached the helicopter. He remained in his vehicle.

"Because of the weather, Robben Island has been closed to the public," he called forcefully. "The ferries have all stopped running. No vessel can come to the port area here and no helicopters are allowed to land. You should have known about this! *You should not be here!*" the officer emphasized, adding, "Who are you people?"

The guard did remain professional at all times. But he was visibly surprised. And obviously mildly shaken, perhaps imagining that the occupants of the aircraft had planned some kind of ground assault. And thinking the unexpected visitors had illicit intentions.

"All is good here," the pilot said with a firmness and confidence not often seen. He was now standing outside the helicopter and began to walk slowly toward the man in the truck, first adjusting his shirt then arranging his helmet, which he kept on. The pilot was not young. You could detect this from the way he walked.

"This is a special day for them," remarked the pilot, his voice getting louder. "These people have come a long way to see the prison cell where Nelson Mandela was jailed. They have come to view the limestone quarry where he was forced to hack away at stones for over a decade, in the torturous sun that reflected off the rock to the point where it damaged his eyesight permanently. They want to view the courtyard where the statesman would exercise and throw tennis balls with confidential messages inside to his fellow political prisoners in the next cellblock. They need to go to the spot where Nelson Mandela's manuscript for *Long Walk to Freedom*, his autobiography, would be secretly buried in the dirt after he'd spent many hours working on it. They need to experience—at least a little—the suffering Mr. Mandela endured over his eighteen grueling years here. And they must learn about how, even though he was so viciously treated—a theft of many of the best years of his life—once he was released, he chose to forgive all those who had been so cruel to him."

The pilot stopped in front of the pickup truck. "These people want to be genuine heroes themselves, I hear. In their professional and in their private lives. They wish to be leaders of their productivity, icons in full-on expression of their mastery and perhaps even path blazers in the fulfillment of a better humanity. Our world has never been so in need of pure heroes as it is today. And, as I always teach when I present from the platform: *Why wait for them when you have it in you to become one of them?*

"Wouldn't you agree, Stone?" asked the pilot, turning to speak to the billionaire, whose mouth instantly fell completely open.

The pilot then, ever so gingerly, almost in slow motion, took off his face guard. Next, he shed his sunglasses. And, finally, he removed his helmet.

The billionaire, the entrepreneur and the artist were astonished by what they saw.

It was The Spellbinder.

———

Sterile and calculating fluorescent lighting kept the prison on Robben Island hauntingly eerie, even during the daytime. And feeling frugal, brutal and unsparing.

A set of invisible hands seemed to be guiding the members of The 5 AM Club on that fantastic South African morning because, by some precious symphony of synchronicity—the billionaire would call it "the magic"—the security guard who had raced up in the dusty pickup truck was a huge follower of The Spellbinder's. An "I'm your #1 fan" kind of fan. He loved The Spellbinder's work that much.

And so—you won't believe this but it really did happen—the head of housekeeping, after receiving a green light from the guard, started the tour bus that was out of commission that day because of the bad weather and drove it to where the visitors stood. She also asked one of the few guides still on the island to raise the flag and open the prison for a totally private tour. Just for the billionaire, the entrepreneur, the artist and The Spellbinder.

In every life, especially the hardest ones, doorways of possibility and gateways into the miraculous swing open, revealing the reality that everything that each one of us experiences is part of some intelligent—and yes, often illogical—plan meant to draw us nearer to our greatest powers, most wonderful circumstances and highest good. Everything we go through as we travel through a life is, in truth, a fantastic orchestration designed to introduce us to our truest talents, connect us with our most sovereign selves and deepen our intimacy with the glorious hero that lives inside each of us. Yes, *within every single one of us*. And that does mean you.

The tour guide, who also happened to be a former political prisoner, was a large man with a gruff voice. As he led his guests toward the cell where Nelson Mandela was forced to live for so many long and harsh years, he answered each of the questions they asked.

"Did you know Nelson Mandela?" queried The Spellbinder thoughtfully.

"Yes, I served with him for eight years here on Robben Island."

"What was he like as a person?" asked the artist, appearing overwhelmed by the emotions that he was feeling as they walked down the main corridor of the jail that had been home to so many atrocities during the apartheid era.

"Oh," said the guide gently with a gracious and even wise smile across his face, "that man was a humble servant."

"And what was Nelson Mandela like as a leader?" pressed the entrepreneur.

"Tremendous. Dignified. Inspirational by the way he handled himself and all he went through. Every time he met one of his fellow leaders, often it was here in this courtyard," commented the guide as he stepped into the area where the political prisoners would walk, talk, plan and stand, "he would ask, 'Are you learning?' He'd also often say, 'Each one, teach one,' in this way mentoring his associates on the importance of sharing their daily learning to increase the leadership capability of all those around them. Mr. Mandela understood that education is the ultimate highway into freedom.

"That man was treated so poorly. All those hours of back-breaking work in the limestone quarry. All the degradation and humiliation. A few years after he came here, he was ordered to dig a grave in the prison yard—and then to lie in it," the tour guide added.

"He must have thought that was the end," reflected the billionaire, softly.

"Probably," replied the guide. "Instead, the guards unzipped their pants. And urinated over him."

The Spellbinder, the billionaire, the entrepreneur and the artist all looked down.

"We all have our own Robben Islands that can keep us imprisoned, I guess," the billionaire mused.

"As we go through life we endure our own trials and injustices. Nothing as severe as what went on here, of course. I read that Nelson Mandela said his greatest regret was not being allowed out of this prison to attend the funeral of his eldest son after he was killed in a car accident," expressed the billionaire. He looked up to the sky. "I guess we all have our regrets. And no one gets out without their own ordeals and tragedies."

The tour guide pointed to the fourth window, to the right of the entrance into the courtyard. "There," he stated. "That's Nelson Mandela's cell. Let's go in."

The cell was incredibly small. No bed. A small wooden table that the prisoner would kneel at to write in his journal as there was no chair, a concrete floor and a brown woolen blanket, with green and red flecks in it.

"For the first year of his imprisonment, Nelson Mandela wasn't even permitted to wear long pants, though it was freezing over the South African winter. He was given only a thin shirt and flimsy shorts. When he showered, the guards stood and watched this elderly man standing naked, an attempt to humiliate—and break—him. When it was time to eat, he was given food unfit for an animal. When letters would arrive from his wife and children, often they wouldn't be delivered. Or if they were, they would be significantly censored. All this was carefully done to crush Mr. Mandela's spirit," the guide explained.

"It seems to me all that he endured in this shoebox of a jail cell, on this desolate island encircled by a raging ocean, developed him, strengthened him *and opened him*. The prison became his crucible. The mistreatment became his salvation, leading him into his natural power, highest humanity and fullest state of unstained heroism. In a world of such selfishness, apathy and people disconnected from what it means to be human, he used what he was presented with to grow into an advanced soul on the planet—a man who would show the rest of us what leadership, fortitude and love look like. And in so doing, he became one of our great emblems of forgiveness. And finest symbols of peace," The Spellbinder offered.

"Yes, indeed," replied the tour guide. "When Mr. Mandela was ultimately released from Robben Island, he was transferred to what is now called Drakenstein Correctional Centre, between Paarl and Franschhoek. His ascension to the presidency of South Africa was inevitable, so he was being prepared to assume the position and to lead a free yet enormously divided nation. During that final period of his incarceration, he was given the warden's home. And on the day of his release, he walked out of this residence, over to a long paved road with a guard post and a white gate at the end of it. Nelson Mandela was asked by prison personnel if he'd prefer to be driven down this road to freedom. He refused and indicated simply that he would rather walk. And so, this transformational leader and history-maker who has left a legacy that will inspire many generations took halting steps toward his long-awaited liberation."

The tour guide took a long, weary breath. Then he carried on.

"Mr. Mandela was given a country on the cusp of a civil war. Yet, somehow, he managed to become a unifier instead of a destroyer. I still remember the words from the famous speech he gave during one of his trials:

During my lifetime I have dedicated myself to this struggle of the African people. I have fought against white domination, and I have fought against black domination. I have cherished the ideal of a democratic and free society in which all persons will live together in harmony and with equal opportunities. It is an ideal for which I hope to live for and to see realized. But . . . if it needs be, it is an ideal for which I am prepared to die.

Mr. Riley cleared his throat. He kept looking at the cement floor of the tiny cell.

"Mr. Mandela was a true hero," confirmed the guide. "After his release he invited the prosecutor who demanded the death penalty for him to dinner. Can you believe that? And he asked one of the jailers who watched over him here on Robben Island to attend his inauguration as the president of South Africa."

"Really?" the entrepreneur asked quietly.

"Yes, that's a fact," responded the tour guide. "He was a real leader, a man of genuine forgiveness."

The Spellbinder raised a finger to signal he wished to share another point: "Nelson Mandela wrote, 'As I walked out the door toward the gate that would lead to my freedom, I knew if I didn't leave my bitterness and hatred behind, I'd still be in prison.'"

"He also said that 'to be free is not merely to cast off one's chains, but to live in a way that respects and enhances the freedom of others,'" the guide added. "And that 'no one is born hating another person because of the color of his skin or his background or his religion. People must learn to hate, and if they can learn to hate, they can be taught to love, for love comes more naturally to the human heart than its opposite.'"

"I read he'd often get up around 5 AM and run on the spot for forty-five minutes, then perform two hundred sit-ups and then do one hundred fingertip push-ups. That's the reason I'm always doing my push-ups," the billionaire contributed, somewhat awkwardly.

"Hmm," said the tour guide before continuing, "Mr. Mandela came into this cell as a hot-headed, angry, hostile and militant young man. It was who he grew into here in this prison that made him the icon we all now revere. As Archbishop Desmond Tutu taught us, 'suffering can either embitter us or ennoble us.' Thankfully, Madiba—which was his clan name—chose the latter."

"All the best men and women of the world have one thing in common," said The Spellbinder: "extreme suffering. And each of them evolved into their greatness because they chose to leverage their circumstances to heal, purify and uplift themselves."

The Spellbinder then pulled out a learning model from his jacket, the final one that the two students would see. It was called *The Heroic Human Circle*. Here's what it looked like:

THE HEROIC HUMAN CIRCLE

"These are the virtues each of us must aspire to, to become world-changers and heroes for the benefit of a better society," said The Spellbinder, his voice filled this morning with hints of both melancholy and immense strength.

"Leadership is for everyone. Each of us, no matter where we live, what we do, what's happened to us in the past and what we're experiencing right now, must release the shackles of blame, chains of hate, leg irons of apathy and prison bars of ordinary that keep us in slavery to the dark forces of our lowest nature. Every one of us must rise each morning—yes, at 5 AM—and do everything we can possibly do to unfold our genius, develop our talents, deepen our character and escalate our spirits. Each of us must do this, across our world."

The Spellbinder began to cry as he went on. "We all must break free from our private jails that incarcerate our glory and keep our nobility in bondage. Please remember that gifts and talents neglected become curses and sorrows."

The Spellbinder paused.

"It's your time," he stated, looking directly into the eyes of the entrepreneur and the artist.

The *Heroic Human Circle* framework had been placed on the small table in the chamber that sat under the window with bars. The Spellbinder dragged it to the center of the space, so it became the focus in the prison cell, on that very special day.

The Spellbinder then asked the billionaire, the entrepreneur, the artist and the tour guide to crowd around the diagram. They held one another's hands.

"Yes, no matter what struggles we face and what adversities we will endure. No matter what attacks, humiliation and violence are visited on us. We must persist. We must continue. We must stay strong. We must live our luminous nature. And magnify our sovereign selves. Even if it feels the whole world is against us. This is truly what makes us human beings. Even if it seems the light will never transcend the darkness, keep making *your* walk to freedom. Model what's highest for the rest of us. Exemplify grace, for the majority of us. Demonstrate actual *love*, for all of us.

"Now is your moment," said The Spellbinder, raising a hand and placing it on the arm of the artist. He gently rested the other one on the shoulder of the entrepreneur.

A quiet smile stretched across his face. He looked poised. And serene.

"Time for what?" wondered the artist.

"To start your pilgrimage," was the simple reply.

"To where?" asked the entrepreneur, looking a little confused.

"To a territory called Legacy," indicated The Spellbinder. "A lot of people are tourists at this place. For fleeting minutes of their precious mornings, they think about the body of work they've built and what it is that they'll leave behind, once they die. For brief intervals, before they get distracted, they reflect on the quality of their productivity, the degree of their decency and the depth of their impact. For mere short stints, before the bustle of being busy consumes them again, they pause to contemplate how beautifully they've lived and how helpful they were. They are mere visitors to this realm."

Mr. Riley lifted his arms high as he listened to his mentor's words. "I love my life. I will become an even better leader. I will make an even greater contribution. And I'll upgrade into a much more inspirational human being," he whispered, mostly to himself.

"The distinguished heroes of humankind," resumed The Spellbinder, "were citizens and lifetime inhabitants of this Territory of Legacy. It was their homeland. And this is what ultimately made them legendary. The mighty mission they constructed their lives around was to exist for a cause that was larger than themselves. So, when they died, they left our world brighter than they found it."

"We all come with an expiration date," added the billionaire. "None of us knows how long we get to live."

"True," agreed the entrepreneur.

"Today," The Spellbinder declared, "and this very moment, deserves and demands your commitment to become sublimely creative, pristinely productive, decadently decent and of service to many. Please stop postponing your mastery. No longer resist your primal power. Refrain from allowing the shadow forces of fear, rejection, doubt and disappointment to dim the light of your most luminous self. This *is* your time. And now *is* your day: to make your leap, in your original way, into the rare-air of the finest leaders who have ever lived. And to enter the universe of the true masters, eminent virtuosos and authentic heroes who have been responsible for all progress of civilization."

All five were still huddled in the circle. Mr. Riley began to yodel, a little—before The Spellbinder's strong stare helped him to tone it down. They smiled at one another. A clear gesture of mutual respect.

"To lead is to inspire others by the way that you live. To lead is to walk through the fires of your hardest times to step up into forgiveness. To lead is to remove any form of mediocrity from infiltrating the quarters of your life in a dazzling celebration of the majesty that is your birthright. To lead is to turn your terrors into triumphs and translate each of your heartbreaks into heroism. And more than all else, to lead is to be a force for good on this tiny planet of ours. Today, you get to accept this grand call to raise the standard by which you live out the remainder of your life."

"Or at least starting tomorrow," the billionaire suggested with a mischievous grin.

"Starting at 5 AM," they all said together. "Own your morning. Elevate your life!"

Five Years Later

A few months after his time on Robben Island, Stone Riley passed away.

He died peacefully in his sleep in a small apartment in the historic center of Rome. His loving daughter was at his side. As was The Spellbinder.

On the day of the titan's death, more doves and butterflies took flight over the Eternal City than ever before. There was even a double rainbow that extended all the way from the Spanish Steps to the Colosseum.

You would have been impressed, if you had been there to see it.

The billionaire had been suffering from a rare and incurable disease which he had told no one about, except for The Spellbinder. Because he was his best friend.

You'll be happy to know that, during his last days, the eccentric tycoon completely liquidated the various ventures of his vast business empire. And gave the entire amount to charity.

Mr. Riley did decide to leave his oceanside compound in Mauritius to the entrepreneur and the artist, as he knew how much they loved being there.

Allow me to share what has happened to the entrepreneur and the artist since the time of that most surreal adventure they had with the billionaire. I know you're probably wondering.

The entrepreneur has become a fabulously wealthy woman, having grown the company she founded into an iconic enterprise. She has let go of the demons of her past that haunted her for so long and absolutely loves the life she shares with her husband, the artist. She still works hard, but she also enjoys her time off a lot. She just completed her fourth marathon, has taken a great liking to gardening and volunteers at a shelter for homeless people every Tuesday night. She no longer cares much about fame, fortune and worldly power, even though she now has all these things.

The artist, you'll be fascinated to learn, has become one of the most celebrated painters in his field. He completely beat his procrastination issues, is widely considered a master of his craft and is an extraordinary husband. He ran two marathons with his wife and has now become a vegan. He goes to yodeling classes on Wednesday nights.

And get this: the couple has a wonderfully handsome and ever so intelligent little boy. They named him Stone.

The entrepreneur and the artist are still members of The 5 AM Club, running *The 20/20/20 Formula* every morning well before daybreak. They still practice most of the disciplines Mr. Riley taught them. And they've kept the promise they made to their mentor to tell as many people as possible about the transformational value of rising early.

As for The Spellbinder, he's still alive. In many ways, he's going stronger than ever. He's based out of Tokyo but still spends much of his life on stages in stadiums across the planet, on airplanes and in hotel rooms.

He still loves fishing.

What's Next on Your Heroic Adventure?

The end of this book is the beginning of your own journey into The 5 AM Club. To help you lock in the early rising habit as a lifetime practice as well as install *The 20/20/20 Formula* as your morning routine so you experience world-class results, Robin Sharma has created the following tools for you, all being made available absolutely free:

The 5 AM Habit Installer

A remarkable app that will help you track your daily progress over the next sixty-six days so waking up before daybreak becomes automatic. You'll also receive full access to worksheets for integrating the frameworks you've now learned, music playlists to fuel your confidence and an amazing support platform so you connect with other members of The 5 AM Club.

The 5 AM Club Challenge

You'll receive two months of content-rich and enormously practical coaching videos, mentoring encouragement and fast shots of inspiration from Robin Sharma so you stay with your commitment. And maximize your victories as someone who rises early.

The 5 AM Club Morning Mastery Meditations

To help you start your day feeling calm, focused and positive, Robin Sharma has carefully created and meticulously calibrated a series of guided meditations for you to run through each morning so you optimize your Mindset, purify your Heartset, fortify your Healthset and escalate your Soulset.

The Secret Lost Chapter

In a blaze of creative fire early one morning, the author wrote an alternate (and most unexpected) final chapter to this book. It's intriguing, enchanting and intensely dramatic.

To get your full access to all of these beautiful and valuable resources
being made available to you at zero cost, go to:
robinsharma.com/The5AMClub

Fuel Your Rise by Reading All of Robin Sharma's Worldwide Bestsellers

Have you ever noticed that the most thoughtful, articulate, successful and graceful people you've met all have a common practice? They read everything they can get their hands on.

Whether you're at your mountaintop or just starting your climb, reading is one of the masterhabits of the great ones.

So here's a complete list of the author's internationally acclaimed books to support your ascent into peak productivity, total craft mastery and living beautifully—while you make your mark on history.

[ ] The Monk Who Sold His Ferrari
[ ] The Greatness Guide
[ ] The Greatness Guide, Book 2
[ ] The Leader Who Had No Title
[ ] Who Will Cry When You Die?
[ ] Leadership Wisdom from The Monk Who Sold His Ferrari
[ ] Family Wisdom from The Monk Who Sold His Ferrari
[ ] Discover Your Destiny with The Monk Who Sold His Ferrari
[ ] The Secret Letters of The Monk Who Sold His Ferrari
[ ] The Mastery Manual
[ ] The Little Black Book for Stunning Success
[ ] The Saint, the Surfer, and the CEO

ABOUT THE AUTHOR

Robin Sharma is a globally respected humanitarian and the founder of a not-for-profit venture that helps children in need lead better lives.

Widely considered one of the world's top leadership experts, this pathblazer's clients include many Fortune 100 companies, famed billionaires, professional sports superstars, music icons and members of royalty.

Organizations that have engaged Robin Sharma to help them build employees who lead without a title, produce exceptional work and master change in these complex times include NASA, Microsoft, NIKE, GE, FedEx, HP, Starbucks, Oracle, Yale University, IBM Watson and the Young Presidents' Organization.

He is also one of the most in-demand keynote speakers in the world. To inquire about his availability for your next conference, visit robinsharma.com/speaking.

The author's #1 bestsellers, such as *The Monk Who Sold His Ferrari*, *The Greatness Guide* and *The Leader Who Had No Title*, have sold millions of copies in over 92 languages, making him one of the most broadly read writers alive today.

DATE DUE